Praise for START SEEING & SERVING UNDERSERVED GIFTED STUDENTS

"Enormous kudos to the authors! Many have written on the *need to* 'see and serve' underserved and underresourced gifted students, including English language learners, culturally and linguistically diverse students, economically disadvantaged students, and twice-exceptional students. But this book is unique; it is practical and strategic in that it extends to the *how to* 'see and serve' these students by providing a plethora of classroom-friendly steps and activities *any* teacher can take to create an environment of equity and excellence for all students in their classes. The abundant strategies, vignettes, checklists, and surveys help teachers home in on all students' diverse learning needs. This book essentially operationalizes NAGC's tenets of *See Me, Know Me, Teach Me,* and *Challenge Me,* which very successfully represent the framework of the book itself. Founded in research, teaching pedagogy, and practical experiences, this resource should be in every teacher's classroom. *Start Seeing and Serving Underserved Gifted Students* poignantly guides us to reflect on our own personal biases and inherent views of others and move toward newfound respect and relationship-building."

—**Dina Brulles, Ph.D.,** director of gifted education, Paradise Valley Unified School District, and School District Representative, National Association for Gifted Children (NAGC) Board of Directors

"*Start Seeing and Serving Underserved Gifted Students* is an easy-to-read, easy-to-use, practical, and much-needed resource for educators. The authors not only demonstrate research- and evidence-based best practices in the field of gifted education, but also give real-world examples from educators who have identified and met the needs of underserved and underrepresented gifted students in their classrooms and schools by using the toolkit strategies. This book is a valuable tool that is greatly needed to identify, understand, and meet the needs of underserved gifted students whose potential, creativity, curiosity, and gifts must be nurtured and developed."

—**Lois Baldwin, Ed.D.,** 2e educational consultant and president and cofounder of the Association for the Education of Gifted Underachieving Students (AEGUS)

"From start to finish, this creatively formatted, multilayered book feels new—unclichéd, generative, and crackling with energy and optimism about caring adults responding to complex needs of diverse students. It is full of practical, personalized strategies, including for engaging families and community, flexibly grouping students according to interests and needs, and attending to social and emotional development. Concepts do not feel 'borrowed' because they are explained through real-world experiences of creative educators, and strategies are often unique to the book. Particularly important is the continual emphasis on teacher and student self-reflection, on incorporating the arts, and on the importance of language development. Fundamentally, the perspective of this book is developmental, with a focus on growth for everyone involved."

—**Jean Sunde Peterson, Ph.D.,** professor emerita, Purdue University, and author of *Counseling Gifted Students* and *Get Gifted Students Talking*

START SEEING & SERVING UNDERSERVED GIFTED STUDENTS

50 Strategies for Equity and Excellence

Jennifer Ritchotte, Ph.D.
Chin-Wen Lee, Ph.D.
Amy Graefe, Ph.D.

free spirit
PUBLISHING®

Copyright © 2020 by Jennifer A. Ritchotte, Ph.D., Chin-Wen Lee, Ph.D., and Amy K. Graefe, Ph.D.

All rights reserved under International and Pan-American Copyright Conventions. Unless otherwise noted, no part of this book may be reproduced, stored in a retrieval system, or transmitted in any form or by any means, electronic, mechanical, photocopying, recording, or otherwise, without express written permission of the publisher, except for brief quotations or critical reviews. For more information, go to freespirit.com/permissions.

Free Spirit, Free Spirit Publishing, and associated logos are trademarks and/or registered trademarks of Free Spirit Publishing Inc. A complete listing of our logos and trademarks is available at freespirit.com.

Library of Congress Cataloging-in-Publication Data
Names: Ritchotte, Jennifer A., author. | Lee, Chin-Wen, author. | Graefe, Amy K., author.
Title: Start seeing and serving underserved gifted students : 50 strategies for equity and excellence / Jennifer A. Ritchotte, , Chin-Wen Lee, Amy K. Graefe.
Description: Minneapolis, MN : Free Spirit Publishing, [2019] | Includes bibliographical references and index. | Summary: "This guide promotes equity in education by providing teachers with flexible tools to see, understand, challenge, and advocate for underserved gifted students. It outlines ways to nurture the academic and affective growth of gifted students from traditionally underserved populations. Includes digital content to aid with professional development"-- Provided by publisher.
Identifiers: LCCN 2019013441 (print) | LCCN 2019980431 (ebook) | ISBN 9781631983283 (paperback) | ISBN 1631983288 (paperback) | ISBN 9781631983290 (pdf) | ISBN 9781631983306 (epub)
Subjects: LCSH: Gifted children--Education. | Gifted children--Identification. | Children with social disabilities--Education. | Educational equalization.
Classification: LCC LC3993.25 .R57 2019 (print) | LCC LC3993.25 (ebook) | DDC 371.95--dc23
LC record available at https://lccn.loc.gov/2019013441
LC ebook record available at https://lccn.loc.gov/2019980431

ISBN: 978-1-63198-328-3

Free Spirit Publishing does not have control over or assume responsibility for author or third-party websites and their content. At the time of this book's publication, all facts and figures cited within are the most current available. All telephone numbers, addresses, and website URLs are accurate and active; all publications, organizations, websites, and other resources exist as described in this book; and all have been verified as of July 2019. If you find an error or believe that a resource listed here is not as described, please contact Free Spirit Publishing. Parents, teachers, and other adults: We strongly urge you to monitor children's use of the internet.

Permission is granted to reproduce the pages included in the list of reproducible pages (on page viii) or in the digital content that goes with this book for individual, classroom, and small group use only. Other photocopying or reproduction of these materials is strictly forbidden. For licensing and permissions information, contact the publisher.

Edited by Christine Zuchora-Walske
Cover design by Shannon Pourciau; interior design and production by Emily Dyer

10 9 8 7 6 5 4 3 2 1
Printed in the United States of America

Free Spirit Publishing Inc.
6325 Sandburg Road, Suite 100
Minneapolis, MN 55427-3674
(612) 338-2068
help4kids@freespirit.com
freespirit.com

Free Spirit offers competitive pricing.
Contact edsales@freespirit.com for pricing information on multiple quantity purchases.

Dedication

To all our former, current, and future students of all ages who inspired us to write this book. And to our friends, families, and loved ones who provided endless encouragement and support throughout this incredible journey. Also, to the educators working with and advocating for gifted learners, particularly underserved gifted learners, thank you for all you do.

★ ★ ★ ★ ★

Acknowledgments

We are forever grateful to our graduate students and colleagues who enriched the pages of this book with examples of their dedication to seeing and supporting underserved gifted learners: Lois Baldwin, Brent Braun, Steve Burch, Lisa Charles, Jodi Church, Dimitra Collier, Heidi James Craycroft, Jennifer Dickey, Thelma Bear Edgerton, Alicia Estis, Mandy Festi, Bertie Fiz, Therese Gilbert, Jessica Huggins, Karen Kendig, Margie Lacy, Jessica Likes, Paula McGuire, Christina Mudd, Rebecca McKinney, Jacquelin Medina, Amber Morman-Burke, Jaimarie Nelson, Daphne Pereles, Allison Rothwell, Jenna Rude, Erin Sciscione, Kelly Ann Stiles, Lisa Turk, Cassie Weber, and Lindsey Young.

Thank you to Judy Galbraith and Brian Farrey-Latz. You believed in us all along and gave us the opportunity to write a book that has the potential to positively impact the lives of so many underserved gifted learners. These words will have to suffice, but they cannot begin to express our gratitude to both of you.

Thank you to Meg Bratsch for guiding us through the process of writing our first book and for lending support whenever we needed it.

Thank you to Christine Zuchora-Walske for your responsiveness, kindness, and professionalism during the editing process.

Thank you to the entire staff at Free Spirit Publishing. You are amazing at what you do!

Contents

List of Figures... viii
Digital Content ix
List of Reproducible Pages ix
Introduction... 1
   A Call to Serve Underserved Gifted Learners....................................... 1
   About This Book 2
   How to Use This Book.. 4

Chapter 1: See Me 6
Toolkit Strategies: Breakfast with Stars • Speak Up • What I Want You to Know About Me • Talent Hunt Inventory • Identification Plan Investigation • Understanding How Implicit Bias Works • Learning More About Myself and Implicit Bias • Learning More About My Classroom and Implicit Bias

   Who Are Underserved Gifted Students? 6
   Determining Underrepresentation 13
   Why Are Some Gifted Students Underserved?................................... 15
   Chapter Summary... 26

Chapter 2: Understand Me 32
Toolkit Strategies: My Memory Timeline • Talent Tree • Family Identity Survey • Recipe for Success • Safe Climate Checklist • Positive Classroom Norms • Empowered-to-Learn Checklist • Honoring Small Requests • Tips to Promote Meaningful Engagement • Opportunities to Lead • Learning Goal Plan • Applying UDL Principles to Create an Inclusive Classroom

   Creating a Culturally Responsive Classroom...................................... 32
   Building Meaningful Connections 33
   Conveying and Supporting High Expectations................................... 37
   Nurturing a Safe Climate 38
   Setting the Stage for Engaged Learning... 41
   Chapter Summary... 46

Chapter 3: Teach Me 63
Toolkit Strategies: Helping Students Connect with the Future • Creating a Plan for Service Learning • Creating Interest Groups • Surveying Learning Needs • Group Work Self-Reflection Checklist • Mini-Lesson Ideas for Culturally Responsive Literature Circles • Student Evaluation of Cultural Connections in Texts • Creating Choice Boards • Building RAFTs • Building Step-by-Step Project Timelines • Process Evaluation Rubric • Higher-Level Thinking Bookmark • Implementing Socratic Seminars

   CARE Strategies: Connect Learning to Students' Lives......................... 64
   CARE Strategies: Ability Group Students Flexibly 69
   CARE Strategies: Respectfully Differentiate for Students 80
   CARE Strategies: Engage Students in Higher-Level Thinking 86
   Chapter Summary... 91

Chapter 4: Challenge Me 104

Toolkit Strategies: Determining Learner Readiness for Challenge • Academic Challenge Support Tips • Mentorship Questionnaire • Mentorship Evaluation Rubrics • Independent Investigation Planning Guide • Independent Investigation Self-Evaluation • Young Chautauqua Presentation Rubric • Choosing Content Acceleration Options Thoughtfully • Choosing Whole-Grade Acceleration Options Thoughtfully • Curriculum Compacting Steps

    ASPIRE Strategies: Add Challenge Thoughtfully 105
    ASPIRE Strategies: Supply the Support Necessary for Success 106
    ASPIRE Strategies: Provide Opportunities for Mentorships 108
    ASPIRE Strategies: Identify Possibilities for
        Independent Investigations 112
    ASPIRE Strategies: Recognize When Acceleration Is Vital 122
    ASPIRE Strategies: Embed Curriculum Compacting into
        Learning Units 130
    Chapter Summary 132

Chapter 5: Advocate for Me 147

Toolkit Strategies: Your Past, Present, and Future Advocacy • Advocacy Focus Finder • Setting SMART Advocacy Goals • Lightning Talks • Designing a Professional Learning Opportunity • Creating a Needs Assessment • Action Planning

    What Does It Mean to Be an Advocate? 148
    Determining Your Main Focus Areas for Advocacy 151
    Advocating Beyond Your Classroom 153
    Putting the Pieces Together: Developing an Advocacy Action Plan 160
    Chapter Summary 161

References 172
Resources 175
Index 177
About the Authors 181

List of Figures

Figure 1-1 Masking in Twice-Exceptionality 12
Figure 1-2 Sample Talent Hunt Inventory 19
Figure 2-1 My Memory Timeline Sample 33
Figure 2-2 Sample Talent Tree 34
Figure 2-3 Recipe for Success Sample Card 35
Figure 2-4 Sample Safe Climate Checklist 39
Figure 2-5 Sample Empowered-to-Learn Checklist 40
Figure 2-6 Sample Learning Goal Plan 44
Figure 3-1 Sample Student Evaluation of Cultural Connections in Texts 79
Figure 3-2 Sample Choice Board 83
Figure 3-3 Sample RAFT 84
Figure 5-1 Teacher Learning Cycle 156
Figure 5-2 Professional Learning Questionnaire:
    Cultivating Creativity in Your Classroom 157
Figure 5-3 Sample Needs Assessment 159
Figure 5-4 Sample Action Planning Template:
    Implementing UDL Guidelines 161

Digital Content

See page 180 for instructions for downloading sample lesson plans and digital versions of all reproducible forms.

List of Reproducible Pages

Talent Hunt Inventory	27–28
Best Practices in Identification Checklist	29–30
"See Me" Checklist for Inclusive Identification	31
My Memory Timeline	47
Talent Tree	48
Family Identity Survey	49–50
Recipe for Success	51
Sample Lesson Plan: Self-Awareness and Identity	52–53
Safe Climate Checklist	54–55
Empowered-to-Learn Checklist	56–58
Learning Goal Plan	59
UDL Strategies Checklist	60–61
"Understand Me" Checklist	62
Learning Needs Survey	92
Becky Block Letter	93
Beatriz Block Letter	94
Building Supply Costs and Order Form	95
Group Work Self-Reflection Checklist	96
Student Evaluation of Cultural Connections in Texts	97
Project Timeline	98
Process Evaluation Rubric	99
Higher-Level Thinking Bookmark	100
Sample Lesson Plan: Using Higher-Level Questioning to Guide Inquiry	101–102
"Teach Me" Checklist	103
Mentorship Questionnaire	133–135
Mentorship Evaluation Rubric 1: For the Mentor	136
Mentorship Evaluation Rubric 2: For the Mentee	137
Independent Investigation Planning Guide	138
Independent Investigation Self-Evaluation Rubric	139
Sample Curriculum Unit: Not Just Math	140–144
"Challenge Me" Checklist	145–146
Your Past, Present, and Future Advocacy	163
Advocacy Focus Finder	164
SMART Advocacy Goal Worksheet	165
Professional Learning Opportunity Design Template	166
Sample Needs Assessment	167–168
Action Planning Template	169–170
"Advocate for Me" Checklist	171

Introduction

Late one afternoon several years ago, a teacher from a Title I school contacted our university office where we housed a summer program for more than two hundred gifted children in preK through grade 12. Earlier in the year, she had helped one of her students apply for the program, and we had awarded that student a full scholarship to attend. She was excited that her student would be able to participate, and she wanted to let us know how excited he was too. As she continued talking, she shared that she would be the one driving him to and from the program, about an hour each way. She said, "His mother doesn't drive, so he's actually never been outside the town he lives in." She asked what she should tell her student to pack for the dance on the program's final night: "Will the kids be dressed up? Should he bring his church clothes?" She concluded the conversation by telling us she had collected money for her student from the teachers at her school, since she didn't want him to feel left out if the other kids brought spending money for lunch and snacks.

This student was not the first or the last gifted student from an underresourced community we have worked with, but his story illustrates how educators so often go above and beyond to support their students. Most teachers lack the capacity to drive students to and from additional classes or to collect money for them, but this is one example of a teacher's steadfast commitment. There are countless other examples. The importance of caring and committed teachers who see the potential in their underserved gifted learners and who support them in fulfilling that potential cannot be overstated. Yet many of the teachers we've worked with over the years have had no training, either preservice or professional development, designed to help them recognize and develop the intellectual and creative strengths that exist in their diverse student populations. So even with the best intentions—which we believe all teachers have—the teachers had limited strategies for meeting gifted students' needs.

We wrote this book for you, the educators who wake up every day with your hearts and minds set on making a positive difference in your students' lives. And we wrote it for your students, who are counting on you never to stop seeing and believing in their potential.

A Call to Serve Underserved Gifted Learners

The term *underserved* is traditionally used in educational research to describe individuals from certain groups whose needs are not consistently met in K–12 schools. From our experience, underserved gifted students reflect the diversity of public school students: they are students from culturally and linguistically diverse (CLD) backgrounds, students who are English language learners (ELL), students from a range of socioeconomic backgrounds, and twice-exceptional (2e) students. This book's chapters are organized according to the four pillars of the Giftedness Knows No Boundaries campaign of the National Association for Gifted Children (NAGC): "See Me," "Understand Me," "Teach Me," and "Challenge Me," followed by a fifth chapter titled "Advocate for Me." One of the primary goals of the NAGC campaign is to bring awareness to the unique learning needs of gifted students.

Using the pillars of this campaign as a framework, the intent of this book is to promote equity and excellence in schools by giving you a variety of teaching tools. You can use these tools to recognize the potential and foster the academic, social, and emotional growth of the underserved gifted learners you care so deeply about. Although the primary focus of this book is gifted learners, the teaching and learning activities can be adapted easily for other learners in your classrooms and for any age group, ranging from kindergarten through high school.

As you read this book, we hope that you will begin or continue to:

- recognize the strengths of underserved gifted learners in your schools and classrooms
- become aware of your implicit bias and how it affects your teaching
- understand the academic, social, and emotional needs of your underserved gifted learners
- create a culturally responsive learning environment
- provide high-quality instruction that shows how much you care about your students' learning
- carry out challenging instruction to help your underserved gifted leaners soar
- advocate for your underserved gifted learners on a micro and macro scale

We hope this book inspires you to become a change agent for your underserved gifted learners. Meanwhile, we also hope this book fills your teaching toolkit with many new strategies that you can use right away to better meet the unique needs of all your students.

About This Book

Chapter 1: See Me focuses on the need to identify and cultivate *potential* (as opposed to developing talents). It provides proactive strategies to help you spot evidence of high potential in your students. It also confronts issues that hinder identification of underserved gifted learners and their access to gifted programming.

Chapter 2: Understand Me includes strategies to help you create a culturally responsive learning environment in which your underserved gifted learners can thrive. Creating such an environment begins with knowing and appreciating who your underserved gifted learners are and what they need to feel engaged and excited to learn. We also provide tips for involving both students and their families in the learning process.

In **Chapter 3: Teach Me,** you will find an abundance of strategies to support not only the learning of your underserved gifted students, but also the learning of *all* the students in your classroom. We use the acronym CARE to represent the strategies in this chapter. To recognize and develop our students' strengths, we must:

Connect learning to their lives

Ability group them in flexible ways

Respectfully differentiate their learning

Engage them in higher-level thinking activities

In **Chapter 4: Challenge Me,** we share toolkit strategies that focus on advanced learning options for underserved gifted learners. You will want to embed challenge thoughtfully into your students' learning experiences and provide supports to help them accomplish difficult tasks. We chose the acronym ASPIRE to sum up the strategies in this chapter, because we want underserved gifted learners to aspire to reach their fullest potential, and we want you to aspire to provide your students with learning experiences that help them shine their brightest. You can accomplish this goal when you:

Add challenge thoughtfully

Supply the support necessary for success

Provide opportunities for mentorships

Identify possibilities for independent investigations

Recognize when acceleration is vital

Embed curriculum compacting into learning units

In the final chapter, **Chapter 5: Advocate for Me,** we help you prepare to become a change agent for your underserved gifted learners. We provide toolkit strategies for advocacy at the micro and macro levels, including finding your advocacy focus, setting SMART goals (goals that are specific, measurable, attainable, relevant, and timebound), designing professional learning activities, and creating an action plan that incorporates the strategies from chapters 1 through 4 that you are most excited to try.

Throughout the book, you will find the following recurring elements:

Toolkit Strategies. You will find fifty strategies for promoting equity and excellence for underserved gifted learners throughout the five chapters of this book. Many of these strategies are best practice for working with gifted leaners. However, we have adapted some strategies and created new strategies to address the unique learning needs of underserved gifted learners.

Real-World Examples. In each chapter, we present real stories from our classroom experiences and from those of educators we have worked with through the years. The purpose of these snapshots is to give you practical, authentic ideas for applying many of the strategies you will find in each chapter.

Spotlights. Throughout this book, you will find several Spotlights written by educators who care deeply about underserved gifted learners. In these in-depth features, educators share insights from their personal experiences in supporting and advocating for underserved gifted learners.

What I Want You to Know About Me. Over the years, author Amy Graefe has asked her gifted students to write down what they want their teachers to know about them—beyond what their test scores and other data reveal. Amy has used these notes to get to know her students better and to personalize learning opportunities and supports for them. She has also shared these notes with the students' other teachers, so they, too, could understand and serve the students better. We've included quotes from Amy's students throughout this book, so you can hear from actual underserved gifted learners what they wish their teachers knew about them.

How to Use This Book

We created many of the strategies in this book from our own experiences as educators and researchers, with underserved gifted learners specifically in mind. We chose not to align specific strategies with specific groups of underserved learners, because that would be a nearly impossible task given the unique and diverse individual needs that exist within special populations of learners. Additionally, many strategies may benefit multiple populations of underserved gifted learners, so we don't want to limit your use of them. Although we wrote this book with underserved gifted learners in mind, we believe that *all* students need culturally responsive teaching and *all* students can benefit from gifted-education strategies. We also believe that at different points in time, *all* students require targeted supports to develop their potential. We believe that one-size-fits-all teaching is inappropriate for any student—and especially for underserved gifted learners, who come to school with diverse skill sets, ability levels, supports outside the classroom, and lived experiences that need to be honored in the classroom and school communities. Therefore, we've adapted many strategies that represent good teaching for all learners to make them even more beneficial for underserved gifted learners, in addition to creating new strategies with underserved gifted students specifically in mind.

We'd like you to begin reading this book with the goal of transforming learning experiences for *each and every* student in your classroom, focusing on how you can improve the education your underserved gifted students are currently receiving and will receive in the future. This focus will require you to pause and reflect constantly on current practices in your classroom and school. We do not want you to feel discouraged by what's not happening in your classroom and school, but rather to feel empowered by all the strategies in this book that you can use right away to improve the educational experiences of your underserved gifted learners.

We strongly recommend that you complete the reproducible checklist provided at the end of every chapter to help you identify your areas of strength in supporting underserved gifted learners and your areas for improvement. These checklists are based on the strategies presented in each chapter. They point you toward topics you might want to revisit in this book. Consider these checklists as progress checkups that tell you where you are in terms of applying the strategies in this book: beginning, developing, or leading.

You may choose to read this book from cover to cover, comprehensively learning ways to see, understand, teach, challenge, and advocate for underserved gifted learners. Or, you may choose to go straight to strategies that you feel could benefit your students right now. This book is designed to be read either way, and its strategies can be adapted easily for any grade level and subject area.

If you decide to pick and choose specific strategies, please be sure to visit chapter 5; we share concrete steps for turning the knowledge you've acquired from this book into an action plan you can carry out to make a positive impact on the lives of your underserved gifted learners. We believe that the pursuit of equity and excellence for underserved gifted learners requires a commitment not only to learning who these students are and how educators can best support them, but also to advocating on their behalf.

Although you can pick strategies to use depending on your classroom and school needs, please keep in mind that even if you were to implement all fifty strategies in this book, achieving equity and excellence for your underserved gifted students will be an ongoing journey. This book is a starting point for many of you and a midpoint for others, intended to provide you with information to consider and ideas to help your underserved gifted students realize and achieve their full potential.

We trust that you'll gain valuable insights from reading this book, and we hope you'll feel inspired to advocate for your underserved gifted learners like never before. Let's get started!

Jennifer Ritchotte
Chin-Wen Lee
Amy Graefe

1

SEE ME

*Every day in a hundred small ways our children ask,
"Do you see me? Do you hear me? Do I matter?"
Their behavior often reflects our response.*
—L. R. Knost

★★★★★

At some point in your career, you may have overheard statements similar to this one: "I've been teaching for many years. I know what I'm doing, and I treat all students equally. I don't know why we need to focus on diversity so much. I just don't get it." On the surface, the teacher who says this may seem to be doing the right thing by striving to teach all her students equally. However, the phrase *treat all students equally* implies that the teacher is giving all her students the exact same learning opportunities and supports. This approach runs counter to best practice in education.

Equity, not equality, needs to be the teacher's goal. Treating students equitably means providing all students with learning opportunities and supports according to their unique needs. Treating students equitably is the best way to ensure students have opportunities to demonstrate and cultivate their potential. Educating students in an equitable manner means that teachers must recognize and honor the diversity of their students. Teachers must make meaningful efforts to see who students are and what they are capable of contributing and achieving.

It takes courage to examine honestly what you believe about educating gifted students from underserved populations and to reflect on how your thinking and actions support or contradict these beliefs. Throughout this chapter, as you consider your beliefs, thoughts, and behaviors, you may feel uncomfortable at times, and *that is okay*. When it happens, stop and ask yourself this question: "What's best for my students?"

Let's begin our journey toward seeing underserved gifted learners more clearly.

Who Are Underserved Gifted Students?

What does it mean to be underserved, or underrepresented, in gifted education? Underserved gifted students are those whose needs are not being met in general education settings. Underrepresentation can be evaluated by examining the data on who is identified—and being served—as gifted in a given setting. For example, if most of the students at a school identify as Latinx, but most of the students receiving gifted or advanced academic programming are *not* Latinx, then Latinx students are underserved in that particular gifted-education program.

In this chapter, we talk specifically about four groups of students who often fall into the category of underserved gifted learners:

- students from culturally and linguistically diverse (CLD) backgrounds
- English language learners (ELL students)
- learners who are economically disadvantaged
- twice-exceptional (2e) learners (students who are both gifted and have one or more other special needs)

> **A Note About Gifted Students in Underresourced Rural and Urban Areas**
> Gifted students living in rural and urban areas do not fit into the underserved category by virtue of geographical location alone. It would be inaccurate to say that *all* gifted students attending schools in rural and urban areas are *underserved* by existing gifted programs and services in the same way that students from historically underserved populations are. The term underresourced is an important distinction to use when referring to these geographical areas, because many—but certainly not all—inner-city schools and rural schools are located in low-income areas lacking educational infrastructure, such as libraries, community centers, youth programs, and gifted services.
>
> Although we must be careful not to assume that all gifted students living in urban and rural areas are from CLD backgrounds, are ELL students, are economically disadvantaged, or are twice-exceptional, these underserved groups of students certainly do attend schools in these geographical regions. Further, due to limited resources and lack of teacher training in many of these districts, other students attending these underresourced schools also might not have the opportunity to be identified for gifted programming. Because of these overlapping challenges, the strategies in this book will prove useful to teachers in underresourced rural and urban schools too.

Culturally and Linguistically Diverse Learners

Culturally and linguistically diverse (CLD) learners are students growing up in households that differ in some way from the system-normed, white, middle-to-upper-class North American household. This group includes, but is not limited to, students whose cultural heritage is African, Hispanic, Asian, American Indian, Middle Eastern, Russian, or Alaska Native. It also includes students who are proficient in English but whose home language is not English.

According to a report from the National Center for Education Statistics (NCES), roughly 80 percent of public school teachers and administrators in the United States are white, while fewer than half of public school students are white (Snyder, de Brey, and Dillow 2019). In 2018, NCES projections for the 2018–2019 school year indicated that the 50.7 million public school students entering preK through grade 12 would include 26.6 million students of color: 14.0 million Hispanic students, 7.8 million black students, 2.6 million Asian students, 0.2 million Pacific Islander students, 0.5 million American Indian/Alaska Native students, and 1.6 million students of two or more races. Meanwhile, the percentage of white students enrolled in public schools was projected to continue declining through at least fall 2027 (National Center for Education Statistics 2018).

With changing demographic realities, it becomes increasingly important for educators to understand how their cultural experiences and backgrounds influence how they "see" their students. As Jean Sunde Peterson, professor emerita and former director of school counselor preparation at Purdue University, has pointed out, "The concept of giftedness appears to be bound to context. Each culture sees goodness through its own cultural lens, including the dominant culture, which has its own particular value orientation" (Peterson 1999). Various cultural groups often see giftedness through distinct lenses. White, middle-class teachers, who are heavily represented in K–12 classrooms, may place too much emphasis on IQ, achievement, intense interest in topics in the cultural mainstream, precocious verbal ability, and motivation when they are nominating students for gifted programming. However, the cultures of individual groups of underserved students may not value overt displays of ability, achievement, and talents; competing with peers; promoting individual accomplishments; or respectfully challenging authority figures and peers during learning opportunities. Rather, some cultural groups place more value on collaboration, listening, humility, selflessness, family support, and community service. Further, underserved students may not show interest in subject matter that teachers personally value as important, and as a result, these students unknowingly miss opportunities to demonstrate their capability to their teachers. It is only through assimilating to what the dominant culture values that many underserved students are eventually identified as gifted. Due to these realities, it is important to choose culturally sensitive and relevant options when assessing these students for gifted programming.

Pause and ask yourself these questions:

- Having learned (or been reminded) that giftedness may manifest differently in each culture, what have I observed about the way in which my CLD students express their learning?

- What difficulties might I encounter in evaluating my CLD students' strengths if they are hesitant to share their accomplishments, don't enjoy competing academically, or avoid disagreeing with others?

- In thinking about CLD students in my classroom, who has exhibited strengths in collaboration, listening, humility, selflessness, family support, and community service?

- If my CLD students had the opportunity to nominate themselves for accelerated or enrichment programs, what would they say their strengths were?

English Language Learners

For our purposes, English language learning (ELL) students are students whose lack of English proficiency could negatively affect their academics in some way. Perhaps the student doesn't speak English at all, or the student does speak English, but not at the level needed to succeed independently without support in the classroom. ELL students could be children born inside or outside the United States or Canada. They might speak fluently in Spanish, Mandarin, French, Russian, Arabic, or any other language that is not English. ELL students may also include Alaska Natives and American Indians.

English language learners deserve our attention for two important reasons:

1. This population is growing every year with an estimated 4.9 million students in total (National Center for Education Statistics 2019b).
2. Lack of English proficiency may create barriers to success for learners not only in school, but also in their social communities and other areas of their lives.

You may teach some ELL students who are able to communicate well in some instances. You might note that your ELL students can be kind, diligent, and helpful, especially since many of these students act as translators and become the primary source of communication between teachers and families. These qualities might cause some confusion when ELL students do not perform well academically. You might wonder, "How can such a competent child be doing so poorly in my class?"

Often, teachers mistakenly assume that because students can carry on a conversation in English, they should have no problem with English in an academic setting. It's important to understand that *social* language skills (basic interpersonal communication skills) are different from *academic* language skills (proficiency with language in intellectual contexts). Social language proficiency takes one to three years to develop, whereas academic language proficiency can take four to six years. Until gifted ELL students develop academic language mastery, they may struggle to perform at a level considered "proficient" on various academic activities and assessments—including gifted and talented assessments—that focus heavily on language.

Due to these challenges, it is important to incorporate nonverbal or performance-based options when assessing these students for gifted programming. While it may take time for ELL students to develop English proficiency, many gifted ELL students learn languages at an accelerated pace. This is a primary indicator of giftedness you may see in ELL students: children who are learning English (both social and academic) at a much faster rate than other ELL students. You may see gifted ELL students being very articulate during role-playing and storytelling activities; being able to understand jokes in English; or learning in both English and their first language. Pay attention to these clues. They will help you "see" your underserved gifted ELL students more clearly.

> **REAL-WORLD EXAMPLE**
>
> Maria was a sixth-grade ELL student who rarely asked questions and never seemed to need teacher assistance. This led her to "disappear" in most of her classes, except Ms. Nelson's science class. That year, Ms. Nelson decided to increase the challenge of her class by establishing a new grading system. In the new system, performing at an A level meant "exceeding grade-level expectations," performing at a B level meant "meeting grade-level expectations," performing at a C level meant "approaching grade-level expectations," and performing at a D or F level meant "not meeting grade-level expectations." Most students performed at a B level, because they chose not to push themselves to exceed sixth-grade science standards. Maria was one of three students in the class who consistently performed above grade-level expectations. Her writing used scientific language, she expanded on her ideas, and she learned new concepts quickly. This caught Ms. Nelson's attention early in the school year. Maria's performance was not typical compared to that of

her same-age peers, and definitely not typical of other ELL students Ms. Nelson had taught in the past.

Ms. Nelson thought that Maria might be gifted and asked the ELL teacher at her school, Mr. Ku, for more information. Mr. Ku said that when he had worked with Maria the first quarter, he'd noticed the same high level of aptitude and achievement. He had placed Maria in a sixth-grade advanced language arts class instead of the ELL classes she'd been assigned to at the beginning of the school year. Mr. Ku and Ms. Nelson saw potential and talent in Maria that had never been noticed in elementary school and might have continued to be unseen as Maria progressed through the school system, quiet and labeled as an ELL student.

—Contributed by Jaimarie Nelson, gifted and talented coach, Milliken Middle School, Milliken, Colorado. Used with permission.

Pause and ask yourself these questions:

- What are the languages spoken by the students and families at my school?
- Having learned (or been reminded) about the difference between social language and academic language, what difficulties might I find in evaluating ELL students using commonly held views of gifted traits and characteristics?
- What opportunities can I provide my ELL students to demonstrate their strengths?
- Which of my students in intensive ELL programs might be demonstrating gifted behaviors in some way even without academic English proficiency?

Who Are Long-Term English Language Learners?

Long-term English language learners are students who have not attained English language proficiency in K–12 schools after five years. As a result of struggling to attain English language proficiency, many long-term ELL students face postsecondary challenges, such as graduating from college. State and local educational agencies are putting in place initiatives to increase support for long-term ELL students in schools and to increase the number of students attaining English language proficiency within five years (US Department of Education 2016).

Economically Disadvantaged Learners

Consider the following economic data on children in the United States (Carson, Mattingly, and Schaefer 2017):

- Of all US children, 20.7 percent are living in poverty.
- Typically, black children experience the highest rates of poverty (36.5 percent), followed by Hispanic children (30.5 percent).
- Regionally, students living in urban areas experience the highest rates of poverty (27.2 percent), followed closely by students living in rural areas (24.3 percent).

Being economically disadvantaged contributes to physical and emotional stressors for students. Economically disadvantaged students may lack basic necessities like adequate food, housing, clothing, and supplies, and may also struggle with poor nutrition, poor health, lack of emotional support, and an unstable home environment. Eric Jensen, an internationally recognized expert on student poverty, cautions educators that economically disadvantaged students face multiple risk factors, which may result in chronic stress and place them at greater risk for academic failure (Jensen 2016).

Although economically disadvantaged gifted students may be able to use the positive attributes of their giftedness to help them overcome obstacles, these students still face significant challenges. Like other groups of underserved gifted learners, economically disadvantaged students may lack cultural capital, which hinders their ability to reach their full potential. In a school situation, having cultural capital may mean having parents who know who in the district to call to advocate for something the child needs. It may just mean having parents who know it's okay to contact someone to advocate for their child. Economically disadvantaged gifted students often face challenges such as limited exposure to career possibilities and fewer educational opportunities outside school. Even in the most supportive families, providing any type of additional academic support or enrichment that requires financial resources is often impossible. These challenges may directly affect the academic achievement of economically disadvantaged gifted students.

Nonverbal and performance-based options may prove helpful in identifying students from low-income households for gifted programming. Additionally, you may also consider the following research-based identification approaches: universal screening, local norming (such as by school, district, or county), early identification, multiple criteria, and portfolios of student accomplishments. Please keep in mind that gifted students from all underserved groups are likely to benefit from these research-based approaches to identification.

Pause and ask yourself these questions:

- What community resources are available to help students gain knowledge and support outside the school? Which of these resources do the families of my students use?

- How can I help provide resources that are not easily accessible to the families of my students?

- What school or community resources are available to assist families with basic necessities, health care, and emotional support?

- How have I observed economically disadvantaged students using their strengths to overcome challenges?

TOOLKIT STRATEGY

Breakfast with Stars
Teachers of underserved gifted learners need to make genuine efforts to get to know their students and their students' families well. Invite students, their families, and community members to breakfast at school. At the breakfast, you can present a talent show or other types of activities, such as project presentations or poetry readings, in which students have the opportunity to shine.

Twice-Exceptional (2e) Learners

Twice-exceptional (2e) learners are gifted students with one or more additional special needs. The National Twice-Exceptional Community of Practice (2e CoP) created the following definition (Baldwin et al. 2015):

> Twice-exceptional individuals evidence exceptional ability and disability, which results in a unique set of circumstances. Their exceptional ability may dominate, hiding their disability; their disability may dominate, hiding their exceptional ability; each may mask the other so that neither is recognized or addressed.
>
> 2e students, who may perform below, at, or above grade level, require the following:
>
> > Specialized methods of identification that consider the possible interaction of the exceptionalities
>
> > Enriched/advanced educational opportunities that develop the child's interests, gifts, and talents while also meeting the child's learning needs
>
> > Simultaneous supports that ensure the child's academic success and social-emotional well-being, such as accommodations, therapeutic interventions, and specialized instruction
>
> Working successfully with this unique population requires specialized academic training and ongoing professional development.

What does this mean? Basically, this definition means that it can be really difficult to identify students who are both gifted and have a disability. Sometimes these students' strengths are so significant that they hide the disability, so the students receive gifted-education services but not the appropriate special education services. Other times, the reverse is true: the disabilities are so distinct that they hide the giftedness, so the student receives special education services but not gifted-education services. In yet another scenario, a child's giftedness and disability balance each other, so the child looks like a typical student, and neither need gets addressed. Ideally, educators recognize and address both needs. The table in **figure 1-1** provides a visual of the aforementioned scenarios:

Figure 1-1 Masking in Twice-Exceptionality

GIFTEDNESS & **DISABILITIES** Characteristics in both areas are evident.	**GIFTEDNESS** & disabilities Gifted characteristics hide or compensate for disabilities.
giftedness & **DISABILITIES** Disabilities hide gifted characteristics.	giftedness & disabilities Neither gifted characteristics nor disabilities are evident or addressed.

Many twice-exceptional students may not be identified due to the masking phenomenon mentioned in the 2e CoP definition. The US Department of Education Office for Civil Rights reports that students with disabilities served under the

Individuals with Disabilities Education Act (IDEA) make up 2.7 percent of enrollment in gifted and talented programs nationwide. Given that students with identified disabilities represent approximately 14 percent of the entire student population in K–12 schools, their 2.7 percent share of gifted enrollment is low (National Center for Education Statistics 2019a; US Department of Education Office for Civil Rights 2018). This low percentage raises the concern that schools are not only failing to identify 2e students but also failing to meet their educational needs (Kena et al. 2015).

To see twice-exceptional learners in the classroom, teachers need to continue educating themselves and others in their schools and districts about the characteristics of these students and ways in which to meet their needs. Sometimes this might take the form of graduate-level coursework or professional learning opportunities. Other times, simple conversations between colleagues may be useful in identifying strengths of 2e students. A multidimensional approach to identification is critical for 2e students. Data need to be collected (beyond achievement and aptitude test scores) that demonstrate students' strengths. In addition to traditional identification measures, student products, behavior rating scales (completed by teachers and parents), classroom observations, and portfolios may help educators more clearly see a 2e student's gifted potential.

Pause and ask yourself these questions:

> Having learned (or been reminded) that 2e students may perform below, at, or above grade level, what difficulties might I find in evaluating 2e students using commonly held perceptions of giftedness?

> How many of my students in special education programs may be demonstrating gifted behaviors that their teachers are not seeing?

> How might I use available technology at my school to help my 2e students compensate for their learning difficulties?

Determining Underrepresentation

Now that you have a better understanding of who we are talking about when we say "underserved gifted learners," let's discuss how to determine whether certain groups of students truly are underrepresented in your school's gifted program. One common way of determining underrepresentation is to look at the percentage of a specific student population within the general student population and compare this to the percentage of that same specific student population within the gifted program. For example, if economically disadvantaged students make up 35 percent of a school's population, but they make up only 12 percent of the gifted-identified population, economically disadvantaged students would be considered underrepresented in the school's gifted-education program.

Sometimes when talking about students who have been historically underserved in gifted programs, people will use the term *minority*. You might hear a gifted-education coordinator say, "We'd like to do a better job of identifying and serving our minority students." However, the meaning of *minority* depends on the context in which it's used, so this word can be unclear or even inaccurate. Also, whether a particular "minority" is underserved depends on the group. For example, Asian and Pacific Islander Americans make up about 5 percent of the entire US student population, so they are considered a minority group (National Center for Education Statistics 2017). However, Asian Americans have been historically *over*represented in gifted programs. This means that *more* than 5 percent of gifted-identified students are Asian and Pacific Islander Americans. In other words, not all minority groups are underrepresented in gifted education. Gifted students who are underserved are those who are not equitably represented in gifted programming; they form a smaller percentage of the gifted-identified population than they form within the general population.

> **Diversity Within Cultural Groups**
> Of course, a great deal of diversity exists *within* cultural groups. For example, within the group Asian and Pacific Islander Americans, Asian Americans vastly outnumber Pacific Islanders; combining these subgroups hides that fact. Viewing Asian Americans as a homogeneous group is problematic, too, because East Asian Americans differ culturally and linguistically from South Asian Americans. Therefore, when examining potential underrepresentation, educators need to disaggregate data by subgroups.

So, what's a clear sign of underrepresentation that needs attention? Dr. Donna Ford, a prominent researcher in the field of gifted education and leading expert on multicultural gifted education, proposes using a 20 percent threshold to examine students' access to gifted-education programs (Ford 2014). For example, if Hispanic students compose 60 percent of a school district's student population, ideally Hispanic students should also compose 60 percent of the district's gifted population. But if it's not 60 percent, at the very least, Hispanic students should compose 48 percent of the gifted population (which is 20 percent smaller than 60 percent).

You can examine possible equity issues in your state and your school district by visiting the Civil Rights Data Collection website of the US Department of Education (ocrdata.ed.gov) and using the 20 percent threshold. Let's take two school districts for examples.

- The two largest student groups in a Kentucky school district are white students (48 percent of the student population) and black students (37 percent). Using the 20 percent threshold, the district's gifted program enrollment should include 38 to 48 percent white students (because 38 percent is roughly 20 percent less than 48 percent). The gifted program enrollment should include 30 to 37 percent black students (because 30 percent is roughly 20 percent less than 37 percent). The reported enrollment numbers for gifted programs in this district are 65 percent white (overrepresentation) and 20 percent black (underrepresentation).

- A Colorado school district's student population includes 21 percent white students and 58 percent Hispanic students. Using the 20 percent threshold, the gifted program enrollment should be 17 to 21 percent white students and 46 to 58 percent Hispanic students. The reported enrollment numbers for gifted programs in this district are 38 percent white (overrepresentation) and 43 percent Hispanic (underrepresentation).

An interactive map in *Education Week* shows the following data (Sparks and Harwin 2017):

- In California, the percentage of English language learners at schools that offer gifted education is 23 percent. The gifted enrollment should include at least 18 percent ELL students; however, the reported number is 8 percent.

> Nevada is another state that has a huge gap in meeting its equity goal. The percentage of English language learners at schools that provide gifted education is 15 percent. The gifted enrollment should include at least 12 percent ELL students, but the reported number is 3 percent.

You can also use the 20 percent threshold to examine the gifted enrollment of twice-exceptional students. The US Department of Education Office for Civil Rights reports that 12 percent of students in schools that offer gifted and talented programs are students with disabilities served by IDEA. However, students with disabilities make up less than 3 percent of gifted and talented enrollment. We have a long way to go before that number reaches what it should be: at least 10 percent (US Department of Education Office for Civil Rights 2018).

Underrepresentation of certain groups of students in gifted programming is a problem of equity that needs to be addressed. The "Speak Up" toolkit strategy below can help you better understand the issue of equity and give you more information to help you advocate for underserved gifted learners in your school and district.

TOOLKIT STRATEGY

Speak Up

1. Visit the US Department of Justice Case Summaries website: justice.gov/crt/case-summaries. These court cases are associated with educational opportunities and are sorted by protected class: disability (including special education), national origin (including English language learners), race, religion, and sex.
2. Search the text for the word *gifted*.
3. Review court cases in which underserved students have been denied access to gifted programs.
4. Share this information with your colleagues (classroom teachers, principal, or district or state leaders) and discuss the following questions:
   > What are the implications of these cases on practice?
   > What are the implications of these cases on policy?
   > How can we provide adequate access to students who are historically underserved in gifted and talented programs? (To help you answer this question, keep reading!)

Why Are Some Gifted Students Underserved?

So why does inequity exist in gifted education? Although educators and researchers have made great strides toward equity in K–12 gifted programming, much work remains to be done. Understanding the causes of inequity can help educators move toward equity. The following sections discuss factors that contribute to the underrepresentation of some students in gifted programming and strategies for addressing these factors:

- Giftedness may look different in underserved populations than it does in traditionally served student populations.
- Gifted learners from underserved groups face unique challenges in formal gifted assessment and identification.
- All educators have implicit biases that affect their ability to see all students clearly.

Giftedness May Look Different in Underserved Populations

Giftedness can be found in all student populations, including students with disabilities (twice-exceptional or 2e students) and students from all socioeconomic, ethnic, and cultural groups. In your own teaching experience, you may have noticed that giftedness can look different in underserved student populations than it does in traditionally served student populations.

> **REAL-WORLD EXAMPLE**
>
> Javier, a Latino student whose family recently immigrated to the United States, changed schools several times and was not formally identified as gifted in reading until eighth grade. His identification surprised his language arts teacher, because she felt his writing was average and filled with grammatical issues, and his discussion skills were poor. He would mutter short, nondescriptive responses to the questions she asked in class. She contended that even though Javier's aptitude and achievement test scores were in the 99th percentile, she just did not see him succeeding in an advanced language arts class. The school's part-time gifted coordinator continued to advocate for Javier, providing him and his teacher with extra support and resources throughout the school year. Once Javier caught up with his peers who had been in advanced language arts classes throughout middle school, his language arts teacher started to question not only her initial perception of Javier, but also what she thought she knew about giftedness in general.

When students do not show "typical" gifted characteristics, such as knowing and sharing all the answers to teachers' questions and completing work at a level that surpasses teachers' expectations, teachers and parents may not see them as gifted and may fail to nominate them for participation in gifted programs. This is what happened to eighth grader Javier in the Real-World Example. Likewise, a precocious fourth grader who has emotional outbursts in class, argues with her teacher, and runs out of the classroom when she is upset may never appear gifted to teachers who associate studiousness and compliance with giftedness. Educators' personal observations are subjective and prone to implicit bias. (See page 21 for more information on implicit bias.)

In addition, many checklists used in the nomination process pose barriers to gifted nomination of underserved students. For instance, Mikayla, an undergraduate student in a preservice teacher preparation program, shared this experience: "When I was in elementary school, my teacher gave me a nomination form for the gifted program to give to my mom. I was so excited—until I started reading the questions on the form: 'Does your child like to go to the museum? Does your child like to go on adventure trips? Does your child like to build or use technology programs?' We couldn't afford these things, and I thought this would embarrass my mother, so I threw the form in the trash and made up an excuse when my teacher asked about it."

Following is an abbreviated list of potential characteristics of underserved gifted learners. While it's rare for a gifted child to exhibit all these characteristics, the presence of any one of them could indicate giftedness and should be documented as evidence that might be used to support formal identification. At the very least, these characteristics may indicate the need for appropriately differentiated curriculum to challenge and build upon the child's strengths:

- is inquisitive, often asking unexpected or unconventional questions
- is observant
- expresses ideas well
- easily recalls information
- is interested in how things work
- likes novelty
- sees complex relationships and makes connections
- displays creativity in a variety of ways
- exhibits unique sense of humor
- has depth of knowledge about specific topic or has wide range of interests
- likes puzzles and games of strategy
- is persistent and determined when interested in an activity or a project
- is a good problem solver
- demonstrates leadership among peers and/or in community

It is important to understand that, even after a student is identified as gifted, the development of potential is an ongoing process. (This is true for all gifted learners.) For this process to work well—meaning that students are supported in developing toward their full potential—educators must really be able to see their underserved gifted learners. This means educators need to realize that each and every student has many facets—not only the academic facet, which is the one that's easiest to observe daily in the classroom, but also the cognitive, emotional, social, and physical facets. When teachers address a student's strengths and needs in *all* these domains, they are supporting the whole child. Awareness of and responsiveness to the strengths and needs of the whole child helps establish an equitable classroom.

According to Dr. George Betts, professor emeritus at the University of Northern Colorado and former president of the National Association for Gifted Children (NAGC), it is important for teachers to support the development of the whole gifted child. To reach their full potential, gifted learners need to learn to embrace a strong sense of self, develop a love of lifelong learning, and find a purpose that ties to their strengths and passions. They also need to develop unconditional positive regard toward themselves and others and learn to work collaboratively toward goals that have personal meaning, as well as those that have the potential to make the world a better place (Betts 2016).

> **TOOLKIT STRATEGY**
>
> **What I Want You to Know About Me**
> Ask your students what they want you to know about them that you wouldn't necessarily know from looking at their test scores or from having them in class every day. You'll be surprised by the thoughtful, insightful information they will share with you. This request will help you see your students much better.

Identification Issues

In addition to not showing characteristics of giftedness that educators might expect, gifted learners from underserved groups may face some unique challenges when it comes to formal gifted identification. Often, educator misconceptions about how giftedness manifests itself leads to under-identification. For example, high IQ scores and high achievement scores are well-known indicators of giftedness, but these are certainly not the only indicators. For many students from underserved populations, neither type of score is the primary indicator, especially when students have not had opportunities for a wide range of early academic and enrichment experiences.

> ★ ★ ★ **What I Want You to Know About Me**
> "I want to be encouraged to reach my potential, because I sometimes don't see it."

What is more, underserved gifted learners often have strengths in areas that the educational system doesn't fully value or even recognize as potential signs of giftedness, such as excellent visual-spatial thinking skills. (For help spotting these signs, see the toolkit strategy "Talent Hunt Inventory.") To make things even more complicated, when such strengths *are* recognized and valued, it is often difficult to measure these strengths. It's fairly simple to analyze IQ test scores. It's clear when a student scores in the most advanced category on a year-end state assessment. However, it is much more difficult to measure, for example, how well a child intuitively understands how things work. Because we don't have great tests to tell us definitively whether a child is gifted in certain ways, we must find other methods to uncover underserved gifted learners' strengths and identify them for appropriate programming.

> **TOOLKIT STRATEGY**
>
> **Talent Hunt Inventory**
> To use this inventory, you'll begin with the left column. With a particular student in mind, read through the characteristics and behaviors listed. Then compare the student's characteristics and behaviors, one at a time, with those of their peers. Use the blank rows to add characteristics or behaviors you've noticed in your student that are not listed in the inventory. It is always helpful to write down specific examples when doing the comparison, since these clarify your ratings. The following example shows responses from a social studies teacher at the secondary level. At the elementary level, one teacher could respond to multiple content areas. You'll find a reproducible version of this form on pages 27–28.

Figure 1-2 Sample Talent Hunt Inventory

Talent Hunt Inventory

To use this inventory, begin with the left column. With a particular student in mind, read through the characteristics and behaviors listed. Then compare the student's characteristics and behaviors, one at a time, with those of their peers. Use the blank rows to add characteristics or behaviors you've noticed in your student that are not listed in the inventory. It is always helpful to write down specific examples when doing the comparison to clarify your ratings.

Student: Mike Date: September 15, 2021
Observer: Ms. Garces Relationship to student: social studies teacher

	Not Presently	Emerging	Exceptional (compared with peers)	Examples (especially for Exceptional rating)
1. Is inquisitive, often asking unexpected or unconventional questions			X	He wants to understand the "why" behind every historical event.
2. Is observant		X		
3. Expresses ideas well			X	Both verbally and in writing.
4. Recalls information easily			X	Particularly in American history.
5. Is interested in how things work		X		
6. Likes novelty		X		He loves to explore new ideas/concepts but seems much more grounded when his schedule follows a regular routine.
7. Sees complex relationships and makes connections			X	Regularly connects topics and concepts from American history to sociological theories and to current events.
8. Shows creativity in a variety of ways		X		

Talent Hunt Inventory continued

	Not Presently	Emerging	Exceptional (compared with peers)	Examples (especially for Exceptional rating)
9. Displays a unique sense of humor	X			
10. Has depth of knowledge about a specific topic or has a wide range of interests			X	Depth of knowledge regarding history, sociology, current events (see note on #7).
11. Likes puzzles and games of strategy				I don't feel like I have enough information to answer this one.
12. Is persistent and determined when interested in an activity or a project			X	Spent many more hours than anyone else in the class on his History Day project. Took second place at state competition.
13. Is a good problem solver		X		
14. Demonstrates leadership among peers and/or in the community		X		Is good at leading discussions in class but don't see evidence of this elsewhere.
15. Has excellent visual-spatial skills	X			I haven't observed this in my class (but I also haven't observed that he has poor visual-spatial skills).
16.				
17.				
18.				

Tips:
- Provide as many specific examples as possible.
- Invite your colleagues on a talent hunt! Other teachers may have observations that differ from your observations of the same student.

REAL-WORLD EXAMPLE

Sydney was a nine-year-old fourth grader. Based on testing done outside school, Sydney was diagnosed with inattentive attention deficit hyperactivity disorder (ADHD). Her doctor told her parents that despite this diagnosis, Sydney was "highly creative, with an advanced intellect." A different doctor had previously diagnosed Sydney with a delay in processing information into a written format. Her teachers explained to her parents that her verbal answers to questions were extraordinary, but she struggled to put them into writing. Sydney's strengths lay in verbal expression and music. Her music teacher mentioned to Sydney and her parents how impressed she was by Sydney's ability to play music by ear (without seeing the notes). Sydney was not receiving any gifted and talented services because her Cognitive Abilities Test (CogAT) scores did not meet her school district's cutoff. Unfortunately, the school district relied only on the CogAT for gifted identification.

—Contributed by Amber Morman-Burke, teacher at Tully Elementary, Louisville, Kentucky. Used with permission.

Do you have students like Sydney who have been denied advanced learning opportunities due to restrictive identification criteria? In the following toolkit strategy "Identification Plan Investigation" on page 20 you will find key issues hampering gifted identification of underserved students and the best practices that address these issues. Educators need to honestly examine the identification practices in their schools and districts. Next, educators need to determine if, when, and how consistently their schools and districts are using best practices to identify underrepresented students for gifted programming. To identify strengths and areas for growth in the current identification procedures used by your school or district, complete the Best Practices in Identification Checklist on pages 29–30 at the end of this chapter.

TOOLKIT STRATEGY

Identification Plan Investigation

Identification Issue	Best Practice
Misconceptions about giftedness hamper referrals and nominations for gifted identification in underserved populations. These misconceptions include: › low academic expectations for students from underserved populations › expectation of fully developed talent rather than recognition of potential	Teachers, administrators, and families regularly receive information about all the various potential characteristics and behaviors of gifted students, including how these characteristics and behaviors may differ in underserved populations. Districts and schools offer universal screenings that give all students at a particular grade level the opportunity for an initial gifted assessment.
Districts and schools use narrow definitions of giftedness (for example, only high IQ) or a single assessment (for example, only a cognitive score) to identify students for gifted programming.	Gifted-education teams use a holistic approach to identification, incorporating multiple measures that are culturally sensitive and relevant. This approach could include rating scales from teachers, family members, and community members; performance evaluations; and nonverbal assessments. Schools work with a statistician to develop current local norms for gifted assessments and rating scales. Gifted identification and services for underserved populations are then based on these local norms rather than national norms.
Districts and schools use cutoff scores (or minimum scores) to eliminate students from gifted identification and/or programming.	Gifted-education teams collect a body of evidence that represents many aspects of the learner. They do not eliminate students from the gifted-identification process simply because students do not achieve a certain score on a single assessment, if other measures indicate giftedness. When possible and appropriate, the school or district provides gifted programming to students who show particular strengths in certain areas and who could benefit from services, even if they have not been formally identified as gifted. (For example, a child who scores in the advanced category in mathematics on a state assessment may benefit from gifted

	mathematics programming even if there is not enough evidence to formally identify that child as gifted.)
Students get one opportunity in their entire K–12 schooling to qualify for gifted programming.	Districts and schools provide a universal screening at the elementary level and another one at the middle school level.
	Districts and schools continue to accept referrals for gifted identification and programming through high school.
	Districts and schools continue to monitor and collect a body of evidence for students who scored well on the universal screening or who were nominated for gifted identification, even if they did not qualify initially. Districts and schools assess students for formal identification multiple times if the body of evidence supports this.
As a result of low academic expectations, classroom curriculum and instruction does not develop potential and therefore does not put students in a position to be formally identified for gifted programming.	Districts and schools provide all students from an early age with academic and enrichment experiences that broaden background knowledge.
	Districts and schools offer all students appropriately challenging curriculum.
	Districts and schools provide additional supports for students who are motivated to succeed in advanced academic programming but have not yet developed all the necessary foundational skills.

Implicit Bias

Implicit bias in educators is perhaps the most important factor contributing to inequity in gifted education. While underserved gifted students may not appear gifted in ways you might expect and their talents can be more difficult to measure and identify, often these students belong to groups that many people are biased against, either explicitly or implicitly. Explicit bias is conscious and deliberate. For example, a high school AP civics teacher may consciously believe that his black students are less capable than his white students. Implicit bias, on the other hand, consists of unconsciously held attitudes that people may not realize exist in their minds or manifest through their actions. Implicit bias is more challenging to understand yet is equally harmful to students. Two examples of implicit bias follow. In the first example, Ms. Thompson catches herself in an implicit bias. In the second, Mr. Hawes does not realize he has an implicit bias.

> **REAL-WORLD EXAMPLE**
>
> Ms. Thompson was white. She grew up in an upper-middle-class suburb and attended affluent schools with little diversity. She eventually became a high school gifted coordinator, providing instruction in a school with a large population of students who received free and reduced lunch. At first, she mused, "These poor kids have so much to worry about outside school that academics are probably not a big priority for them. Wouldn't being in a gifted program only add to their stress?" After saying this in her head, she immediately stopped herself and felt terrible. She wondered if thoughts like this had ever led her to be unfair toward her economically disadvantaged students. She decided to make a concerted effort to learn more about her students as individuals so she could really see their potential and not just their life circumstances.

> **REAL-WORLD EXAMPLE**
>
> Keisha, a talented black student in Mr. Hawes's fifth-grade class, was constantly getting sent to the principal's office, bumped to other classrooms, or given disciplinary referrals for her "disrespect" and "rudeness." Frustrated, Mr. Hawes, who is white, exclaimed to the principal and other teachers that Keisha's parents couldn't care less about her loud, disruptive behavior in class; they didn't even pick up the phone when he called. He felt that while he was trying to "save" Keisha from going down a "bad path" in middle school like "most of the girls like her" that he'd taught, her parents were enabling her.
>
> When Mr. Hawes wouldn't call on Keisha to share her creative ideas during discussions or when he cut her off in the middle of sharing and told her to "calm down," she felt invalidated and spoke even louder, voicing her opinions more passionately. She knew Mr. Hawes would just end up disciplining her, as he did every week, but she refused to back down. She continued to advocate for herself—in what Mr. Hawes believed was a socially unacceptable manner. Mr. Hawes never stopped to reflect on his implicit bias. Reflection might have helped him realize that he had mistaken Keisha's passion and sense of justice for rudeness and disrespect, based on past experiences he'd had and assumptions that he'd made.

First, it's important to understand that everyone has implicit biases and that having them does not mean you outwardly resent particular groups of people. What it does mean is that at some point in your life, you unconsciously developed stereotypes about particular groups of people, and those stereotypes are so deeply ingrained in your mind that you may act on them without even realizing it. Ms. Thompson, for example, at some point in her life—whether through messages in movies, conversations overheard as a child, or early personal experiences—began to unintentionally (and incorrectly) believe that economically disadvantaged people did not value education. This led her to dissociate poverty and academics when she became a teacher, without even realizing she was doing it.

> TOOLKIT STRATEGY
>
> ## Understanding How Implicit Bias Works
> To help you more fully understand how implicit biases work, try the following exercise. What is the first thing you think of when someone says the following phrases?
>
> - *peanut butter and . . .*
> - *bread and . . .*
> - *stars and . . .*
> - *peas and . . .*
> - *hot and . . .*
> - *salt and . . .*
>
> While these responses may vary depending on past experiences, for many people who grew up in the United States, their immediate responses would be *jelly*, *butter*, *stripes*, *carrots*, *cold*, and *pepper*. These associations are so culturally ingrained for many Americans that it takes no thought at all to come up with the "correct" answers. (If people pause to think for a moment, though, they could come up with other answers, such as *peanut butter and bananas*.) This is similar to the way implicit bias associations, or stereotypes, work.

Implicit bias consists of unconscious attitudes, associations, and beliefs or unconscious stereotypes that cause you to react either positively or negatively toward a person who is a member of a particular social group. These unconscious biases may differ from what you *consciously* believe and profess. Implicit bias may affect the way in which you see or don't see underserved gifted learners. The good news is that you can work to overcome and minimize the impact of your implicit biases—just as you can come up with alternate word pairs in the toolkit strategy above if you pause to think about it, and just as Ms. Thompson was able to shift her train of thought. Overcoming bias is a long process, but it is necessary to break down barriers to the identification of underserved gifted learners. Beginning somewhere, even with a simple word-association activity, is an important first step. To reflect further on your potential unconscious biases, fill out the reproducible "See Me" Checklist for Inclusive Identification on page 31.

> TOOLKIT STRATEGY
>
> ## Learning More About Myself and Implicit Bias
> A simple audit of your social media accounts and an online test may reveal hidden biases.
>
> ### SOCIAL MEDIA AUDIT
> 1. Look through all your social media accounts. Who are your friends? Who do you follow? Make a list of names of the top twenty most frequent interactions on each of your social media accounts.

2. Do you see any patterns in the type of people you most often interact with on social media?

3. Reflect on possible reasons for these results. Might they reflect biases for or against certain groups of people?

IMPLICIT ASSOCIATION TEST
Researchers from the University of Washington, the University of Virginia, and Harvard University have developed an Implicit Association Test to help individuals uncover potential hidden biases they may have. You can take this test by visiting their Project Implicit website: implicit.harvard.edu/implicit. You'll receive an individualized report based on your results. Reflect on the purpose of the test, your results, and why you might have scored the way you did.

TOOLKIT STRATEGY

Learning More About My Classroom and Implicit Bias
POTENTIAL BIAS RECOGNITION
It can be hard—even painful—to acknowledge biases you may have about your own students. The purpose of this activity is not to make you feel bad. Rather, its purpose is to help you become more aware of your biases to ensure you are educating your students in the fairest possible manner.

1. Write down the name of the student who immediately pops into your mind for each descriptor in the following list. Remember that your answers aren't good or bad or right or wrong. This is just an exercise to help you identify potential biases, so try not to filter your responses.

    a. most dependable

    b. most likely to forget homework

    c. most creative

    d. most charismatic

    e. most brilliant

    f. most neat, clean, and ready for learning

    g. best sense of humor

    h. best leadership skills

    i. best attitude

    j. most respectful

    k. most likely to be referred for a discipline issue

    l. most likely to attend a top college in the future

2. Write down the following for each student named above, if you know these details:

    a. gender

    b. socioeconomic status

c. job(s) of parent(s) or guardian(s)
   d. racial or ethnic background
   e. disability or special needs
   f. English language proficiency

3. Reflect on whether your responses to step 1 show a pattern based on the students' gender, socioeconomic status, parents' or guardians' jobs, race or ethnicity, disability or special needs, English language proficiency, or any other characteristics.

4. Note the student whose name popped into your mind for the negative descriptor in step 1 ("most likely to be referred for a discipline issue"). Reflect on one positive trait or strength this student has to help you see the student more clearly.

5. Reflect on one or more of your students who may not have come to mind immediately for several of the positive traits. What might you do to see these traits in them and to offer these students opportunities to shine?

PEER OBSERVATION: LEVEL ONE

Your peers may be able to give you valuable insights into your teaching practices. Use this activity to cultivate your awareness of how you interact with students.

1. Ask a trusted peer to observe a discussion in your class and tally who you call on most often. (Try to do what comes naturally.)

2. Reflect on the tally. Did you call on a certain gender most often? Did you call on more extroverted students than quiet ones? Did you call on students from a particular racial background or culture more often than other students? Did you call most often on students at the front or back of the room or at the right side or left side of the room?

3. If you notice any inequitable patterns, reflect on how you might address these inequities consciously during your next class discussion.

PEER OBSERVATION: LEVEL TWO

1. Ask a trusted peer to observe a discussion in your class and tally the complexity level of questions you ask of specific students (using Bloom's Revised Taxonomy or another taxonomy with which you and your peer are both familiar).

2. Reflect on the tally. Which students were asked more complex, higher-level questions?

3. If you notice any inequitable patterns, reflect on what you can do to question students more equitably during class discussions.

Implicit bias exists in people unconsciously and can be detrimental to students and society. The good news is that you can become more cognizant of your own unintentional biases by constantly reflecting on your personal beliefs and the interactions you have with your students from marginalized populations. We strongly encourage you to keep returning to the activities in this section and checking your progress in this area. Acknowledging that you have biases and holding yourself accountable may be challenging and uncomfortable at times; however, doing so is necessary to identify and break down barriers to equity for your underserved gifted learners.

Chapter Summary

Taking steps toward achieving equity for underrepresented gifted learners, whether it be in your classroom, school, or district, deserves your best effort. Seeing your underserved students' unique characteristics and understanding how your beliefs and values, as well as those held by other educators and staff, may serve as barriers to equity, are necessary first steps to cultivating your students' gifts and talents. The strategies in this chapter will help you examine your implicit biases, recognize potential indicators of giftedness, and understand best practices for identifying giftedness in diverse student populations. These strategies are intended to help you see giftedness where you or others may have failed to see it in the past. Using them will help you ensure that your underserved gifted learners get the opportunities they deserve to maximize their learning potential.

★ ★ ★ ★ ★

Talent Hunt Inventory

To use this inventory, begin with the left column. With a particular student in mind, read through the characteristics and behaviors listed. Then compare the student's characteristics and behaviors, one at a time, with those of their peers. Use the blank rows to add characteristics or behaviors you've noticed in your student that are not listed in the inventory. It is always helpful to write down specific examples when doing the comparison to clarify your ratings.

Student: _____ Date: _____

Observer: _____ Relationship to student: _____

	Not Presently	Emerging	Exceptional (compared with peers)	Examples (especially for Exceptional rating)
1. Is inquisitive, often asking unexpected or unconventional questions				
2. Is observant				
3. Expresses ideas well				
4. Recalls information easily				
5. Is interested in how things work				
6. Likes novelty				
7. Sees complex relationships and makes connections				
8. Shows creativity in a variety of ways				

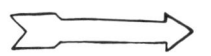

From *Start Seeing and Serving Underserved Gifted Students: 50 Strategies for Equity and Excellence* by Jennifer A. Ritchotte, Ph.D., Chin-Wen Lee, Ph.D., and Amy K. Graefe, Ph.D., copyright © 2020. This page may be reproduced for individual, classroom, or small group work only. For all other uses, contact Free Spirit Publishing Inc. at freespirit.com/permissions.

Talent Hunt Inventory continued

	Not Presently	Emerging	Exceptional (compared with peers)	Examples (especially for Exceptional rating)
9. Displays a unique sense of humor				
10. Has depth of knowledge about a specific topic or has a wide range of interests				
11. Likes puzzles and games of strategy				
12. Is persistent and determined when interested in an activity or a project				
13. Is a good problem solver				
14. Demonstrates leadership among peers and/or in the community				
15. Has excellent visual-spatial skills				
16.				
17.				
18.				

Tips:

- Provide as many specific examples as possible.
- Invite your colleagues on a talent hunt. Other teachers may have observations that differ from your observations of the same student.

Best Practices in Identification Checklist

Take a look at your school's or district's gifted-identification practices and note strengths and areas for improvement.

Best Practice	Strengths	Areas for Improvement
Teachers, administrators, and families regularly receive information about the potential characteristics and behaviors of gifted students, including how these characteristics and behaviors may differ in underserved populations.		
The district or school offers universal screenings that provide all students at a particular grade level the opportunity for an initial gifted assessment.		
Gifted-education teams use a holistic approach to identification, incorporating multiple measures that are culturally sensitive and relevant. This approach could include rating scales from teachers, family members, and community members; performance evaluations; and nonverbal assessments.		
Gifted-education teams collect a body of evidence that represents many aspects of the learner. Students are not eliminated from the gifted-identification process simply because they do not achieve a certain score on a single assessment, if other measures indicate giftedness.		
When possible and appropriate, the school or district provides gifted programming to students who show particular strengths in certain areas and who could benefit from services, even if they have not been formally identified as gifted. (For example, a child who scores in the advanced category in mathematics on a state assessment may benefit from gifted mathematics programming even if there is not enough evidence to formally identify that child as gifted.)		

From *Start Seeing and Serving Underserved Gifted Students: 50 Strategies for Equity and Excellence* by Jennifer A. Ritchotte, Ph.D., Chin-Wen Lee, Ph.D., and Amy K. Graefe, Ph.D., copyright © 2020. This page may be reproduced for individual, classroom, or small group work only. For all other uses, contact Free Spirit Publishing Inc. at freespirit.com/permissions.

Best Practices in Investigation Checklist continued

Best Practice	Strengths	Areas for Improvement
The district or school provides a universal screening at the elementary level and another one at the middle school level.		
The district or school continues to accept referrals for gifted identification and programming through high school.		
The district or school continues to monitor and collect a body of evidence for students who scored well on the universal screening or who were nominated for gifted identification, even if they did not qualify initially. The district or school assesses students for formal identification multiple times if the body of evidence supports this.		
The district or school provides all students from an early age with academic and enrichment experiences that broaden background knowledge.		
The district or school offers all students appropriately challenging curriculum.		
The district or school provides additional supports for students who are motivated to succeed in advanced academic programming but have not yet developed all the necessary foundational skills.		

Note: Identification and programming must go together. The NAGC suggests that the identification process and the assessments used must align with the program's definition of giftedness.

From *Start Seeing and Servving Underserved Gifted Students: 50 Strategies for Equity and Excellence* by Jennifer A. Ritchotte, Ph.D., Chin-Wen Lee, Ph.D., and Amy K. Graefe, Ph.D., copyright © 2020. This page may be reproduced for individual, classroom, or small group work only. For all other uses, contact Free Spirit Publishing Inc. at freespirit.com/permissions.

"See Me" Checklist for Inclusive Identification

Use this checklist to reflect on your implicit biases and inclusive identification practices. Review your results to become more aware of your areas of strength and your areas for growth.

Key:
Beginning: You're aware and want to try.
Developing: You have tried or are trying.
Leading: You are consistently aware, implementing changes, and making others aware.

Implicit Bias Awareness	**Beginning**	**Developing**	**Leading**
I acknowledge that implicit biases are learned and that they affect my interactions with students.			
I acknowledge that everyone has implicit biases and that mine may be opposite of my conscious beliefs.			
I recognize that implicit bias may influence the academic expectations I hold for my students.			
I carefully process situations in the classroom before reacting to them to minimize the impact of my implicit biases.			
I regularly examine my curriculum to determine if it might be reinforcing inaccurate stereotypes or misconceptions about certain groups of students.			
I regularly reflect on what my implicit biases might be and the ways my implicit biases manifest in my classroom.			

Inclusive Identification Practice	**Beginning**	**Developing**	**Leading**
I consistently use multiple criteria to nominate or identify students for gifted programming.			
I teach others in my school about how giftedness may look in underserved populations.			
I share with students, families, and community members how giftedness may look in underserved populations.			
I encourage family and community members to partner in the process of nominating students for gifted identification and programming.			
I periodically ask about the identification process to ensure it reflects best practices in the field.			

From *Start Seeing and Serving Underserved Gifted Students: 50 Strategies for Equity and Excellence* by Jennifer A. Ritchotte, Ph.D., Chin-Wen Lee, Ph.D., and Amy K. Graefe, Ph.D., copyright © 2020. This page may be reproduced for individual, classroom, or small group work only. For all other uses, contact Free Spirit Publishing Inc. at freespirit.com/permissions.

2 UNDERSTAND ME

Every child deserves a champion—an adult who will never give up on them, who understands the power of connection, and insists that they become the best that they can possibly be.
—Rita F. Pierson

★★★★★

Seeing underserved gifted students is an important first step. Once we become aware of who these students are in our classrooms and schools, we then need to work toward *understanding* their unique learning needs. We must know and appreciate who our students are academically, culturally, socially, and emotionally.

Creating a Culturally Responsive Classroom

It is critical that underserved gifted students perceive they are valued and respected in their learning environment. Educators need to establish a safe space where teaching is student-centered, where there are high expectations of success for *all* students, and where the strengths of everyone involved in the educational process (students, teachers, families, and administrators) are recognized, appreciated, and utilized. This type of positive and respectful learning environment is often called a "culturally responsive classroom."

A culturally responsive classroom is one in which the teacher strives to create connections by focusing on the similarities among students, while also recognizing, valuing, and honoring their inherent diversity—including family history and traditions, cultural background, and home language. In a culturally responsive classroom, the teacher models and encourages respect for and collaboration with others and shows an openness to learning about and from students and their families. References and connections to students' backgrounds, lives, and cultures are evident in the classroom and are seamlessly interwoven into the curriculum.

You will recognize a culturally responsive classroom because its students are engaged. Isn't that what all educators want—to have students who are actively involved in their own learning, who are growing academically and socially, and who are happy to be part of the classroom community? To engage students, educators need to find ways to tap into students' internal motivation. You can start by embedding opportunities in your classrooms for students to connect meaningfully with their learning environment.

> ★★★ **What I Want You to Know About Me**
> "I'm quiet when I don't know or when I just don't want to speak out, so sometimes it seems that I don't know. Also, I'm sometimes shy to ask for help, but I will try and find help because I don't like not knowing."

Building Meaningful Connections

For educators, creating meaningful connections with all students is critical. You need to take special steps to know your underserved gifted students and to develop positive relationships with them. Positive student-teacher relationships strongly support increased academic and emotional growth for underserved students (Ritchotte and Graefe 2017). Getting-to-know-you worksheets, posters, and writing prompts are staples in most classrooms at the beginning of the school year. These activities often elicit only basic information about students, such as their favorite color, sport, hobby, or school subject. In the first four toolkit strategies that follow, you'll find activities to help you learn more about your students, so you can start building the relationships needed for success. The "What I Want You to Know About Me" toolkit strategy introduced in chapter 1 (see page 18) is also great for better understanding your gifted students.

To lay the groundwork for establishing deep, meaningful connections with underserved students, consider using a memory timeline like the sample shown in the "My Memory Timeline" toolkit strategy. (You'll find a reproducible version of this timeline on page 47.)

TOOLKIT STRATEGY

My Memory Timeline

This timeline activity gives your students an opportunity to share important moments in their lives, both in and out of school, that they believe have shaped who they are, while offering you rich information that will help you understand and connect with your students. Students may complete the timeline at home with family support, or you may choose to have parents and guardians complete a separate timeline about their child to capture various perspectives. You could revisit the timeline throughout the school year to give students opportunities to add to it.

Please be mindful that this activity may lead to sensitive revelations. If you choose to have students present their timelines to the class, let them know that they may share only what they feel comfortable sharing. For example, students may choose to share only one or two timeline moments with their classmates. Encourage students who feel comfortable sharing with the class to explain how each moment they listed has influenced who they have become. This will give you an even deeper look into the lives of your students and show them that you genuinely want to understand all the facets of their identity beyond just academics.

Figure 2-1 My Memory Timeline Sample

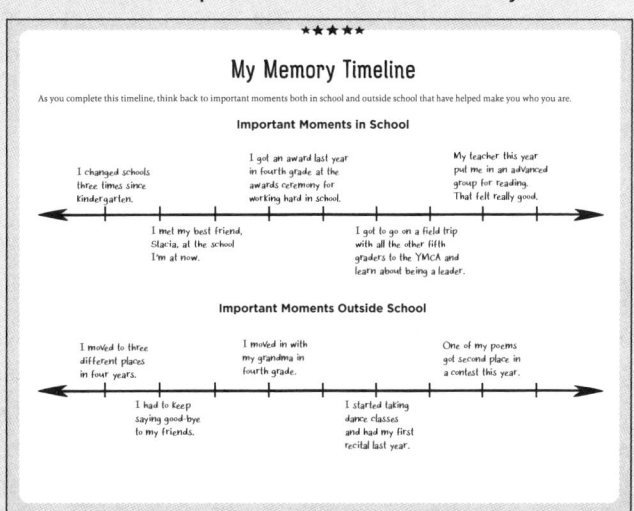

In addition to asking students to reflect on important moments, you can develop personal connections with your students by offering them opportunities to showcase their strengths, passions, goals, and diverse backgrounds through an activity like the "Talent Tree" toolkit strategy. (You'll find a reproducible version of the "Talent Tree" on page 48.)

TOOLKIT STRATEGY

Talent Tree

The "Talent Tree" encourages students to reflect positively on environmental factors like culture, family, friends, and community that give them strength (the roots); their individual strengths, talents, and gifts that make up the core of who they are (the trunk); the goals they aspire to reach (the branches); and their interests and passions that may continue to grow or change over time (the leaves). This activity's focus on strengths reinforces a positive self-concept and builds classroom community through honoring every student's uniqueness and potential for excellence.

Figure 2-2 Sample Talent Tree

Building respectful, meaningful relationships between school and home is critical. Understanding your students' home lives will help you understand students' in-school behaviors and what they need to succeed in school. Just as you must strive to validate the strengths of your underserved gifted learners, you must also focus on family strengths. Family is anyone who plays a significant role in a student's life outside school. Family could include aunts, uncles, grandparents, cousins, and so forth. What's most important is not formally defining the word *family* but understanding the outside influences on each student's life and figuring out who you can partner with to best support the child.

TOOLKIT STRATEGY

Family Identity Survey

You can use the reproducible "Family Identity Survey" on pages 49–50 to better understand a student's home life. You can interview family members in person or send home the survey and follow up with a phone conversation. You could also have the survey translated into languages used by your students at home if needed. The goal of the survey is to acquire a deep and respectful understanding of a student's home life that centers on strengths instead of deficits, and to open the lines of communication between home and school in a positive, constructive manner.

SPOTLIGHT

I worked in a district with lots of diversity and over 60 percent of students on free and reduced lunches. As a gifted-education specialist, it was important to me to get to know the families of my underserved gifted learners. I used recipe cards as a first contact with parents or grandparents at back-to-school night or during the first open house of the year. Recipe cards are an informal, familiar, almost neighborly way to learn more about another person. I recognized that only the families really knew what "ingredients" made up their child, and they're also the ones who knew which ingredients were key, which were secondary, and which really added the flavor!

The format of the recipe card was not intimidating or overwhelming—it was quick and fun. And it assumed the parents or other family members had something positive to share about their child. It was a great way for me to begin to connect with both my underserved gifted learners and their families.

—*Contributed by Therese Gilbert, veteran teacher and former gifted education specialist in Greeley-Evans Schools, Colorado. Used with permission.*

TOOLKIT STRATEGY

Recipe for Success

This is a great way to get important information about your gifted students and connect with your families. Ideally, at a school event early in the year, you would hand the recipe card to family members and have them fill it out so you could have a brief conversation immediately. Another option is to mail (or email) the card to families and ask them to bring it to a school event. If they cannot attend, they can mail (or email) the card back to you. (You'll find a reproducible version of this recipe-style questionnaire on page 51.)

Figure 2-3 Recipe for Success Sample Card

SPOTLIGHT

Each year, Denver Public Schools (DPS) grows closer to its goal of equitably serving gifted students from all racial backgrounds and helping families of underserved gifted learners know that they are seen, appreciated, heard, and understood. This work began by first listening to the needs of parents throughout the district. Family focus groups were held across the district, in which the gifted and talented director and her team took the time to hear from families what was working with gifted identification and programming for their students and what was not working. These focus groups helped drive changes to existing practices.

Given the growing number of Spanish-speaking families in the district, DPS designs events with Spanish-speaking families' needs specifically in mind. It offers meetings in Spanish (with English translation available) about gifted and talented programming options. Meals and child care are available at all district events to remove some of the barriers that may prevent families from attending. District events often consist of informational sessions about the characteristics and needs of gifted children, with an emphasis on how these characteristics may differ for children from culturally diverse backgrounds. These sessions also include information on nurturing the whole gifted child and what ideal programming should look like for children in the district. The sessions offer families various avenues for advocating for their gifted and talented children within district schools.

The DPS gifted and talented team has also begun to build family nights targeted at supporting the needs of diverse families. These nights bring together families to have conversations and build community. Experts both from the district gifted and talented team and nationally have been brought in to engage with families. The efforts began by focusing on black families and will be expanded in future years to ensure the diverse families within DPS have opportunities to come together and give voice to their needs and provide a community of support for one another.

Members of the DPS gifted and talented team collaborate with a parent volunteer from the state gifted organization to further support their family outreach efforts in the Latinx gifted community. Together, they communicate with families in Spanish via social media about information and supports specific to gifted education in the district. They also provide families with information on community and educational resources.

Gifted and talented specialists in DPS work behind the scenes every day to support Latinx gifted learners and their families. They often use the district's Spanish-language radio station to communicate with families about important information pertaining to their gifted children's education. They make sure videos posted on the district's gifted and talented department website are available in both English and Spanish. Further, gifted and talented specialists and teachers regularly reach out to Spanish-speaking families in the district through personal phone calls and face-to-face meetings whenever possible. They want families to know they are valued, respected, and appreciated and that their voice in their gifted children's education is important.

—*Contributed by Bertie Fiz, highly gifted and talented program specialist, Morey Middle School, and Dr. Rebecca McKinney, director, Gifted and Talented Department, Denver Public Schools, Colorado. Used with permission.*

Conveying and Supporting High Expectations

To develop meaningful relationships with underrepresented gifted students, you need to believe genuinely in their potential and make sure they know that you are a caring adult who believes in their potential. Underserved gifted students may question their giftedness. You must make sure students know that being labeled "gifted" does not mean that they are expected to know everything or that school should not require effort from them. While some underserved gifted students are very aware of their strengths, in general, students should not rely solely on their own perceptions of what they are capable of, because these perceptions may be low and inaccurately derived from past experiences. Building underserved gifted students' academic self-concept means conveying high expectations for them—and supporting them as they strive toward these expectations.

> **REAL-WORLD EXAMPLE**
>
> Throughout elementary school, Sam always heard that he needed to improve in writing and that his writing skills were at least a grade level below those of his peers. His parents told him he had a learning disability. His parents also told him he was identified gifted in reading, and writing was a big part of his targeted literacy instruction. Sam was confused. He assumed that the gifted label must be wrong. He couldn't write like his peers. He knew it and his teachers knew it—that was why they always gave him shorter writing assignments and so much extra time to complete them. It wasn't until sixth grade, when he joined a language arts class for gifted students, that a teacher finally explained to him what it meant to be twice-exceptional. The teacher helped him understand why he was identified as gifted in reading and that the label was not a mistake.

Conveying high expectations to underserved gifted students, while also providing the support they need for success, demonstrates respect for them and shows them that an adult believes they are capable of achieving at high levels. High expectations also boost their academic achievement, motivation to learn, and belief in their ability to succeed (Ford 2015; Jensen 2013). It is imperative that you set high expectations for your students and ask them to hold the same expectations for themselves. It is also important to realize that high expectations without the necessary scaffolding and support to help students attain learning mastery isn't beneficial. This approach sets up students to fail. It helps perpetuate their—and others'—belief that they might be incapable of succeeding at high levels.

You'll also want to be careful about sending mixed messages. While you publicly state that you have high expectations for underserved gifted learners, take care not to undermine these expectations by signaling inadvertently that you don't fully believe in them. For example:

- Are you asking underserved gifted students only lower-level questions during discussions?
- Are you giving students too much guidance on assignments or modifying challenging assignments unnecessarily?

> **What I Want You to Know About Me** ★★★
>
> "There are many things that are bringing down my self-esteem and have been embarrassing me or putting me under stress. For example, I have trouble getting enough sleep to get to school on time, and I tend to wait until passing period to go to school, so that I do not have to walk into a class that has already started."

- Are you swooping in too quickly to help students when they are trying to solve academic problems?
- Are you editing students' classwork to the point where their voice and original thoughts are no longer present?
- What are other ways you might inadvertently convey low expectations of your underserved gifted students?

On pages 52–53 at the end of this chapter is a sample lesson plan on self-awareness and identity that helps underserved gifted students get to know themselves. You can also find a digital version of this sample lesson plan and others by using the URL and password on page 180.

> ★★★ **What I Want You to Know About Me**
> "My teachers should know that I'm a hardworking, dedicated student. I'm a very bad speller. I'm not a very social person."

Nurturing a Safe Climate

All students need to learn in an environment that feels safe to them. This is especially true of underserved gifted students. These students are more likely to disengage from learning when they perceive that others do not value their cultural backgrounds and do not believe they can succeed. Creating a safe climate that supports and includes all students' lived experiences is critical to students' educational success.

> **REAL-WORLD EXAMPLE**
>
> Angel was not identified as gifted in language arts until seventh grade, likely due to his classification as an English language learner. On the first day of school, he walked into a class of thirty-one mostly white gifted students and sat at a desk by the door. Students ignored him as they talked about how difficult this class would be and how nervous they were to have to memorize three hundred Latin roots, an increase of one hundred words from their sixth-grade language arts class. Angel felt insecure in this environment, both socially and academically. He did not feel that he belonged or that he was smart enough to succeed. He began to question whether he should be in a class for gifted students.

TOOLKIT STRATEGY

Safe Climate Checklist

If students do not feel safe in your classroom, you will never really have the opportunity to get to know them and understand them. To create a safe climate, it's important to assess your classroom through your students' eyes. One way to do this is to use the "Safe Climate Checklist" reproducible on pages 54–55.

Figure 2-4 Sample Safe Climate Checklist

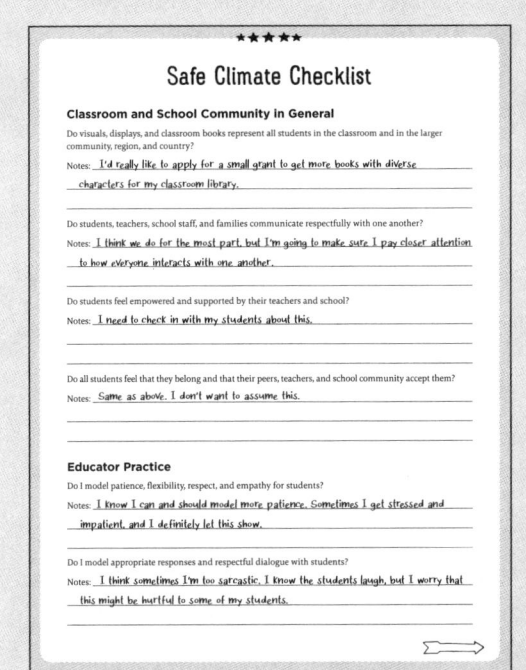

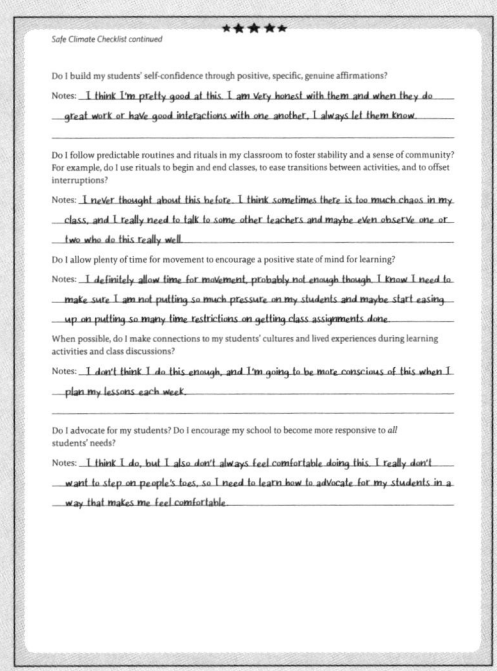

Safe Climate Checklist

Classroom and School Community in General

Do visuals, displays, and classroom books represent all students in the classroom and in the larger community, region, and country?
Notes: I'd really like to apply for a small grant to get more books with diverse characters for my classroom library.

Do students, teachers, school staff, and families communicate respectfully with one another?
Notes: I think we do for the most part, but I'm going to make sure I pay closer attention to how everyone interacts with one another.

Do students feel empowered and supported by their teachers and school?
Notes: I need to check in with my students about this.

Do all students feel that they belong and that their peers, teachers, and school community accept them?
Notes: Same as above. I don't want to assume this.

Educator Practice

Do I model patience, flexibility, respect, and empathy for students?
Notes: I know I can and should model more patience. Sometimes I get stressed and impatient, and I definitely let this show.

Do I model appropriate responses and respectful dialogue with students?
Notes: I think sometimes I'm too sarcastic. I know the students laugh, but I worry that this might be hurtful to some of my students.

Safe Climate Checklist continued

Do I build my students' self-confidence through positive, specific, genuine affirmations?
Notes: I think I'm pretty good at this. I am very honest with them and when they do great work or have good interactions with one another, I always let them know.

Do I follow predictable routines and rituals in my classroom to foster stability and a sense of community? For example, do I use rituals to begin and end classes, to ease transitions between activities, and to offset interruptions?
Notes: I never thought about this before. I think sometimes there is too much chaos in my class, and I really need to talk to some other teachers and maybe even observe one or two who do this really well.

Do I allow plenty of time for movement to encourage a positive state of mind for learning?
Notes: I definitely allow time for movement, probably not enough though. I know I need to make sure I am not putting so much pressure on my students and maybe start easing up on putting so many time restrictions on getting class assignments done.

When possible, do I make connections to my students' cultures and lived experiences during learning activities and class discussions?
Notes: I don't think I do this enough, and I'm going to be more conscious of this when I plan my lessons each week.

Do I advocate for my students? Do I encourage my school to become more responsive to *all* students' needs?
Notes: I think I do, but I also don't always feel comfortable doing this. I really don't want to step on people's toes, so I need to learn how to advocate for my students in a way that makes me feel comfortable.

TOOLKIT STRATEGY

Positive Classroom Norms

It is important for students to create collectively a list of positive classroom norms. Doing so requires students to reflect on the type of classroom community they believe supports learning and consider how their treatment of classmates *and* their attitudes toward themselves promote such a community. Positive norms set an optimistic and supportive tone for the class. You can display them and refer to them regularly both to redirect and to celebrate students' behaviors. Following is an example of positive classroom norms. Your own classroom norms should be generated by your students. Student ownership of these norms is key.

In our classroom community:
› We learn together and from one another.
› We value and learn from our mistakes.
› We show unconditional respect for ourselves and for one another.
› We put forth our best effort.
› We honor our differences.
› We encourage one another's successes.

In a safe classroom climate, students feel empowered to learn. Educators need to embrace a proactive, affirming mentality. Students who do not manifest "typical" characteristics of giftedness should not be viewed as problems to overcome but as potential that needs to be cultivated. You can affirm various ways of thinking, behaving, and learning on a daily basis. You can view teaching through an additive lens that tries to build on students' existing knowledge, skills, interests, and strengths. And you can gather input on classroom climate directly from your students.

TOOLKIT STRATEGY

Empowered-to-Learn Checklist

Districts often send out climate surveys to families; however, it is just as important (and potentially more valuable) to gather feedback directly from your students. Asking them about their perceptions and then validating those perceptions through discussions or changes in the classroom helps students feel not only safe and supported, but also empowered. And this ultimately leads to student engagement and growth.

As a starting point in this process, ask your students to complete the "Empowered-to-Learn Checklist." You'll find a reproducible version of this checklist on pages 56–58. You may have to change some of the wording in the checklist, depending on the age of your students. Let students complete this checklist anonymously.

Figure 2-4 Sample Empowered-to-Learn Checklist

Many school districts face issues with retention of underserved students in gifted programming. Learner empowerment is key to retaining these students in gifted programs. When students like Angel (see page 38) feel they belong in gifted-education classes, they are more likely to embrace the gifted label and welcome the challenge that gifted programming can provide. Educators must always remember the following:

› Underserved gifted students need to feel valued, respected, and supported. If they don't feel this way, they will find it difficult to learn. This is especially true for gifted students from historically marginalized populations.

› Underserved gifted students are more likely to feel isolated when most of their peers do not share their cultural backgrounds or lived experiences. Nurturing a safe, supportive classroom climate is critical to reducing isolation.

> **TOOLKIT STRATEGY**
>
> **Honoring Small Requests**
> Occasionally throughout the school year, ask your students to list small requests, such as the one described in the real-world example that follows, that would help them learn better in your classroom. Try honoring as many of the requests as possible—any that seem reasonable within the context of your classroom—and validate your students by letting them know you're doing so.

REAL-WORLD EXAMPLE

Ms. Gray, a high school teacher completing graduate coursework in gifted education, shared the following experience: "It was the third time we'd met as a small group when Kate, a tenth grader with autism spectrum disorder who was also identified as gifted, made a simple request during a timed essay-writing activity: 'If you don't mind, could you please take the clock off the wall? I'm bothered by the noise. I just can't concentrate.' 'No problem! I can do it,' I said. 'Oh, thank you,' she replied, looking surprised. When I took out the batteries, she said, 'I asked my (homeroom) teacher to do the same thing, and she refused.' This surprised me for two reasons. First, a ticking clock can be annoying—to anyone. Second, why wouldn't a teacher want to help a student concentrate on a learning activity by simply removing a distraction in the background? I wondered: How many small requests of this kind have been voiced by students? And how many of them have been addressed by teachers?"

Setting the Stage for Engaged Learning

When underserved gifted students feel meaningfully engaged in school, their learning potential is maximized. "Children who are meaningfully engaged willingly participate in learning activities, feel connected to what they are learning, and embrace the opportunity to be challenged in school" (Ritchotte, Zaghlawan, and Lee 2017, 9). Researchers have distinguished three types of engagement—behavioral, emotional, and cognitive (Fredricks et al. 2011):

> *Behavioral* engagement focuses on participation in academic, social, and out-of-school activities.

> *Emotional* engagement centers on how connected children feel to their teachers, peers, and what they are learning in school.

> *Cognitive* engagement occurs when children are invested in their learning and put effort into understanding challenging material.

Meaningful engagement includes all three types. We must strive to engage underserved gifted learners behaviorally, emotionally, and cognitively. You'll find tips to promote meaningful engagement in the following toolkit strategy.

TOOLKIT STRATEGY

Tips to Promote Meaningful Engagement

Practices and Approaches	Tips
Collaborative teaching requires individual accountability from students and helps them develop positive interdependence and interpersonal skills.	› Use the jigsaw strategy. Break an assignment into pieces and break the class into groups. Sometimes these can be mixed-ability groups, but it's also important for gifted students, including underserved gifted students, to have the opportunity to work together. In each group, students collaboratively complete an assignment piece. The groups then come together and collaborate to complete the entire assignment. › Encourage students to generate questions when they do not understand content due to lack of prior knowledge. Students can discuss these questions later with teachers.
Culturally responsive feedback helps teachers foster student self-esteem, monitor their understanding, and challenge their thinking.	› Incorporate students' ideas, language, and experiences into individualized feedback. › Provide both affective and cognitive feedback. › Create multiple opportunities for students to share their thoughts and ideas regarding class assignments, including individualized teacher-student conferences.
Modeling benefits students who learn through observation better than through other methods.	› Explicitly show students how to meet expectations for assignments. Take time to model how to complete assignments in front of them. › Provide varied exemplars of student assignments demonstrating various ways to complete assignments. Try to include exemplars that resonate with students' cultural, linguistic, and lived experiences.
Instructional scaffolding promotes deeper understanding.	› Use various types of questions. › Provide appropriate wait times and take turns. › Acknowledge and extend students' responses. › Use supporting instructional materials, such as visual organizers and story maps.

Practices and Approaches	Tips
A problem-solving approach promotes higher-level thinking skills.	› Engage students in real-world, open-ended problems. › Use examples from students' daily lives and communities.
Student-centered instruction creates learner autonomy.	› Provide opportunities for choice in what students learn, how they learn it, and how they demonstrate their learning. › When appropriate, let your students shine and teach the class what they have learned. This will provide them with an even greater opportunity to take ownership of their learning.

While positive interdependence and interpersonal skills are important for all students, be aware that working in groups can be frustrating for gifted learners. They often feel that their own learning needs don't get met in group work. When you are structuring group work, plan for individual accountability. Each student must take responsibility for a certain aspect of the assignment, so the gifted student doesn't end up carrying an unfair load. Make sure that gifted students aren't penalized for other students' not completing their portions of the assignment. Group gifted students thoughtfully. To grow academically, they need opportunities to work with other students who have similar interests and abilities. As psychologist Lev Vygotsky pointed out, students learn best in the zone of proximal development (ZPD). The ZPD lies between what a student can do without help and what a student can do with a little help from an adult or a capable peer (Vygotsky 1978). If gifted students are always the ones providing answers and support to others in the group, they do not have the opportunity to work in their own ZPD.

What I Want You to Know About Me ★★★
"I'm not a big fan of group projects when the rest of the group doesn't share similar motivation or work ethic. I usually prefer working alone to ensure my work is to my standard."

Opportunities to lead within the classroom and share authority with the teacher may promote meaningful engagement in underserved gifted students. Research has found that gifted students' motivation and engagement increases when teachers are willing to share authority in the classroom (Graefe 2017). Teachers can do this by first developing students' leadership ability and then providing regular opportunities for them to lead in the classroom.

TOOLKIT STRATEGY

Opportunities to Lead

Consider taking the following steps:

› Provide students with opportunities to share their expertise on unit topics with the entire class.
› Embed opportunities for students to make choices regarding what they learn and how they learn it.
› Allow students to hone their leadership skills through leading small-group projects. Hold each member of the group responsible for individual tasks. Do not penalize others for group members who don't follow through with their responsibilities.

You can help students continually cultivate leadership skills through goal-setting and self-regulation activities. Underserved gifted students need opportunities to discuss their goals and dreams for the future and to reflect on how school can help them achieve those goals and dreams. This strategy can engage and empower the students in your classroom by helping them connect their learning meaningfully to their lives.

TOOLKIT STRATEGY

Learning Goal Plan

The "Learning Goal Plan" strategy helps students learn the process of chunking, or breaking down a goal into manageable steps. (You'll find a blank reproducible version of this plan on page 59.) Rarely can people simply think of a goal and then go out and achieve it; teaching students how to set realistic goals and self-regulate to achieve their goals needs to start early, in elementary school. By doing this, educators give underserved gifted learners opportunities to feel successful. When students see that they can achieve their goals—short-term, long-term, affective, and cognitive—their motivation, self-efficacy, and engagement increase.

★★★★★

Learning Goal Plan

Learning Goal Plan: Part 1

What is my goal?	Why do I want to do this?	How will I do this?	Who will help me if I need help?	How will I know I met my goal?
I want to get a B or higher in math at the end of this quarter.	I really like math but haven't focused much on my grade lately. I'd like to make sure that I'm understanding all my math now, because I might want to study architecture when I get to college, and that's going to require some really advanced math classes.	I am going to check in with my teacher every day to make sure I understand what I'm doing and get extra help if I need it. I'm also going to turn off the TV and not rush through my math homework at home.	My teacher said he would help me. One of the kids in my class gave me her phone number in case I need help.	I'll get Bs or higher on my homework and tests. This will mean I understand what I'm doing.

Learning Goal Plan: Part 2

Did I meet my goal?	Did I really do my best to meet my goal?	Did I do the things I said I was going to do to meet my goal?	Did I ask for help?	Was this a good goal for me?
Yes! I got As and Bs on all my work and tests and ended up with an A in math.	Yes, I worked really hard. I feel like I have a really strong foundation for future math classes I might need if I study architecture.	Most of the time. Sometimes I forgot to check in with my teacher after class, but most days I did.	I didn't end up needing that much help. I just really needed to focus more and pay attention.	Yes. I feel really proud of myself for doing so much better in math this quarter.

Figure 2-6 Sample Learning Goal Plan

Setting the stage for more meaningful learning means providing the opportunity for *all* students not only to access learning, but to do so in a way that maximizes their full potential. You can use Universal Design for Learning (UDL) principles, which are based on neuroscience research, to guide development of curriculum that sets up all students for success.

UDL is guided by the philosophy that there is no such thing as a one-size-fits-all approach to learning. In other words, students are unique individuals who have unique learning needs. When learning experiences are designed with UDL in mind, the following three principles are embedded into learning activities when appropriate:

- *Multiple means of representation:* Students are given various ways to access new information and knowledge.
- *Multiple means of expression:* Students are given opportunities to demonstrate what they've learned in various ways.
- *Multiple means of engagement:* Students are given learning experiences that ignite their interests, offer appropriate challenges, and thereby increase their motivation to learn.

UDL principles give students more equitable access to learning and have been shown to increase learner engagement, achievement, and positive post-school outcomes. The UDL toolkit strategy helps you apply UDL principles by offering questions that correspond with each principle.

TOOLKIT STRATEGY

Applying UDL Principles to Create an Inclusive Classroom

Principles	Learners Ask	Teachers Should Ask
Provide multiple means of engagement.	Why am I learning this?	› What is the purpose of students learning about this topic? › Is this something students are interested in? › If students cannot see the value, how will I explain it to them? › How am I going to keep students interested in this topic that I need them to learn? › How can I help students take ownership of their learning?
Provide multiple means of representation.	What is this? What am I learning?	› How can I present information in various ways, visually or audibly? › How can I present information in various forms (for example, video, picture, audio recording, and diagram)? › Have I made key concepts or vocabulary words available in English and students' first languages? › How will I activate students' prior knowledge to help them see connections between past and current learning?
Provide multiple means of action and expression.	How am I going to complete this task?	› Will my students have opportunities to demonstrate their learning in multisensory modalities? › How will I help students develop fluency and independence while performing tasks? › What strategies can I use to improve students' executive function to help them become more independent, strategic learners?

On pages 60–61, you'll find a reproducible "UDL Strategies Checklist" you can use to evaluate your current teaching practices, lesson plans, and teaching environment against UDL principles. You may discover that you've been applying UDL strategies without even realizing it. If you find areas that you still need to work on, that's okay. Give yourself permission to master one strategy at a time.

Chapter Summary

The information and strategies in this chapter will help you more fully understand and appreciate who your underserved gifted learners are. You show your students that you value them as individuals and care about their learning when you create a safe, culturally responsive learning environment. This means you model unconditional positive regard for one another, encourage positive collaboration, convey high expectations, and consistently honor cultural heritage and experiences. The tools presented in this chapter can be used as is or adapted to engage not only your students in the wonderful learning that happens in your classroom, but also to engage their families. Following the tips in this chapter will help you build or continue to cultivate the type of supportive learning environment that all your students, especially your underserved students, need and deserve. To reflect on your progress at building meaningful connections, nurturing a safe climate, and setting the stage for engaged learning, fill out the reproducible "'Understand Me' Checklist" on page 62.

My Memory Timeline

As you complete this timeline, think back to important moments both in school and outside school that have helped make you who you are.

Important Moments in School

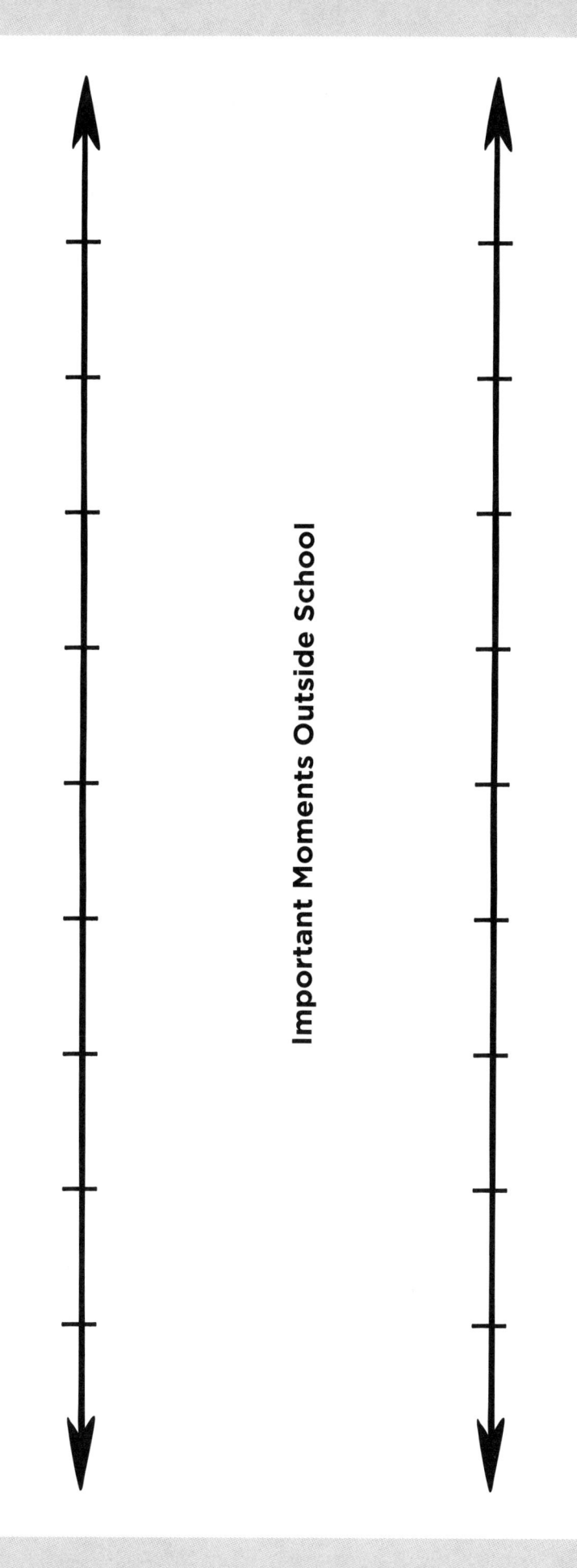

Important Moments Outside School

Talent Tree

Leaves (your interests and passions)
Branches (your goals)

Trunk (your strengths, talents, and gifts)
Roots (origin of your strengths)

From *Start Seeing and Serving Underserved Gifted Students: 50 Strategies for Equity and Excellence* by Jennifer A. Ritchotte, Ph.D., Chin-Wen Lee, Ph.D., and Amy K. Graefe, Ph.D., copyright © 2020. This page may be reproduced for individual, classroom, or small group work only. For all other uses, contact Free Spirit Publishing Inc. at freespirit.com/permissions.

Family Identity Survey

Please write your answers to the following questions.

1. How do you define the word *family*? _____
   _____
   _____

2. Based on your personal definition of *family*, who are the members of your family? Please describe each family member in as little or as much detail as you'd like. _____
   _____
   _____
   _____
   _____

3. Which family members does the student spend the most time with? _____
   _____

4. What do you value as a family? _____
   _____
   _____
   _____

5. What are some of your family traditions? Do you know where any of these traditions come from? Please explain. _____
   _____
   _____
   _____

6. What holidays do you celebrate as a family? How do you celebrate these holidays? _____
   _____
   _____
   _____

7. What are you proud of as a family? _____
   _____
   _____
   _____

From *Start Seeing and Serving Underserved Gifted Students: 50 Strategies for Equity and Excellence* by Jennifer A. Ritchotte, Ph.D., Chin-Wen Lee, Ph.D., and Amy K. Graefe, Ph.D., copyright © 2020. This page may be reproduced for individual, classroom, or small group work only. For all other uses, contact Free Spirit Publishing Inc. at freespirit.com/permissions.

Family Identity Survey continued

8. What rules exist within your family? _____
_____
_____
_____

9. How are important decisions made within your family? _____
_____
_____
_____

10. Where does your family meet and interact with members of your community (for example, church, clubs, organizations, and so on)? _____
_____
_____
_____

11. In what ways is your family involved in school activities (such as attending parent-teacher conferences or sporting events)? _____
_____
_____
_____

12. What do you value most about school? _____
_____
_____
_____

13. What concerns or questions do you have about school? _____
_____
_____
_____

14. Is there anything else you would like to share about your family? _____
_____
_____
_____

From *Start Seeing and Serving Underserved Gifted Students: 50 Strategies for Equity and Excellence* by Jennifer A. Ritchotte, Ph.D., Chin-Wen Lee, Ph.D., and Amy K. Graefe, Ph.D., copyright © 2020. This page may be reproduced for individual, classroom, or small group work only. For all other uses, contact Free Spirit Publishing Inc. at freespirit.com/permissions.

Recipe for Success

～ Recipe for Success ～

Name: _____

Parent or guardian: _____

Email: _____

Phone: _____

Key Ingredients: What Should I Know About Your Child?

Strengths: _____

Challenges: _____

Interests: _____

Key ingredients of your child's character—your child is: _____
_____

-- fold here --

_____
_____
_____
_____
_____
_____
_____
_____

Getting to know your child requires more than looking at test scores and grades. Could you help me? Tell me a story about the first time you realized your child had unique gifts or abilities.

From *Start Seeing and Serving Underserved Gifted Students: 50 Strategies for Equity and Excellence* by Jennifer A. Ritchotte, Ph.D., Chin-Wen Lee, Ph.D., and Amy K. Graefe, Ph.D., copyright © 2020. This page may be reproduced for individual, classroom, or small group work only. For all other uses, contact Free Spirit Publishing Inc. at freespirit.com/permissions.

Sample Lesson Plan: Self-Awareness and Identity

Overview and Objectives

Middle school students (grades 6–9) will reflect on the labels that others have placed on them and create identity statements that speak to their individual brilliances and what makes them who they are.

- Students will be able to reframe negative labels with the support of their peers.
- Students will be able to see similarities among themselves and articulate what makes them individually unique.

NAGC Gifted Programming Standards*

Standard 1: Learning and Development

1.1. Self-Understanding. Students with gifts and talents demonstrate self-knowledge with respect to their interests, strengths, identities, and needs in socio-emotional development and in intellectual, academic, creative, leadership, and artistic domains.

1.3. Self-Understanding. Students with gifts and talents demonstrate understanding of and respect for similarities and differences between themselves and their peer group and others in the general population.

Standard 4: Learning Environments

4.1. Personal Competence. Students with gifts and talents demonstrate growth in personal competence and dispositions for exceptional academic and creative productivity. These include self-awareness, self-advocacy, self-efficacy, confidence, motivation, resilience, independence, curiosity, and risk taking.

*National Association for Gifted Children (NAGC). 2010. *NAGC Pre-K–Grade 12 Gifted Programming Standards.* Washington, DC: NAGC. nagc.org/resources-publications/resources/national-standards-gifted-and-talented-education/pre-k-grade-12.

Materials/Resources Needed

- short video: "Don't Label Me" (youtube.com/watch?v=1vkkFDg7UEc)
- blank paper (one sheet per student)
- writing utensils
- markers, glue sticks, pencils, scrapbook paper, or other art supplies

Sequence of Learning

1. Students watch a short video titled "Don't Label Me."
2. Students discuss the negative labels that we place on people and others place on us, as well as the negative labels we place on ourselves.
3. On slips of paper, students write down some of these negative labels.

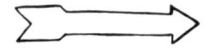

Sample Lesson Plan: Self-Awareness and Identity continued

4. Students trade their labels with classmates and have their peers reframe the negative labels into positive ones, writing the reframed labels on the backs of the originals.
5. Students retrieve their original labels from their peers with the reframed, positive labels written on the back.
6. Students discuss with one another similarities and differences in how they are labeled and why reframing can be a helpful strategy.
7. Students create identity statements that reinforce who they are through their own eyes, in any format or art media they choose (lists, sentences, paragraphs, images, and so on).
8. Students share their identity statements if they feel comfortable doing so.

Reflection/Assessment

Students reflect on what makes them individually unique, why their unique identity matters, and how they can protect their identity.

Used with permission from Jessica Likes, middle school math teacher. From *Start Seeing and Serving Underserved Gifted Students: 50 Strategies for Equity and Excellence* by Jennifer A. Ritchotte, Ph.D., Chin-Wen Lee, Ph.D., and Amy K. Graefe, Ph.D., copyright © 2020. This page may be reproduced for individual, classroom, or small group work only. For all other uses, contact Free Spirit Publishing Inc. at freespirit.com/permissions.

Safe Climate Checklist

Classroom and School Community in General

Do visuals, displays, and classroom books represent all students in the classroom and in the larger community, region, and country?

Notes: _____
_____
_____

Do students, teachers, school staff, and families communicate respectfully with one another?

Notes: _____
_____
_____

Do students feel empowered and supported by their teachers and school?

Notes: _____
_____
_____

Do all students feel that they belong and that their peers, teachers, and school community accept them?

Notes: _____
_____
_____

Educator Practice

Do I model patience, flexibility, respect, and empathy for students?

Notes: _____
_____
_____

Do I model appropriate responses and respectful dialogue with students?

Notes: _____
_____
_____

Safe Climate Checklist continued

Do I build my students' self-confidence through positive, specific, genuine affirmations?

Notes: _____
_____
_____

Do I follow predictable routines and rituals in my classroom to foster stability and a sense of community? For example, do I use rituals to begin and end classes, to ease transitions between activities, and to offset interruptions?

Notes: _____
_____
_____

Do I allow plenty of time for movement to encourage a positive state of mind for learning?

Notes: _____
_____
_____

When possible, do I make connections to my students' cultures and lived experiences during learning activities and class discussions?

Notes: _____
_____
_____

Do I advocate for my students? Do I encourage my school to become more responsive to *all* students' needs?

Notes: _____
_____
_____

From *Start Seeing and Serving Underserved Gifted Students: 50 Strategies for Equity and Excellence* by Jennifer A. Ritchotte, Ph.D., Chin-Wen Lee, Ph.D., and Amy K. Graefe, Ph.D., copyright © 2020. This page may be reproduced for individual, classroom, or small group work only. For all other uses, contact Free Spirit Publishing Inc. at freespirit.com/permissions.

Empowered-to-Learn Checklist

Directions: Respond to each statement by writing an *X* in the appropriate box ("Always," "Sometimes," or "Never"). If you'd like to comment on your response, you can do that in the box below the statement, but you do not have to write a comment.

		Always	Sometimes	Never
1.	My teacher encourages and supports me to learn as much as I can.			
	Comment:			
2.	Our classroom is structured so that I can learn best (for example, materials available, good classroom management).			
	Comment:			
3.	There are times I can choose what I learn (for example, choice of topic, independent study).			
	Comment:			
4.	There are times I can choose how I learn (for example, with a partner, by myself, on the floor).			
	Comment:			
5.	There are times I can choose how I demonstrate what I have learned (for example, written paper, presentation).			
	Comment:			
6.	I feel comfortable asking for what I need to help me learn better (for example, different seating, modification on assignment).			
	Comment:			
7.	Students and teachers in our classroom treat one another with respect.			
	Comment:			

From *Start Seeing and Serving Underserved Gifted Students: 50 Strategies for Equity and Excellence* by Jennifer A. Ritchotte, Ph.D., Chin-Wen Lee, Ph.D., and Amy K. Graefe, Ph.D., copyright © 2020. This page may be reproduced for individual, classroom, or small group work only. For all other uses, contact Free Spirit Publishing Inc. at freespirit.com/permissions.

Empowered-to-Learn Checklist continued

		Always	Sometimes	Never
8.	I feel important; I feel like a valuable member of this class.			
	Comment:			
9.	My teacher recognizes and appreciates what I have to offer.			
	Comment:			
10.	My teacher is interested in me and likes me for who I am.			
	Comment:			
11.	The other students in my class recognize and appreciate what I have to offer.			
	Comment:			
12.	The other students in my class are interested in me and like me for who I am.			
	Comment:			
13.	There are times I participate in making decisions in our classroom.			
	Comment:			
14.	I feel comfortable asking questions in our classroom.			
	Comment:			
15.	I feel comfortable making suggestions in our classroom.			
	Comment:			

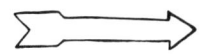

From *Start Seeing and Serving Underserved Gifted Students: 50 Strategies for Equity and Excellence* by Jennifer A. Ritchotte, Ph.D., Chin-Wen Lee, Ph.D., and Amy K. Graefe, Ph.D., copyright © 2020. This page may be reproduced for individual, classroom, or small group work only. For all other uses, contact Free Spirit Publishing Inc. at freespirit.com/permissions.

Empowered-to-Learn Checklist continued

		Always	Sometimes	Never
16.	What we learn in this class is important (important information for everyone to have or important to me in some way).			
	Comment:			
17.	What we learn in this class is interesting to me.			
	Comment:			
18.	What we learn in this class is meaningful to me (for example, because of my personal interests or my future plans).			
	Comment:			
19.	What we learn in this class is relevant to me.			
	Comment:			
20.	I see and learn about people like me in the content we study and the books we read.			
	Comment:			
21.	I have opportunities to be the best "me" I can be in this class.			
	Comment:			

From *Start Seeing and Serving Underserved Gifted Students: 50 Strategies for Equity and Excellence* by Jennifer A. Ritchotte, Ph.D., Chin-Wen Lee, Ph.D., and Amy K. Graefe, Ph.D., copyright © 2020. This page may be reproduced for individual, classroom, or small group work only. For all other uses, contact Free Spirit Publishing Inc. at freespirit.com/permissions.

Learning Goal Plan

★★★

Learning Goal Plan: Part 1

What is my goal?	Why do I want to do this?	How will I do this?	Who will help me if I need help?	How will I know I met my goal?

Learning Goal Plan: Part 2

Did I meet my goal?	Did I really do my best to meet my goal?	Did I do the things I said I was going to do to meet my goal?	Did I ask for help?	Was this a good goal for me?

UDL Strategies Checklist

Use this checklist to evaluate your current teaching practices, lesson plans, and teaching environment against UDL principles.

UDL Strategies to Improve Engagement	I Do This	I Need to Work on This
1. I invite students to participate in designing classroom activities.		
2. I invite students to participate in designing assignments and assessments, such as creating rubrics.		
3. I incorporate self-evaluation or self-reflection into assessments.		
4. I have students write their own academic and behavioral goals.		
5. I use culturally responsive teaching practices.		
6. When applicable, I identify an authentic audience for my students' work.		
7. I create a classroom culture where students feel safe to take risks.		
8. I ask students about distractions in the classroom, such as extra lighting and background noise, and remove those distractions if possible.		
9. I explain and display learning objectives or outcomes.		
10. I vary levels of difficulty in learning tasks and give students choices for how they practice new skills.		
11. I set clear goals, norms, and responsibilities for group work.		
12. I provide timely feedback that focuses on effort, progress, and perseverance.		
13. I promote self-regulation skills.		
14. I teach coping strategies.		
15. I encourage the use of data to monitor academic or behavioral progress.		
UDL Strategies to Improve Representation of Information	**I Do This**	**I Need to Work on This**
1. I provide visual aids when possible, such as descriptions, captions, diagrams, and charts.		
2. I allow the use of text-to-speech or speech-to-text software when needed.		
3. I provide pictures or graphic symbols when teaching new vocabulary words.		
4. I use underlines or highlights to explain syntax, big ideas, or relationships in texts.		
5. I make key concepts or vocabulary words available in English and my students' first languages.		
6. I present key concepts in various forms, such as video, picture, diagram, dance, or music.		
7. I activate students' prior knowledge to help them make connections between past and current learning.		
8. I use graphic organizers, such as KWL charts and concept maps, to help students with abstract concepts.		
9. I chunk information for more challenging concepts and assignments.		
10. I help students with generalization by presenting new problems that can be solved using the same principle or strategy used for a previous problem.		

From *Start Seeing and Serving Underserved Gifted Students: 50 Strategies for Equity and Excellence* by Jennifer A. Ritchotte, Ph.D., Chin-Wen Lee, Ph.D., and Amy K. Graefe, Ph.D., copyright © 2020. This page may be reproduced for individual, classroom, or small group work only.
For all other uses, contact Free Spirit Publishing Inc. at freespirit.com/permissions.

UDL Strategies Checklist continued

UDL Strategies to Improve Demonstration of Learning	I Do This	I Need to Work on This
1. I vary the sensory form of learning tasks: visual (poster, slide presentation), oral (storytelling, monologue), audio (recordings), tactile (models, sculptures), or taste/smell (edible/aromatic plant samples).		
2. I provide access to assistive technology.		
3. I encourage the use of "assistants," such as spelling or grammar checks, graph paper, or sentence strips.		
4. I break a task into smaller steps. Students practice and master each step before moving on to the next step.		
5. I provide timely feedback during practice.		
6. I help students write attainable goals with actionable steps.		
7. I provide mentors (community volunteers, family members, or students in higher grades) to help with goal planning and strategy development.		
8. I model strategies, such as how to solve problems and how to prioritize and sort information in texts.		
9. I provide prompts or checklists for students to practice self-monitoring skills.		
10. I include student self-reflection and self-monitoring as part of my instructional routine.		

From *Start Seeing and Serving Underserved Gifted Students: 50 Strategies for Equity and Excellence* by Jennifer A. Ritchotte, Ph.D., Chin-Wen Lee, Ph.D., and Amy K. Graefe, Ph.D., copyright © 2020. This page may be reproduced for individual, classroom, or small group work only. For all other uses, contact Free Spirit Publishing Inc. at freespirit.com/permissions.

"Understand Me" Checklist

Use this checklist to reflect on your progress at building meaningful connections, nurturing a safe climate, and setting the stage for engaged learning. Review your results to become more aware of your areas of strength and your areas for growth.

Key:
Beginning: You're aware and want to try.
Developing: You have tried or are trying.
Leading: You are consistently aware, implementing changes, and making others aware.

Building Meaningful Connections	Beginning	Developing	Leading
I make a special effort to know the underserved gifted students in my classroom, both in and out of school.			
I recognize and cultivate my students' evolving strengths, interests, and passions throughout the school year.			
I take extra steps to know my students' family members and respectfully communicate with them.			
I set high performance expectations for my underserved gifted students and hold them accountable for meeting those expectations.			

Nurturing a Safe Climate	Beginning	Developing	Leading
I consistently model patience, respect, and empathy for my students.			
I believe in the potential of all my students and affirm this to them regularly.			
I have predictable routines and rituals in my classroom.			
I encourage interdependence by giving students opportunities to work collectively toward shared success. *I know that these opportunities require individual accountability, and I am willing to honor requests by students to work individually, when applicable.*			
I foster a supportive classroom community that honors students' unique characteristics and encourages learner empowerment.			

Setting the Stage for Engaged Learning	Beginning	Developing	Leading
I consistently strive to meaningfully engage all students behaviorally, cognitively, and emotionally.			
I regularly provide students with opportunities to lead through sharing their expertise and making decisions about their learning.			
I support students in developing and attaining realistic learning goals.			
I provide equitable access to learning by providing multiple means of engagement and multiple means of representation, and by letting students choose how they express what they know.			

From *Start Seeing and Serving Underserved Gifted Students: 50 Strategies for Equity and Excellence* by Jennifer A. Ritchotte, Ph.D., Chin-Wen Lee, Ph.D., and Amy K. Graefe, Ph.D., copyright © 2020. This page may be reproduced for individual, classroom, or small group work only. For all other uses, contact Free Spirit Publishing Inc. at freespirit.com/permissions.

TEACH ME

I think there is too much emphasis on deficits and not enough emphasis on developing abilities.
—Temple Grandin

★ ★ ★ ★ ★

An experienced teacher educator once asked a group of preservice teachers a seemingly simple question: "What will you teach next year?" Many of the preservice teachers offered answers like "poetry," "pre-algebra," "cell structure," "the American Revolution," "musical expression," and "patterns in art." The veteran teacher followed up his first question with another question: "What will you do to ensure your students care about the topics you will teach?" A long silence ensued, and then one of the preservice teachers said, "Show them that *we* care about *them*."

Teaching underserved gifted students to the best of your ability requires that you care deeply. That is why we've chosen the acronym CARE to organize the strategies in this chapter. When you care, you:

> **Connect learning to students' lives.** You may accomplish this through creating lessons that have real-world applications, allowing students to create projects that are intended for an authentic audience, and by representing and honoring students' unique experiences in learning activities.

> **Ability group students flexibly.** You can group your students for learning in many ways, but it's important to give your underserved gifted learners opportunities to work with others of similar ability or potential. Underserved gifted students need to interact with peers who not only can grasp their ideas, but also challenge them intellectually and academically. Grouping should be intentional and flexible. You may base grouping on demonstrated strength, interest, learning preference, or need. Individual accountability for group work is essential to ensure every student takes an active and equitable role. Further, you should offer supports for underserved gifted learners who are capable of working at a higher level but may lack some of the fundamental skills needed to engage confidently in group work with their like-ability peers.

> **Respectfully differentiate for students.** Students in your classroom have various strengths, needs, background experiences, and interests. The focus of differentiation for underserved gifted learners should be to provide them with opportunities to feel successful and to shine. You may incorporate more choices into how your students learn and how they demonstrate their learning; you may develop grading rubrics that honor the learning process, effort, and growth; and you may chunk larger projects into smaller steps to build your students' self-efficacy.

> **Engage students in higher-level thinking.** You will never truly know your underserved gifted leaners' capabilities unless you offer opportunities for them to

engage in complex thinking activities. Incorporating higher-level questions into discussion and inquiry-based activities can be a powerful way to engage students in learning at a deeper level. Further, incorporating depth and complexity into your lessons will empower your students to become more self-directed learners as they meaningfully engage in and take responsibility for their learning.

Although we selected the strategies in this chapter specifically with underserved gifted learners in mind, we believe these strategies represent good teaching and can benefit *all* students in your classroom.

CARE Strategies: <u>C</u>onnect Learning to Students' Lives

One of the most valuable strategies for teaching your underserved gifted learners is to connect the learning that happens in your classroom to students' lives—in as many ways as possible. This connection is also a key component of culturally responsive teaching. Connect learning to your students' background experiences; make sure that the books you have in your library, the visuals in your room, and the curricula you teach represent your students' cultural heritages; and provide opportunities for students to create authentic products for real audiences. This type of connection helps students find meaning in what you ask them to do. It can also be an opportunity to offer choice to students—both in the types of product they design and the audiences to whom they present. Creating something for (and hopefully also presenting to) a real audience challenges students and helps focus their work. It allows them to identify an audience important to them. (For an example of a real audience, see the community center cleanup project on pages 66–67.)

> ★★★ **What I Want You to Know About Me**
> "Sometimes it takes more than just textbook explanations for me to understand. It's easier to learn things visually. Please be understanding and patient of the way I learn."

TOOLKIT STRATEGY

Helping Students Connect with the Future

In addition to creating authentic products for real audiences, it is also important that students have the opportunity to learn about authentic skills used in real-life disciplines. Many underserved gifted learners have limited exposure to the wide array of careers available. The environments in which students grow up often define the career opportunities they see.

Consider Homer Hickam, the famous astronaut and writer whose life is chronicled in the movie *October Sky*. He grew up in a poverty-stricken West Virginia coal-mining town. Most people he knew were miners, and his father was a mine superintendent. Hickam easily could have followed his father's footsteps into the mine. But his imagination was sparked by reading science fiction novels as a young boy and by hearing of the Soviet Union's 1957 Sputnik satellite launch when he was fourteen. He and five friends formed a rocket-building club, which eventually led him to college and a career in rocket science.

Like Hickam, your underserved gifted students need the opportunity to learn about career fields and to see themselves as professionals. You can help students connect with their futures by showing them the relationship between their classroom learning and careers that excite and interest them.

Set aside time for students to visit the Bureau of Labor Statistics Career Exploration website for K–12 students (bls.gov/k12/content/students/careers/career-exploration.htm). This US government website provides a wealth of data to help students understand various careers, including duties, work environment, pay, job outlook, and similar occupations.

Give students ample time to explore the website. If possible, you may consider pairing high school or college students with younger students to support them during this activity and provide extra engagement. This could turn into a mentorship project. If students want to continue career exploration outside school hours, help them plan for this. Who can help them with their exploration outside school? Where can they work on this? Do they have access to a computer and the internet at home? If not, how might they get around these obstacles?

Encourage students to keep their search results in an online or paper portfolio. Students' interests may evolve over time. Encourage them to revisit the website and any notes or information they collected on careers as they get older.

Service Learning

Service learning provides a unique opportunity for students to engage in authentic work. It helps them see a link between what they do in the classroom and real life. For underserved gifted learners, participation in service learning may enhance psychosocial skills like empathy and self-esteem, as well as boost self-awareness and student confidence in addressing areas of community need (Lee et al. 2007).

REAL-WORLD EXAMPLE

At Renaissance Secondary School in Colorado, service learning helps students meaningfully connect academic knowledge to real-world applications. Students collaborate with one another, their teachers, school staff, and members of their local community to address areas of need. Through this collaboration, students learn civic and social responsibility. This experience also enables them to feel empowered—to believe they can be change agents within their community and make a real difference in people's lives. Service learning at Renaissance is not just a onetime volunteer experience; rather, it is immersive. It requires three important overlapping components: direct service, education, and reflection. Direct service in community settings helps students build connections between their education and real-world experiences. It provides students with a context for learning that is personally meaningful to them. Education is also an integral component of service learning. Students need to delve deeper into the issues they are trying to address through service learning. Education is also needed to ensure community participants are treated respectfully and stereotypes are not unintentionally reinforced. Further, service learning requires time for students to reflect. Individual and group reflection encourages an open dialogue among students and provides them with the opportunity to learn from one another and use that learning to improve the service-learning experience from everyone involved.

High-quality service learning includes student leadership, reflection, and time spent acquiring knowledge about a particular community issue. For example, through observation or through talking to members in their community, students identify a need to keep the space in and around their community center clean. Students collaborate with staff at the community center to help clean the center on the weekends. They keep scientific journals for analyzing and categorizing the trash collected. The students then use this information to create a sustainable recycling plan for the center. With help from the community center staff, the students create and distribute public service announcements (PSAs) to educate their community on the benefits of recycling.

Dr. James A. Banks, a renowned expert on multicultural education, identified four approaches to multicultural education that provide a perspective on service learning that can ultimately empower underserved gifted learners: Contributions, Additive, Transformative, and Decision-Making and Social Action. The Contributions approach is most frequently used in schools. Teachers introduce students to the heroes and holidays of various cultures. After the activities end, students may leave with a partial understanding of a particular culture or even potentially damaging misconceptions. In the Additive approach, although teachers provide students with more exposure to cultural content, typically their learning of this material is filtered through a Western lens. In the Transformative approach, teachers encourage students to view issues from varied perspectives. The oppressed are given voices, and students learn to view social issues from multiple perspectives. In the Decision-Making and Social Action approach, students are supported in choosing a social problem and taking action to make change. For example, what can students do to address prejudice from people outside their school community? Students can take action through the steps of service learning. Through the service-learning process, students not only develop confidence in their ability to make positive changes in their community, they also acquire valuable problem-solving, critical-thinking, and decision-making skills. This is especially important for underserved gifted students, because they often thrive in learning environments where they have meaningful opportunities to cultivate these skills.

TOOLKIT STRATEGY

Creating a Plan for Service Learning

First, help students create a community-wide survey. This survey will help them identify what in their community people believe is the most pressing issue. It will also tell community members that their voices are valued. Share both hard copies and electronic copies of the survey with people in the community. With your guidance, students decide the best, safest way to distribute and collect surveys. (Depending on the location of the school and age of the students, community could be defined as the school community or the local neighborhood.)

Next, have students work individually, in partners, in small groups, or as a class to create an action plan based on survey data. If students work in partners or groups, each pair or group may decide to approach the issue in a particular way, or students may decide that each pair or group should handle a certain part of the action plan. If the data suggest multiple issues are important to the community, each pair or group may focus its action plan on one of the issues. Action plans should include the following components:

- A goal for the service-learning project: What do students hope to accomplish?
- Actionable steps for accomplishing this goal: What projects will students undertake to reach their goal?
- Blueprints for projects: Students need to detail the steps involved in the projects they will undertake in their community and, with your guidance, ensure the steps are feasible and address their goals. In the community center example, the class focused on one project with several steps:
  1. Students arranged to clean up the center on weekends. As a class, they organized various student groups to clean up each weekend.
  2. Students decided what data they wanted to collect during their cleanup initiative and how they would collect and organize the data.
  3. As a class, the students agreed on a system for aggregating and analyzing all the data collected.
  4. A small group of students took responsibility for analyzing the data and sharing the results with the class.
  5. Based on the results, students came together as a class to create a sustainable recycling plan for the center.
  6. A small group of students created and shared a presentation about their plan with community center staff. The students asked for feedback on their plan.
  7. Based on staff feedback, various student groups planned and created individual PSAs about the benefits of recycling for the community.
  8. A separate student group created a plan for distributing these PSAs to the community over the next few months with the help of their teachers, families in the community, and center staff. This group presented its distribution plan to the class and modified the plan based on peer feedback.

Finally, give students time to reflect on the service-learning experience individually, with partners or fellow group members, and as a class. You can use the following questions to guide reflection:

- What are you most proud of from this experience and why?
- What would you change next time, why would you change it, and how would you change it?
- How was this service-learning experience connected to what you have learned and are learning in your classes?
- What type of service-learning project would you like to do in the future and why?

It is our hope that underserved gifted learners will ultimately learn through service learning that no matter what makes them "underserved" in gifted-education programs, this label does not define them. They are active contributors to society. They have the power to make a difference.

You can use service learning in a single class or through collaboration across classes. For example, in middle school, a language arts teacher might partner with a science or math teacher to facilitate the various project components. You can modify action plans to address specific academic standards in various disciplines. Additionally, you might consider seeking out small grant competitions to fund service-learning opportunities. Older students may even help write applications for these grants.

Problem-Based Learning

Problem-based learning (PBL) is another curricular strategy that can help students connect classroom learning to their lives and to real-world applications. PBL focuses just as much on building skills such as communication and critical thinking as it does on the outcome of the problem-solving activity. Moreover, in a five-year study funded by the US Department of Education, PBL was found to be useful in "identifying high-ability middle school students from underserved populations who historically are left out of honors, advanced, and gifted programs" (Cristodero 2018). When you provide underserved students with authentic problems to solve, you give them opportunities to demonstrate their gifts and talents—abilities that might otherwise go unnoticed in general education settings.

PBL offers students the opportunity to learn concepts and content through solving open-ended, complex, real-world problems. Usually, students identify the problem, then they determine what they need to know and attempt to solve the problem. Teachers can help students identify problems they can solve in a short period of time, or the problems can be complex enough to extend for an entire semester (or longer).

Most approaches to PBL include the following steps. Incorporate teacher and peer feedback through the entire problem-solving process.

1. With teacher support, students isolate a problem or an issue that resonates with them.

2. Students identify what they already know about the issue and what knowledge gaps they need to address to generate solutions.

3. Students research the issue using a variety of resources.

4. Students brainstorm and investigate possible solutions. Teachers encourage thinking outside the box.

5. Students list possible solutions to the problem. They may develop and test their hypotheses to isolate a solution.

6. Students present and provide evidence for the efficacy of their chosen solution.

7. Students reflect on the process and evaluate their performance. They note improvements they might make when addressing a different problem in the future.

You could present your students with problems to solve as they learn to work through the PBL process; however, most experts recommend supporting students in identifying problems and issues that interest them instead. Embedding choice allows underserved gifted learners to capitalize on their strengths and interests, and it increases student motivation to engage meaningfully in the problem-solving process.

CARE Strategies: <u>A</u>bility Group Students Flexibly

In this book, the term *flexible ability grouping* means grouping students by interest, need, or ability level (potential or demonstrated). Grouping alone is not enough, however. It is high-quality instruction that makes the difference in these groups.

There are many ways to group your students for learning. Grouping should depend on the educational objectives of the activity. For example, if your goal is for all your students to learn how to work collaboratively with all types of people in all types of settings, it would be appropriate to group students of varying ability levels sometimes. Students live in a technologically connected worldwide community, so learning to communicate well with others, planning together toward a common goal, and just getting along are important skills to develop for success in the real world beyond school. However, if the educational objective is academic growth for your underserved gifted students, consider grouping by ability level so you can provide more targeted activities and support.

That said, when it comes to providing underserved gifted learners with the best opportunity to grow academically, flexibly grouping students based on interest, need, or ability is critical to cultivating students' strengths. It helps ensure students have the opportunity to demonstrate what they know. Flexible grouping means that group members change periodically depending on the lesson or unit. To use this type of grouping well, you must know your students' strengths, interests, and learning preferences (see chapter 2 for ideas on how to gather this information) and plan your lessons accordingly. When educators group students without care and intentionality, underserved gifted learners end up in groups where they do not feel academically challenged or emotionally engaged.

> **What I Want You to Know About Me** ★★★
> "I feel like being in the honors algebra class is a waste of my time. We were put here based on assessment data from last year, but we do the same thing the regular algebra class is doing—same schedule on the calendar even—we just have to complete more worksheets. Doing more of the same thing over and over again is killing me. I'd rather just stay in the regular class and only have to 'practice' the problems once."

Grouping by Interest

Don't underestimate how effectively grouping by interest can motivate underserved gifted learners to challenge themselves and work productively. Opportunities to connect with peers who have similar interests can be extremely engaging. You may find that students grouped by interest are willing to work harder and longer and at a higher level of proficiency than they otherwise would.

> **REAL-WORLD EXAMPLE**
> Marcos, a fourth grader, had picked up a hobby of video game design from his older brother. He spent hours outside his school day building his own games in JavaScript. However, he never mentioned this to his teacher or classmates.
>
> Students at Marcos's school were involved in a yearlong social and emotional development program that focused on kindness and compassion. For one unit project, the students needed to demonstrate their

understanding of compassionate interactions with others who might be struggling with a problem. As Ms. Jones, the fourth-grade teacher, began planning for this unit, she reviewed an interest inventory she'd asked students to complete earlier in the year. One of the questions asked students to share how they spent their time outside class. Ms. Jones saw that Marcos had mentioned video game design on his inventory. She knew of two other students with similar interests: Ashley, who constantly talked about playing video games, and Andre, who often brought board games to share with students when they had choice time. Ms. Jones had been hoping to find a way to better engage Marcos during the school day. She recognized that he had great strengths in problem-solving and logic, but he rarely contributed in class. During recess the next day, she briefly met with the three students and asked if they would be willing to work together to design some type of game that second graders could play to learn about compassionate interactions. All three students agreed.

As Ms. Jones observed and supported Marcos, Ashley, and Andre over the next several weeks, she was pleased to see that Marcos was engaging fully with his groupmates and also taking a leadership role. The group decided to create both a board game and video game. Marcos not only took the lead on the layout of the board game, he also taught Ashley and Andre aspects of video game programming. Marcos was highly engaged in the activity, and Ms. Jones observed strengths she hadn't yet seen in other scenarios. Based on this project, Ms. Jones recommended that Marcos be evaluated for gifted programming services.

Grouping by interest can be engaging and meaningful for all students and can help build a stronger classroom community. In interest groups, underserved gifted learners can share their passions with others who will value them. They can also find commonalities among themselves and students from other economic, social, or cultural circumstances. Take care to group students by interest in a positive, respectful way. Whenever there are options for students to choose their own topics or tasks, make it clear that no topic or task is superior to another. Remind students that it is good to learn about unfamiliar topics or tasks, especially when they are unsure what their interests are. Also, encourage students to learn about each other's interests. Usually students will self-identify a topic of interest quickly and stay with the same peers throughout an entire group project. Discourage students from giving up on a topic and jumping to other groups unless they provide a compelling rationale for doing so. Encourage students to persevere and give a topic a chance. You can use the "Creating Interest Groups" toolkit strategy to help you plan interest groups in your classroom. The strategy describes three types of interest groups, with implementation tips and an example for each.

TOOLKIT STRATEGY

Creating Interest Groups

EXPERT GROUP

Students focus on a topic that interests them and is relevant to a specific unit or lesson; they often teach the class about this topic.

Tips:

- Before grouping, give students time to share topic interests related to the unit or lesson.
- Generate a list of topics on the board.
- Combine similar topics. Students can still focus on the aspect of the topic that they are most excited about.
- Allow students to work alone if they are passionate about a topic that doesn't interest other students.
- Give students an opportunity to evaluate their own roles and their peers' roles in the collaboration.

Example:

Students are studying environmental issues. After allowing students time to circulate and talk with others in the class about their interests, the teacher finds out that students want to examine the following topics more closely in groups: endangered species, recycling, global warming, deforestation, and ocean pollution. Although equal numbers of students are interested in each topic, the teacher could combine similar topics if needed (for example, deforestation and endangered species).

PERSPECTIVES GROUP

Students learn about a topic from a certain perspective that interests them (for example, advocate, writer, or scientist).

Tips:

- As a class, generate several perspectives that would be suitable for the topic at hand.
- Survey students to find out which perspectives interest them most. Leave a blank in the survey for students to write in a perspective that's not listed.
- Consider composing groups representing the various perspectives.
- Let students work alone if you are grouping students by shared perspectives and no one else is interested in their perspective.
- Give students an opportunity to evaluate their own roles and their peers' roles in the collaboration.

Example:

Students are studying the Holocaust in their social studies class. The teacher wants small groups to research the aftermath of the Holocaust from various perspectives. One group assumes the role of documentary makers. Another group chooses to examine the topic through the lens of artists. And the last group assumes the perspective of human rights activists.

> **INDEPENDENT RESEARCH GROUP**
> Students conduct their own research on a passion area of their choice.
>
> **Tips:**
> - Allow students the autonomy to choose a topic they are passionate about.
> - Multiple students may be interested in the same topic or similar topics. Let them work together to research various aspects of the topic.
> - Topics need not be related to academic standards.
> - Ensure that students are investigating a topic that they can share with a real audience, beyond their classmates and teacher.
> - A topic should not only interest the student, but also be researchable and feasible within the time parameters.
> - Help students develop a higher-level thinking question to answer through their research. (See page 87 for guidance on asking higher-level questions.)
> - Create a learning contract for the steps involved in the research investigation, the timeline for completion, ideas for the end product (groups may work on one product or individual products), your role in facilitating and supporting the investigation, and a self- and group-evaluation plan.
> - Let students work alone if other students do not share their passion.
>
> **Example:**
> Several students are constantly finishing their math classwork early. The teacher offers them the opportunity to conduct independent research over the course of the three-week unit once they've completed their classwork. Through an interest survey and informal discussion, the teacher helps the students zero in on a topic they all seem passionate about. They all want to research sports in depth. One student wants to focus on sports medicine, another on Jackie Robinson, another on women's participation in sports over time, and another on European soccer. They decide to create a combined product based on all their research: an interactive sports museum displayed in the library for the entire school.

Keep in mind that some underserved gifted students may have innovative ideas and the motivation to put in great effort but may not yet have developed the academic skills necessary to succeed. These students might need additional targeted support to accomplish the task—even with high levels of interest. To capitalize on their engagement and to mitigate frustration, closely gauge how the interest group is progressing and be prepared to step in with targeted mini-lessons focused on academic, cognitive, or social needs. These mini-lessons will enable the group to proceed confidently with the task at hand, empower them as learners, and ensure that when they face similar challenges in the future, they won't doubt their capabilities.

Grouping by Need

Another effective way to flexibly group your underserved gifted students is by need. This type of grouping can take several forms and can serve multiple purposes. For example, there may be times it makes sense to group students based on who needs targeted mini-lessons on specific academic topics or to obtain a particular academic skill, such as locating information from reliable resources online. There also will be times when it is appropriate to group your students based on social and emotional needs (for example, grouping students who want to practice advocating for themselves). You might also consider grouping your students based on their learning preferences (for example, based on who prefers to gain information via text, who prefers to interview experts on a topic, and who would prefer to watch a documentary to gain the required information).

In certain situations, it will be beneficial for your underserved gifted learners to be grouped with a mix of kids from the classroom. There will be other times when, based on the topic or need, it is more appropriate to put them in a small group just with other gifted students or just with other underserved gifted learners. Through flexibly grouping based on need, your underserved gifted learners have an opportunity to gain targeted academic and social skills to support both their cognitive and affective growth. To use this type of grouping effectively, it is important to know your students well.

There are multiple ways to gain the information you need to successfully group students by need. Sometimes you can get the necessary information through assignments and formal or informal assessments. Conversations with the students themselves and their family members can provide valuable information to help with grouping. You can also use a checklist or survey like the one presented in the toolkit strategy "Surveying Learning Needs" to determine academic needs that can be addressed in small groups with teacher support.

TOOLKIT STRATEGY

Surveying Learning Needs

In chapter 2 (page 44), we introduced the principles of Universal Design for Learning (UDL). You can use these principles to guide curriculum development and modify the learning environment to better meet your students' academic and cognitive needs. Surveying your students' needs will give you a clearer picture of what you need to focus on to improve student engagement, representation of information, and expression of learning. The reproducible "Learning Needs Survey" on page 92 at the end of this chapter provides a safe, nonintimidating outlet for students to express their learning needs to you.

Grouping by Ability

Grouping students with others who have similar strengths or documented achievement is called ability grouping. All available testing data on your students can help you determine how best to ability group your students; but remember, even the best-designed tests may not identify the strengths or potential of underserved gifted learners. You will often need to rely on your own classroom observations. Within-class ability grouping—creating ability groups with your own students in your own classroom—is often the most realistic option because it doesn't require coordinating with other teachers. However, between-class ability grouping may be necessary at times (when possible) to meet the needs of some of your more advanced learners.

Ms. Estis teaches in a Title I elementary school. She has five gifted third graders in her classroom who are Latinx and/or are economically disadvantaged. While the rest of the class is engaged in completing a different unit project, she offers her gifted group the opportunity to engage in an enrichment cluster that will provide them with the freedom to think and display their knowledge in ways that suit them best. During this self-directed investigation, Ms. Estis acts as a facilitator. She wants this group to learn from the experience instead of directly from her. She supports her students in this group as needed while guiding them in setting challenging, attainable goals with actionable steps. You'll find Ms. Estis's description of the enrichment cluster in the following Spotlight and related reproducible forms on pages 93–95. During these activities, third-grade economics standards are more deeply addressed.

SPOTLIGHT

In the middle of our mathematics measurement unit, to provide the opportunity to apply Personal Financial Literacy standards, the entire class receives a letter from Becky Block asking them to build her a home. She wants a square house, exactly 5 inches long and 2.5 inches tall. Each student is given fifteen play dollars to buy interlocking bricks that they will use to physically construct the house. Students are given the option of purchasing a scoop of bricks for five dollars or a single brick of their choice for one dollar. Students must specify the dimensions of the single piece. A week later, the building supply company experiences a shortage of bricks, allowing student construction sites to merge to pool their resources. The merger also encourages teamwork, discussion, and planning among the students. For some students, building Becky's home within their budget is a challenge. Other students can complete the task without much effort. (One student requests a sixteen-by-sixteen piece the second day, a piece that not only exists but is a perfect 5-inch square.) The students who are capable of delving deeper into the unit's objectives receive a new challenge.

Beatriz Block hears about the success of the advanced students in building Becky's home and sends them a letter requesting that they build her a home as well. She doesn't specify dimensions. She says only that the house needs to be twice as long as Becky's house and three times as tall. The width of the house needs to equal half the house's length. The house must be a quadrilateral but not a square like Becky's house. Beatriz also gives requirements for windows, doors, and colors. She requests a detailed blueprint and cost estimate before students begin to build, encouraging students to articulate and plan exactly what will be required to build the requested house.

The enrichment group works together to identify the dimensions requested by Beatriz. They create and label a diagram of the house and fill out an order form detailing the costs of building it. I will accept only one blueprint and order form, so the enrichment-cluster students must work together and agree on both the plan and the execution of Beatriz's house. I allow the enrichment cluster autonomy to work together with minimal interference from me. When needed, I provide guidance and support to help the students successfully complete their more challenging task.

—*Contributed by Alicia Estis, third-grade teacher at Coronado Hills Elementary School in Denver, Colorado. Used with permission.*

At some point in your preservice teacher education program, you probably learned about Vygotsky's concept of the zone of proximal development (ZPD). You may remember that the ZPD is the sweet spot of learning—where students work with support at a level slightly above where they could function on their own. Students learn best when they partner with someone who has the knowledge and skills to move them slightly beyond their current comfort zone. Less learning happens when students can easily accomplish a task on their own or when they're presented with a task that is far too difficult for them to complete.

Students working in their ZPD are potentially working at their highest capacity, increasing their skills and abilities through associating with others more knowledgeable about a particular topic or concept. When your underserved gifted learners are *not* grouped with other students of at least similar ability—when they are always the most knowledgeable or skillful person in a group—they are missing the opportunity for growth provided by working within their ZPD.

> **REAL-WORLD EXAMPLE**
>
> At the beginning of the semester, Juan pretested his physical science students to see who was coming into the class already knowing a great deal about the concepts the class would cover that year. He found that there were at least two distinct groups: one with no apparent knowledge about the upcoming unit and another with a fairly good grasp of the content. Juan decided to structure his lessons so that he could ability group his students. He wanted to make sure each group was meeting the standards while also growing academically.
>
> Juan explained, "I knew that one group was going to need some really foundational knowledge and quite a bit of support from me. I thought the other group could work with more abstract concepts, and that they were similar enough in knowledge about the subject that they could work through some of the material together and push each other at times. However, I also knew that for them to really grow the way I wanted them to, they would need regular interaction with me—so I could model the thinking processes required to work through the higher-level activities." Juan's within-class ability grouping and the support provided by him and by peers allowed the students in his class to work at least a portion of the time in their ZPD.
>
> Juan included one of his underserved gifted learners in the higher-ability group with great success. He explained, "There was one student whose pretest certainly didn't indicate that he should be in the more advanced group, but I'd observed that during previous units, while he didn't know the material coming in, he picked up on it quicker than anyone else. He just seemed to 'get it' as soon as the material was presented. Based on this, I decided to include him in the higher-ability group. I'm so glad I did! He excelled beyond what I expected and seemed to gain additional confidence in his abilities as a scientist."

In chapter 2, we addressed the importance of requiring individual accountability for students working in groups (see page 43). This bears repeating, because there are few things more likely to hamper students' motivation to work in a group than feeling that the process is unfair or at least not personally beneficial. Often in groups, especially when these groups are not created and monitored thoughtfully, the following issues arise:

> Gifted students feel like they have to do all the work to get a good grade.

> High-ability students may do all the work, and then feel dismayed when everyone in the group gets equal credit.

> If gifted students decide not to do all the work, they may be penalized with a bad grade.

When you are planning group work, ensure that each student takes responsibility for a certain aspect of the assignment, so the gifted student doesn't wind up doing all the work. Do not penalize gifted students for other students' lack of follow-through. And remember to group gifted students thoughtfully, placing them with others who have similar interests and abilities.

Sometimes you will want to choose the members of each group carefully, but it's also important to let students choose their own groups sometimes. When you turn over this responsibility, you demonstrate that you trust students to make this decision, and you empower them as learners. This empowerment is important for underserved gifted learners, who may not always feel that they "fit" the educational system or that the educational system fits them. By giving them this choice, you show that you respect their perspective on what works best for them and that you are willing to support them in making important decisions about their own learning.

But be careful. Too much freedom without structure or guidance can be debilitating for your students. Make sure that you are still available to provide support when needed. Also, with freedom comes responsibility. Students must learn to monitor how well their group is functioning and reflect on whether the choices they made were the best possible choices to meet their learning objective. The toolkit strategy "Group Work Self-Reflection Checklist" can help students with this task.

★ ★ ★ **What I Want You to Know About Me**
"I work at a higher level when I work alone rather than in a group or with others. I am a visual learner! Sometimes it takes a little extra explaining before I fully comprehend a subject, but once I learn it, I excel."

TOOLKIT STRATEGY

Group Work Self-Reflection Checklist
Use the Group Work Self-Reflection Checklist at the end of a group project or assignment. (See the reproducible checklist on page 96.) Or, when a project extends over a long period of time, you can ask students to reflect and evaluate themselves at a few points throughout the process.

While many of your students are probably motivated by the opportunity to work with peers, some will prefer to work alone. It is important for students to learn to work collaboratively, but unless there is a specific collaborative learning goal associated with a particular assignment, validate students' learning preferences by letting those who want to work alone do so.

Connecting and Grouping with Culturally Responsive Literature Circles

One especially effective method of flexible ability grouping with underserved gifted learners is to use literature circles. Culturally responsive literature circles, in particular, incorporate both connecting learning to students' lives and ability grouping students flexibly. Literature circles are small student-led discussion groups of about five to six students, organized according to need, interest, or ability level. In a literature circle, students read the same text (ideally, a text that resonates with some aspect of their lived experience) and come together on a predetermined schedule over the course of several weeks to share some aspect of what they have read. One way to approach this is to have students share based on the roles they've been assigned. Roles rotate each time the group meets. These roles help focus students' reading. They commonly consist of the following:

> The *discussion leader* is responsible for the flow of the discussion and prepares questions to help the group interpret the text.

> The *summarizer* provides an oral summary of the assigned reading.

> The *wordsmith* finds and defines interesting, new, or challenging vocabulary words in the text.

> The *key passage locator* selects important passages, provides a rationale for passage selection, and solicits input from other group members.

> The *connector* makes connections between the story's events and real-life events.

> The *artistic interpreter* represents some element of the story visually, provides a rationale for the artistic interpretation or choice, and shares it with the group.

To help students make meaningful connections to their lived experiences and to other cultures, another role you can add to literature circles is the *culture explorer*. The culture explorer is similar to the connector, except that this student focuses specifically on identifying cultural similarities or differences among characters in the text based on personal cultural experience. The culture explorer shares these connections with the group and offers group members an opportunity to make their own cultural connections. (It's important to note that *all* students can serve in this role. It shouldn't be limited to, for example, just your ELL students.)

Literature circles are a great way for underserved gifted learners to become more confident, engaged readers and to cultivate their leadership and collaborative skills in small peer groups. When these groups function well, students are motivated to read, their self-efficacy in reading improves, and they feel safe to express their opinions and interpretations to others.

Short, teacher-facilitated mini-lessons embedded in literature circles can maximize student learning. You can use these mini-lessons to front-load material (such as information about the time period) or skills (such as vocabulary or how to disagree respectfully with another person's opinion) that would enhance the students' reading and discussion of the material. You could also use these mini-lessons while the literature circles are under way, based on teacher observation or student feedback. The toolkit strategy on page 78 offers ideas for mini-lessons that focus on reading and social-skills strategies. You can use these ideas beyond literature circles and English language arts classes too. If you ever group your students or ask them to read independently, consider incorporating one or more of these mini-lessons into your instruction.

TOOLKIT STRATEGY

Mini-Lesson Ideas for Culturally Responsive Literature Circles

READING STRATEGIES

- *Visualizing*: Create pictures in your head of what you are reading.
- *Connecting*: Ask yourself how story elements connect to aspects of your life.
- *Questioning*: Formulate questions about what you don't understand, questions that challenge a character's behavior, or questions about what you wish the author would tell you. Use the "Higher-Level Thinking Bookmark" toolkit strategy on page 87 to help you develop questions.
- *Inferring*: Make predictions about what you are reading based on textual evidence.
- *Evaluating*: Honestly critique parts of the story throughout the reading.
- *Analyzing*: Dig deeper into the author's choices in writing style and storytelling.
- *Recalling*: Practice retelling and summarizing what you read, especially with more challenging passages.
- *Self-monitoring*: Pause and think about your thinking (metacognition). Use context clues or a dictionary to decode challenging vocabulary. Take short breaks from reading as needed, and jot down your thoughts on what you just read. Put a sticky note on a page you struggled with that made you want to stop reading. Move past the page and either come back to it later or ask for support from your teacher or peers.

SOCIAL-SKILLS STRATEGIES

- *Accepting and honoring differences*: Understand that individuals may work differently, especially in groups, and may have varying experiences reading and making sense of texts depending on their backgrounds and life experiences.
- *Communicating clearly and respectfully*: It's okay to disagree with your classmates, but you need to do so in a way that validates their thoughts and makes them feel safe to continue expressing their thoughts in the group. It might be helpful to practice what you want to say in your head or write it down on paper before you say it, to make sure you are stating what you mean clearly. (It's also a good idea, early in the year, for the teacher to model and have students practice how to respectfully disagree with another person's opinion.)
- *Resolving conflicts*: There may be times when disagreements lead to conflict or when some people in the group feel that they are doing more work than others are. In these cases, take steps to ensure every person in the group feels heard and that their concerns are validated.
- *Actively listening*: Instead of actively listening during a conversation, often people are simply waiting to talk. That means they are not listening to understand but

rather to reply. Students need to practice active listening strategies. This will lead to richer, more meaningful discussion of texts.

- *Encouraging and supporting others*: It is important to make all students feel supported in the group, especially if they are struggling with the text or have a connection that is personal or differs from what the other group members have shared.
- *Staying on task and waiting patiently*: When it's not your turn to share, you may start to get distracted or veer off task. This is not fair to other members of your group. Actively listening and taking notes on others' ideas can help you stay focused.
- *Being accountable as individuals and as a group*: All students need to do their part and support others in doing their parts. Simple self-monitoring checklists can foster accountability.

TOOLKIT STRATEGY

Student Evaluation of Cultural Connections in Texts

Another way to infuse culturally responsive teaching into literature circles is to have students evaluate texts for relevant cultural connections. You can use the reproducible "Student Evaluation of Cultural Connections in Texts" on page 97 after students read a literature circle text or class novel, or students can complete the evaluation based on text previews or past texts they've read. You can then use this student feedback to help you select texts for literature circles and other reading activities, to ensure that you give underserved gifted learners the opportunity to connect meaningfully with class readings.

Figure 3-1 Sample Student Evaluation of Cultural Connections in Texts

★★★★★

Student Evaluation of Cultural Connections in Texts

Connections	Yes	A Little	Not at All	Comments (Explain your ratings, give examples from the story, or describe how you wish the story had done this better.)
The characters are similar to me and people I care about.	X			At first I didn't think so, because they were from a completely different part of the world, but the more we read and discussed, the more I realized how similar they were to me in the interests they had and in how they interacted with family members.
The setting of the story is familiar to me. It is like places I know.		X		It wasn't, but I still think it would be good to include this in future classes. It was interesting to learn about a place that was so different from any place I've been and to realize that I can still connect with those characters.
The way the characters talk and act is similar to me and people I know.	X			Especially the way they act.
I've had things happen to me or people I know like what happened to the characters in the story.	X			There were several things, but losing a grandparent was something I could really relate to.
Overall, I felt I shared things in common with at least one of the characters in this story.	X			I was surprised, but I did.
I would recommend this story to my friends.		X		I don't know if some of my friends would appreciate this book, because the reading level was pretty difficult, but I still think I would probably recommend it to some of them. I'd like to be able to talk to them about the things that happened in it.

CARE Strategies: Respectfully Differentiate for Students

In addition to connecting learning to students' lives and ability grouping students flexibly, to both engage and challenge underserved gifted learners, it is important to acknowledge and validate your students' diverse experiences and perspectives. A leading expert on differentiating instruction, Dr. Carol Ann Tomlinson discusses

> ★★★ **What I Want You to Know About Me**
> "I can't learn through lectures and diagrams alone. I need to have an entertaining source and a hands-on experience to learn something. It's not a preference, it's just who I am. I am an extreme visual and physical learner."

ways that teachers can *respectfully* differentiate instruction in their classrooms. This might mean modifying what you teach, how you teach it, what resources you use, the environment where your students learn, or how they demonstrate what they have learned.

Student Choice

Student choice is one way to differentiate in the classroom, and choice is extremely important for underserved gifted leaners. Allowing student choice increases student engagement and shows underserved gifted learners that you care and want them to succeed. Specifically, providing choice in how students demonstrate their learning prevents unnecessary stress and gives underserved gifted leaners—and all students—the opportunity to shine.

> **REAL-WORLD EXAMPLE**
>
> Mr. Jackson had been an eighth-grade English language arts teacher for more than fifteen years. He met with the new gifted coordinator at his school to find out how to really engage his students in learning. He knew that he was a content expert, that he had good classroom management skills, and that he was doing his best to get to know his students. But he was starting to feel that even the students in his more advanced class didn't want to be there.
>
> The gifted coordinator asked Mr. Jackson to describe the unit he was currently teaching. Mr. Jackson said it was a unit he'd taught for years that was part of the eighth-grade curriculum. The students read several dystopian novels, discuss the stories as a class and in groups, take vocabulary quizzes on key terms, watch a dystopian movie, and then write a timed essay connecting the movie to at least two of their readings. The gifted coordinator asked, "Are they learning essay-writing skills during the unit that need to be assessed?" Mr. Jackson shook his head. The gifted coordinator continued, "So, are they able to choose other ways to show you what they've learned about dystopian literature?" Mr. Jackson answered, "No, not really."

How many students in Mr. Jackson's class could have demonstrated their understanding of the unit objectives in other creative ways? Probably almost all of them. Further, how many of his students shut down and felt their self-efficacy crash when they found out they would have to write a timed essay that accounted for a large part of their unit grade? There's no telling—but even one student is too many. Some students might actually prefer to demonstrate their newly acquired knowledge through timed essay writing. But other students, such as gifted students with learning disabilities and ELL students, may find timed essay writing daunting, stressful, and anxiety inducing—especially when essay writing is not part of the unit objectives.

Choice Boards

Choice boards are one way to incorporate choice into learning activities and culminating products. Choice boards empower students by allowing them to choose, within defined parameters, how they learn and how they demonstrate what they know. Choice boards look similar to tic-tac-toe boards. Each square represents a different activity related to lesson or unit objectives.

Students begin by choosing the square they feel most comfortable with or excited about (or you may choose a square they need to complete). Then they select two additional activities. In most cases, their three chosen activities will make a vertical, horizontal, or diagonal tic-tac-toe row.

TOOLKIT STRATEGY

Creating Choice Boards
You can create a choice board by following these simple steps:

1. Identify the educational objective for the choice board. Make sure the activities you choose align with this objective.

2. Decide if the entire class will complete the same choice board or if you would like to design different choice boards based on student need or interest. For example, you may create a choice board for students who need more support with mastering the educational objective, one for students who just need periodic check-ins and limited support to master the educational objective, and one for students who may already have mastered the educational objective and need extra challenge (still with periodic check-ins and support, as needed). This strategy is called *tiering*. Students from underserved backgrounds need exposure to challenging material; however, they may also need to learn and practice foundational skills that will help them complete challenging learning activities successfully. You can flexibly tier assignments and activities to offer underserved gifted learners both types of opportunities, depending on their needs at a given time. One way to begin the tiering process is by designing activities for students who are on grade level and would need limited support in mastering the educational objective. You would then modify those activities for students who need more support and for students who need more challenge. Another way to approach this is to start with your students who need the most challenge and design choice board activities appropriate for them. You would then tier backward from there, attempting to help your other groups get as close to mastering the activities in the highest tier as possible. Tiering assignments and activities helps you ensure that all students are focused on the same educational objective but are able to pursue it at the appropriate level.

3. Design nine learning activities based on what you decide in step 2.

4. Decide how you want to arrange the activities on the choice board.

5. Ask your students to choose three activities to complete. You might decide to require that all students complete the task in the middle. If so, this should be a task that all students could complete successfully. You may also decide that you want to assign a specific activity (not the center square) to each of the groups to ensure that they complete a task appropriate to their specific instructional needs. Students are usually asked to make a vertical, horizontal, or diagonal tic-tac-toe row with their three choices; however, you may decide that students can choose any three activities.

See **figure 3-2** for an example of a choice board. The instructional focus of this unit for seventh graders was how to conduct research. Each student chose a historical person who interested them, conducted research on the most influential time period in that person's life, and then selected three activities from the choice board to demonstrate creatively what they learned about their chosen historical figure. The middle square was a free choice. Students could either select one of the other activities on the choice board or propose their own activity. Students loved having the opportunity to choose not only a historical figure who was personally meaningful to them (Louis Armstrong, Frida Kahlo, Stephen Hawking), but also how they demonstrated their learning. For example, Gabriella, a reticent black student who rarely spoke in class, wrote a beautiful diary entry from Stevie Wonder's perspective and translated it into braille. A simple choice board activity like this empowers underserved gifted learners to make personal connections to content that resonates with them *and* to confidently showcase what they know in engaging ways.

Figure 3-2 Sample Choice Board

Write a poem about the historical person you are researching. Be sure to include important personality traits and key accomplishments. Your poem must include various poetic devices (such as imagery and figurative language).	Make a collage that represents the historical person you are researching. Use 8–10 drawings or pictures that represent the person's personality traits, values, and key moments in their life. You may use words and quotes in addition to images.	Write a diary entry from the perspective of the historical person you are researching. This entry should tell the person's thoughts about an important decision or moment in their life. This entry should give us insight into the person's mindset.
Create a timeline that represents key dates and events in your historical person's life. You should include 8–10 events with brief descriptions, visuals, and dates.	**Your Choice**	Find at least 3 songs that you think reflect an important message from the most influential decade in your historical person's life. Represent the significance of each song using a form of your choice.
Find 6–8 quotes that you feel reflect an important theme or set of beliefs from the time period in which your historical person lived. Visually display the theme or beliefs and place the quotes around it. Be sure to include attributions for your quotes.	Create a work of art that symbolizes an important aspect of your historical person's life or the time period in which they lived. In writing, explain the symbolism behind your creation.	Create a map of a key place during a pivotal decade in your historical person's life. Find a way to help us understand why this place was so significant to this person's life.

RAFTs

Another way to incorporate choice into learning activities and culminating products is by using RAFTs. The acronym stands for **R**ole, **A**udience, **F**ormat, and **T**opic. This strategy enables you to easily offer a variety of relevant and engaging choices to your underserved gifted learners. You can even get suggestions from them on what they would like you to include.

When building a RAFT, you will first need to generate several ideas for roles, audiences, formats, and topics that students can choose from. One effective way to do this is to put a blank RAFT on the board or projector and have the class brainstorm ideas together. You may also share a completed RAFT to give the class more ideas for choices to add to the columns. Once you've generated enough role, audience, format, and topic ideas together, students can begin working on their RAFTs individually, in pairs, or in small groups. You may decide to let students mix and match, choosing any entry they like from each column; however, this will depend on the focus of the RAFT. If the focus of the RAFT is to delve deeper into the lives of historical figures as in the sample on page 84 then it may make more sense to have students select an entire row.

TOOLKIT STRATEGY

Building RAFTs

> **R:** The *role* is the perspective that the student assumes to connect with the topic at hand. For example, the student might take on the role of an investigative reporter to uncover little-known information about a particular historical event.

> **A:** The *audience* is who the student is communicating information to with their project. If, for example, a student is completing a project on fracking, and their audience consists of community members who have voiced strong opinions on fracking, the student will need to share information thoughtfully and respectfully.

> **F:** The *format* is how the student will communicate information to their audience. Format choices may range from podcasts and short films to creative writing, artwork, and more. Format choices may be left blank, so students can propose their preferred format.

> **T:** The *topic* is the focus of the project and is connected to learning objectives. You should strive to choose topics that have real-world applications for your underserved gifted learners. For example, you might select issues that are already relevant to students' lives, or you might help students connect to unfamiliar topics so they become more relevant to students. For example, the novel *To Kill a Mockingbird* may seem dated to students; however, a RAFT can show them how it's relevant to their lives. Harper Lee's novel tackles many timeless topics, such as prejudice, finding courage, and making sense of human nature.

The following sample RAFT asks students to research a renowned scientist from an underserved population. The last row of the RAFT allows students to craft their own choices for the assignment.

Figure 3-3 Sample RAFT

Role	Audience	Format	Topic
Thomas Edison (gifted inventor who also had a hearing disability)	Future inventors	Diary entry (or propose another format)	My disability did not hold me back. It helped me succeed.
Katherine Johnson (black female mathematician whose groundbreaking work for NASA was documented in the film *Hidden Figures*)	Society	Public broadcast (or propose another format)	More black women are needed in STEM fields.
George Washington Carver (innovative botanist and inventor who overcame being born into slavery)	People who doubt their own potential	Speech (or propose another format)	Even through adversity, always keep fighting for the future you deserve.
Michael Faraday (renowned chemist and physicist who grew up economically disadvantaged and had little formal education)	Young children	Blog post (or propose another format)	Poverty shouldn't prevent you from fulfilling your dreams.
Ellen Ochoa (astronaut and first Latina in space)	Future astronauts	TED Talk (or propose another format)	What it was like to become the first Latina in space.
Your choice	*Your choice*	*Your choice*	*Your choice*

Chunking Assignments and Projects

Even though underserved gifted learners may appreciate having choices to demonstrate their learning, large projects may still seem overwhelming to them. For some students, the project they choose may be the first project they have ever been asked to complete. They may seem excited to begin the project, but feelings of frustration may soon take over, especially if students discover that the project requires knowledge or skills they have not yet learned or mastered. You may need to break large projects into smaller components. As students complete each component and receive positive, constructive feedback, they build their self-efficacy and get the message that they can successfully complete the larger project.

> **TOOLKIT STRATEGY**
>
> ## Building Step-by-Step Project Timelines
>
> Usually we can apply a general protocol or framework to breaking a larger project into smaller steps. For example, the engineering design process contains six steps: ask, imagine, plan, create, experiment, and improve:
>
> 1. Ask: Identify the problem, requirements, and limitations.
> 2. Imagine: Brainstorm solutions and ideas. Know what already has been done.
> 3. Plan: Choose a design to prototype.
> 4. Create: Build a prototype.
> 5. Experiment: Test the prototype.
> 6. Improve: Revise the design.
>
> For students planning a design project, you can build a project timeline based on the six steps of engineering design. Remember that going through each step of the design process may not always be necessary but having this framework available as a general guide can help students see how an idea becomes a product.
>
> The creative problem-solving process provides students with another framework for developing solutions to problems while exercising divergent and convergent thinking skills (Isaakson and Treffinger 1985). This process contains the following six steps:
>
> 1. Explore the vision: Clarify the purpose(s) of the project and problem(s) to solve.
> 2. Gather data: Collect and interpret data about the problem(s).
> 3. Formulate challenges: Develop a research question for the project.
> 4. Explore ideas: Generate ideas to find answers to the problem(s).
> 5. Formulate solutions: Expand and evaluate the ideas.
> 6. Formulate a plan: Test the feasibility of the solutions and go back to previous steps if needed.
>
> To help develop students' self-efficacy, incorporate progress monitoring into the project. (For a reproducible project timeline, see page 98.) First, you will need to explain the process to students and help them identify steps, tasks, and expected completion dates for tasks. Students are then charged with checking their progress on the dates they predetermine and writing themselves words of encouragement, as well as noting specific actions they need to take to remain on track for completing their project. You can apply this strategy to both individual and group projects.

Assessment

Assessment is tied in several ways to differentiating effectively for underserved gifted learners. First, preassessments are a great way to determine who has already mastered some or all of what you are getting ready to teach. This information can help you plan differentiated assignments and activities that will foster your students' continued growth. Formative assessments (formal or informal assessments that happen during the learning process) help you modify assignments and activities on the go to provide additional support or challenge for students who need it. Summative assessments help you determine what students have learned at the end of an instructional unit. You can also use information from summative assessments to determine how successful your differentiation efforts during the learning process were and what you might do differently next time. It is important to design your summative assessments to be as equitable as possible, giving students the opportunity to truly show you what they have learned in a variety of ways. Differentiating summative assessments often entails allowing students some choice in how they will document mastery of the learning objectives.

Another important aspect of using summative assessments effectively is making sure students know ahead of time how and on what you will evaluate them. One way to inform students is to give them assessment rubrics early in the unit. While these can be very beneficial, typically assessment rubrics focus on the end product and do not consider students' effort during the learning process—or if they do consider the learning process, it is not weighted heavily. This can be discouraging to underserved gifted learners, especially if they made great strides during the learning process but are assessed only on the end product and how well they completed it to their teacher's specifications. To prevent discouragement, it's important to make sure that your assessments value effort and growth in the learning process and that your students are aware of this.

TOOLKIT STRATEGY

Process Evaluation Rubric

Using a *process* evaluation rubric, in lieu of or in addition to evaluating the final product, can help students reflect on the learning process. They can point out to their teachers process areas that they were particularly proud of and set goals for areas in which they still need to improve. (For a reproducible "Process Evaluation Rubric," see page 99.) Set aside time for a conference in which you and the student can discuss the information they provided in the rubric. You might decide to complete your own separate evaluation of how the student engaged in the learning process. Comparing the student's ratings and your ratings offers a great opportunity for discussion. Be sure to incorporate this information into the final project grading rubric.

CARE Strategies: Engage Students in Higher-Level Thinking

The final CARE strategy for teaching underserved gifted learners involves using higher-level thinking activities in your classroom to engage students. When a question, activity, or assignment is too simplistic, gifted learners may "check out" rather than participate in something they feel is wasting their time and energy. Conversely, embedding an appropriate level of difficulty into lessons can be a huge motivator for your students.

This is as true for underserved gifted learners as it is for other gifted students. If students come to your classroom lacking any foundational skills (such as academic language) needed to complete assignments and activities independently, you might hesitate to challenge them because you do not want to overwhelm them. But as we discussed in chapter 1, teaching underserved gifted students requires you to check your assumptions, dig a little deeper, and provide additional supports. When it comes to engaging your underserved students, these aspects of teaching and all the elements of CARE come together so you can challenge and support their learning.

Asking Higher-Level Questions

Remember that lower-level questions and thinking activities almost always result in lower-level responses from students. Underserved gifted students need opportunities to demonstrate what they are capable of. They can do just that with the proper supports in place to meet their needs when they are engaged in more complex learning.

Bloom's Revised Taxonomy of Educational Objectives describes six levels of thinking: Remembering, Understanding, Applying, Analyzing, Evaluating, and Creating (Anderson and Krathwohl 2001). *Lower-level questions* require students only to remember, understand, and apply knowledge. This boils down to students primarily recalling information from texts or information that they learned. *Higher-level questions*, on the other hand, require students to analyze, evaluate, and create knowledge. Higher-level questions ask students to think and respond more deeply.

Without realizing it, educators tend to ask students far more lower-level questions than higher-level questions. Developing higher-level questions often requires more thought from teachers. That is likely why, without intentional planning for higher-level questioning during instruction, educators tend toward lower-level questions. To better understand your own questioning practices, film yourself during several class periods or have someone you trust observe you during instruction. The "Higher-Level Thinking Bookmark" toolkit strategy can help you become more mindful of the types of questions you ask students during reading, discussion, and other learning activities.

TOOLKIT STRATEGY

Higher-Level Thinking Bookmark

Underserved students, in particular, need opportunities to showcase their potential. Asking higher-level thinking questions is a great way to give them such opportunities. You'll find a reproducible bookmark full of question starters for higher-level thinking on page 100 at the end of this chapter. Simply photocopy the bookmark, cut it out, fold it in half between the two columns, and laminate it. Keep it handy and refer to it when you want to embed more higher-level questions into instruction. You can also make copies of this bookmark for your students. They can use it for discussion-based activities or to develop questions for inquiry-focused projects.

See pages 101–102 at the end of this chapter for a sample lesson plan on crafting higher-level questions based on Bloom's Revised Taxonomy. You can also find this sample lesson plan and others in this book's digital content. (See page 180 for how to download.)

Socratic Seminars

The National Paideia Center, a leading authority on using Socratic seminars in classrooms, defines a Socratic seminar as a "collaborative intellectual dialogue facilitated with open-ended questions about a text" (National Paideia Center, n.d.). Socratic seminars are student-facilitated discussions that foster higher-level critical thinking through the use of thoughtful questions, respectful dialogue, and claims supported with textual evidence. Through questioning and shared discourse, students collectively construct the meaning of what they've read and delve deeper into topics and issues presented in a text.

When done well, Socratic seminars have the potential to increase student motivation for learning. They can cultivate a more supportive classroom culture through improving students' communication skills. Underserved gifted students with strong verbal skills who may have had few opportunities to articulate their ideas and unique perspectives can shine during Socratic seminars.

TOOLKIT STRATEGY

Implementing Socratic Seminars

1. Create discussion norms as a class. Refer to these as needed throughout the Socratic seminar. Norms might include statements about actively listening, questioning respectfully, building on other students' responses, and so on.

2. Choose a text about which you want your students to have a meaningful discussion. Although you can use novels for Socratic seminars, it is often better to start smaller. Consider using poetry, short stories, or specific passages from novels for your initial Socratic seminars. (For example, Aesop's fables are well-known in many cultures and languages and can spark discussion about what students value and why. The poem "Mother to Son" by Langston Hughes may inspire discussion about how the mother's lessons may apply to students' lives.)

3. Formulate questions and discussion starters.

    › Although there may be opportunities for students to write their own Socratic seminar questions, it is usually best if you provide four to six questions at least a day before the seminar, and let the students plan their responses.

    › Stagger questions by complexity. For example, if the first two questions you ask can be answered in a straightforward manner using the text, you might pose these questions first during a Socratic seminar to build students' self-efficacy and encourage them to offer responses to more difficult questions later. This technique is especially important for underserved gifted learners. Seize every opportunity to build their confidence and support them in taking risks.

    › Supply students with dialogue starters they can use when they get stuck, to facilitate respectful discussion. Dialogue starters might include the following:
        ◦ I also think that . . .
        ◦ I agree with you because . . .
        ◦ I really appreciate the point you just made because . . .
        ◦ Although I understand your point about . . . , I disagree because . . .
        ◦ My opinion differs from yours because . . .
        ◦ What is your evidence to support that claim?

> - I'm not sure what you mean by . . . ; can you please clarify?
> - Your comment reminds me of . . .
>
> 4. Although you can use Socratic seminars in many ways, try this one first: Divide students into two groups and set up their chairs in two circles—an inner circle and an outer circle. The inner circle is for students who are discussing the questions. The students in the outer circle take notes on the inner circle students' discussion skills. Circles switch after a predetermined amount of time.
>
> 5. At the end of the seminar, leave time for summarizing the main points students made during the discussion and for allowing students to share their experiences participating in the Socratic seminar. This is also a great time for students to share positive and constructive feedback with one another about what they observed from the outer circle.

Depth and Complexity

Incorporating depth and complexity in your lessons will help you ensure higher-level thinking. As Sandra Kaplan and Bette Gould explained in their classic book *Frames: Differentiating the Core Curriculum*, educators can create depth through examining the following dimensions of a subject:

> - **Big ideas** are the generalizations, principles, and theories that develop from the facts and concepts of the area under study.
> - **Details** are the specific characteristics that describe a concept, theory, or fact.
> - **Ethics** are the controversial issues that surround an area of study.
> - **Language of the discipline** is made up of the specialized and technological terms used in a specific area of study.
> - **Patterns** are traits or events recurring in the details.
> - **Rules** are the natural or person-made structure or order explaining the subject under study.
> - **Trends** are factors that influence events.
> - **Unanswered questions** are ambiguities and information gaps within an area of study.

According to Kaplan and Gould, educators can develop complexity by examining issues (J Taylor Education 2016):

> - **over time,** by understanding time as an agent of change and recognizing that the passage of time changes human knowledge of things
> - **through multiple perspectives,** by understanding that diverse points of view alter the way humans view and value ideas and objects
> - **as interdisciplinary relationships,** by recognizing connections within, between, and among various areas of study

You can examine these dimensions individually (for example, focusing just on details to build a solid foundation for future discussion) or in combination (for example, examining ethical trends over time) to encourage higher-level thinking and meet the learning needs of your students.

One key component of teaching underserved gifted learners well is building teacher capacity to meet the needs of all students through ongoing professional development. The following Spotlight offers an example of how one US state began Depth and Complexity Framework training and support for teachers, so they could then incorporate rigorous programming to better meet the needs of their students.

> **SPOTLIGHT**
>
> Colorado has made it a priority to prepare teachers to provide challenging, high-level instruction for all students—including underserved gifted learners. Colorado public school districts vary greatly in their programming, resources, and number of qualified gifted personnel dedicated to gifted students. For the majority of gifted students in the state, differentiation in the general education classroom is the main programming strategy. To succeed with this strategy, educators must have a common understanding of what differentiation really means. In response to this need and to teacher requests for differentiation strategies for gifted and advanced learners, the Colorado Office of Gifted Education launched a statewide professional development project to increase rigor in the classroom for all students, using any standard and any curriculum.
>
> The project, called Right 4 Rural (R4R), was supported by a grant from the US Department of Education's Jacob K. Javits Gifted and Talented Students Education Program to increase gifted identification among underrepresented populations in rural areas across the state of Colorado. The premise was that rigorous programming must precede identification to provide opportunities for underrepresented populations to exhibit gifted characteristics. To accomplish this goal, regular classroom teachers needed a toolbox of rigorous strategies to pull from on a daily basis in a habitual manner.
>
> A suite of three workshops was offered across the state for schools, districts, Boards of Cooperative Educational Services (BOCES), and R4R sites. Following best practices in professional development implementation theory, the following assurances were in place for every participant:
>
> - commitment to attend the entire suite of workshops
> - support from local administration
> - structures in place for long-range implementation and facilitation of the model
>
> The project also offered a train-the-trainer model to increase capacity across the state by establishing a network of local educators to present and facilitate workshops within their own organizations. The professional development suite combined best practices in gifted education and general education: student academic and teacher effectiveness standards; formative assessment for and as learning; inquiry, gradual release of responsibility, collaboration, and higher-level thinking; differentiation of content, process, and product through tiered tasks; and brain-based, project- or problem-based, and self-directed learning.
>
> Colorado chose the Depth and Complexity model as a differentiation tool that's engaging for both teachers and students. Colorado's adaptation of the Depth and

Complexity Framework has been adopted by large and small school districts in ways that best meet the needs of their student and teacher populations. Teachers who use the Depth and Complexity prompts as thinking strategies with purpose have students who engage in the work with purpose. Implementing the Depth and Complexity Framework promotes a community of engaged teachers and students learning and thinking together in a broader, deeper, and more rigorous context. R4R sites have seen an increase in the number of typically underrepresented populations referred for gifted identification. Teachers in general are more aware of the kinds of behaviors that might reflect gifted potential and report an increased awareness of how deeply and complexly all students can think when given the right opportunities.

—*Contributed by Jacquelin Medina, former Colorado Department of Education director of gifted education, and Karen Kendig, Colorado Department of Education interim director of gifted education. Used with permission.*

Chapter Summary

Teaching underserved gifted learners and helping them maximize their full learning potential requires that you CARE deeply and genuinely about them and their futures. Educators need to **C**onnect learning to students' lives intentionally and thoughtfully, **A**bility group students flexibly, **R**espectfully differentiate for students, and **E**ngage students in higher-level thinking. Although high-quality teaching benefits all students in your classroom, the strategies presented in this chapter are especially effective with historically underserved gifted learners. Used effectively, these strategies give your underserved gifted learners opportunities to engage in meaningful, personalized learning experiences and to demonstrate their gifts and talents—which may not always be visible in traditional educational settings—and will show them that you are their advocate and you believe in their ability to succeed. To reflect on your progress on using these strategies, fill out the reproducible "'Teach Me' Checklist" on page 103.

Learning Needs Survey

To Help Me Understand Why I'm Learning What I'm Learning	Sounds Like Me	Not Really Like Me
I can identify and put into words my own academic and behavioral goals.		
I am comfortable taking risks with my learning (for example, by picking a new topic to work on).		
I know what distracts me, and I have control over it.		
I try to understand the purpose of learning.		
I prefer to find answers to problems with little guidance.		
I am a good partner in group work.		
I persevere no matter what.		
I know how to control my behavior.		
I know how to pick myself up when I feel upset or frustrated.		
To Help Me Understand What I'm Learning	**Sounds Like Me**	**Not Really Like Me**
I rely on visual aids, such as descriptions, captions, diagrams, or charts.		
I rely on text-to-speech or speech-to-text software.		
I rely on pictures or graphic symbols when I'm learning new vocabulary words.		
I use underlines or highlights to capture big ideas or relationships in texts.		
I'd like to have key concepts or vocabulary words available in English and my first language (if English is not my first language).		
I need help making connections between past and current learning.		
I need graphic organizers to understand abstract concepts (for example, KWL charts and concept maps).		
I am overwhelmed by huge chunks of information, and I don't know what to do with it.		
I have trouble connecting what I'm learning in school with my life.		
To Help Me Understand How I'm Going to Complete a Task	**Sounds Like Me**	**Not Really Like Me**
I rely on resources, such as spelling or grammar checks, graph paper, or sentence strips.		
I need instruction to write attainable goals with actionable steps.		
I need help with goal planning and strategy development.		
I need strategies, such as how to solve problems and how to prioritize and sort information in texts.		
I need help with monitoring my behavior or my learning progress.		

From *Start Seeing and Serving Underserved Gifted Students: 50 Strategies for Equity and Excellence* by Jennifer A. Ritchotte, Ph.D., Chin-Wen Lee, Ph.D., and Amy K. Graefe, Ph.D., copyright © 2020. This page may be reproduced for individual, classroom, or small group work only. For all other uses, contact Free Spirit Publishing Inc. at freespirit.com/permissions.

Dear Students:

My name is Becky Block. I was recently hired to work at a company in the city of Blockhaven. I will soon be moving there. The homes there are very nice, but they are not exactly what I **need** to have **harmony**. I know you are learning about measurement, perimeter, and area, so I would like to ask you to construct a new home for me.

I would like a home that is a **perfect square**. The **length of one of the sides** should be exactly **5 inches**. I also request that my home be exactly **2.5 inches tall**. I do not have a preference for color, but I am a very **colorful** person.

I will pay you $5.00 for each requirement you successfully construct. At this time, I am only looking for a simple home. However, if your construction is precise and efficient, I may hire you for additional jobs.

I will give you a **down payment of $15.00** to cover the cost of materials and labor. My new job begins on _____, so my new home must be completed by _____. I know that you are very busy in class, so I must request that your **daily work be completed before you work on my home**. In addition, I require those with whom I do business be of the **highest character**. Therefore, **if you choose to** _____ or fail to _____, I must insist you pay **a fine of $1.00 each day you choose to** _____ and **$1.00 for missing homework**.

Thank you in advance for your hard work.

Sincerely,

Becky Block

Becky Block

Used with permission from Alicia Estis, third-grade teacher at Coronado Hills Elementary School, Denver, Colorado.

Dear Students:

My name is Beatriz Block. My cousin Becky has been raving about your construction abilities and about how much she loves the homes you have built. I would like to contract with you to build my dream home.

My requirements are a bit different from Becky's. I would like a home that is twice as long as Becky's home and three times as tall. The width should be half the length. It would still be a quadrilateral, just not a square.

Unlike my cousin, I prefer a monochromatic color scheme. I would also like a proper door and at least one window on each wall.

If you are willing to construct my dream home, I will pay you three times my cousin's price. Please draw up a well-labeled blueprint that includes size dimensions and color. Also, please calculate the cost to construct my home, so I can adjust my budget accordingly. Once I have received the blueprint and cost estimate, I will send you the money needed to construct my new home.

I am so excited, and I can't wait to hear from you.

Sincerely,

Beatriz Block

Beatriz Block

Used with permission from Alicia Estis, third-grade teacher at Coronado Hills Elementary School, Denver, Colorado.

Building Supply Costs and Order Form

Building Supply Costs

Item	Cost
Structural pieces by the scoop	$5.00 per scoop
Single selected structural piece (You specify the size and color.)	$1.00 each
Basic doors	$3.00 each
Fancy doors (doors with windows)	$3.25 each
Superfancy doors (castle doors)	$4.00 each

Order Form

Item (name, size, shape, and color)	Quantity You Want		Price for One Item		Total Cost
		x		=	
		x		=	
		x		=	
		x		=	
		x		=	
		x		=	
		x		=	
		x		=	
		x		=	
		x		=	
		x		=	
		x		=	
		x		=	
		x		=	
		x		=	
Total cost of all items				=	

Used with permission from Alicia Estis, third-grade teacher at Coronado Hills Elementary School, Denver, Colorado.

Group Work Self-Reflection Checklist

	Definitely	Somewhat	Not Really	My Thoughts
I understood the goals for our group task.				
I held myself accountable for parts of the task I didn't understand and asked clarifying questions.				
I understood my role in making the group successful.				
I understood my teacher's expectations for the group task and felt these were fair.				
I thought group work was appropriate for this task.				
I found the task interesting.				
I felt my contribution to the group was important and showcased my skills.				
I took timelines seriously.				
I felt respected and heard in my group.				
I felt our group members genuinely collaborated with one another.				
I persevered through difficult parts of the task or group experience.				
I asked for peer or teacher support when I needed it.				
I put my best effort into the work I completed in this group.				

Student Evaluation of Cultural Connections in Texts

Connections	Yes	A Little	Not at All	Comments (Explain your ratings, give examples from the story, or describe how you wish the story had done this better.)
The characters are similar to me and people I care about.				
The setting of the story is familiar to me. It is like places I know.				
The way the characters talk and act is similar to me and people I know.				
I've had things happen to me or people I know like what happened to the characters in the story.				
Overall, I felt I shared things in common with at least one of the characters in this story.				
I would recommend this story to my friends.				

From *Start Seeing and Serving Underserved Gifted Students: 50 Strategies for Equity and Excellence* by Jennifer A. Ritchotte, Ph.D., Chin-Wen Lee, Ph.D., and Amy K. Graefe, Ph.D., copyright © 2020. This page may be reproduced for individual, classroom, or small group work only. For all other uses, contact Free Spirit Publishing Inc. at freespirit.com/permissions.

Project Timeline

Steps in the Process	Specific Tasks I Need to Complete	Expected Completion Date	Progress Check Dates	Words of Encouragement and Actions to Make Progress

Process Evaluation Rubric

Parts of the Learning Process	Yes	Kind Of	No	Explanation
I put enough time into planning for and completing this task.				
I asked for help and support when I needed it.				
I didn't give up when I got stuck.				
I learned from my mistakes throughout the process.				
I incorporated teacher and/or peer feedback.				
I turned in my best work.				

From *Start Seeing and Serving Underserved Gifted Students: 50 Strategies for Equity and Excellence* by Jennifer A. Ritchotte, Ph.D., Chin-Wen Lee, Ph.D., and Amy K. Graefe, Ph.D., copyright © 2020. This page may be reproduced for individual, classroom, or small group work only. For all other uses, contact Free Spirit Publishing Inc. at freespirit.com/permissions.

Higher-Level Thinking Bookmark

Lower-Level Question Stems	Higher-Level Question Stems
Remembering • What is . . . ? • When did . . . happen? • Who was . . . ? • Why did. . . . ? • How did . . . ? • How would you explain/describe . . . ? • What was your favorite part? • Describe . . . (the setting and so on)	**Analyzing** • Describe the theme. • What can you infer/guess from . . . ? • What do you think (character)'s reason is for . . . ? Why? • What is the relationship between . . . and . . . ? • How would . . . look in real life? • What was the (funniest, saddest, happiest, most unbelievable) part of the story? And why? • Imagine that you were (character). What would you have been feeling? Why? • What are the important qualities of . . . ?
Understanding • What is the main idea of . . . ? • How would you summarize . . . ? • What do you think . . . means? • What is happening?	**Evaluating** • Do you agree with (character)'s decision to . . . ? Why or why not? • What is your opinion of . . . ? • Why do you think (character) chose . . . ? • What examples can you find to show . . . ? • What would happen if . . . ? Why? • Could this story have happened in real life? Why or why not?
Applying • Predict what would happen if . . . • How is this like . . . ? • How would . . . have handled . . . differently? • How would you . . . ? • How could you use . . . ?	**Creating** • If you could create a different ending for the story, what might that be? Why? • If you could change any part of story, what would you change and why? • Suppose you could . . . What would you do and why? • How would you solve . . . using what you have learned?

From *Start Seeing and Serving Underserved Gifted Students: 50 Strategies for Equity and Excellence* by Jennifer A. Ritchotte, Ph.D., Chin-Wen Lee, Ph.D., and Amy K. Graefe, Ph.D., copyright © 2020. This page may be reproduced for individual, classroom, or small group work only. For all other uses, contact Free Spirit Publishing Inc. at freespirit.com/permissions.

Sample Lesson Plan: Using Higher-Level Questioning to Guide Inquiry

Overview and Objectives

The focus of this lesson is on supporting students in crafting higher-level questions based on Bloom's Revised Taxonomy (analyzing, evaluating, and creating) to guide their individual inquiry into an area of Chinese culture that interests them. (You can adjust the lesson to be about any country or culture.)

- Students will distinguish between higher-level and lower-level questions.
- Students will develop higher-level questions for an area of Chinese culture that interests them.
- Students will identify if they created lower-level questions for their topic of interest and, if so, rework these into higher-level questions.
- Students will answer their questions through self-directed research.

NAGC Gifted Programming Standards

Standard 1: Learning and Development
1.6. Cognitive and Affective Growth. Students with gifts and talents benefit from meaningful and challenging learning activities addressing their unique characteristics and needs.

Standard 3: Curriculum Planning and Instruction
3.4. Instructional Strategies. Students with gifts and talents become independent investigators.
3.5. Culturally Relevant Curriculum. Students with gifts and talents develop knowledge and skills for living and being productive in a multicultural, diverse, and global society.

Standard 4: Learning Environments
4.5. Communication Competence. Students with gifts and talents develop competence in interpersonal and technical communication skills. They demonstrate advanced oral and written skills, balanced biliteracy or multiliteracy, and creative expression. They display fluency with technologies that support effective communication.

(National Association for Gifted Children 2010)

Materials/Resources Needed

- Computers or tablets for student research
- Bloom's Revised Taxonomy chart: cft.vanderbilt.edu//cft/guides-sub-pages/blooms-taxonomy
- Levels of inquiry outline: prodigygame.com/blog/inquiry-based-learning-definition-benefits-strategies

Sequence of Learning

Day 1

1. Present images, topics, and concepts related to China to engage student curiosity for possible research topics.
2. In their social studies notebooks, students document what they wonder about China from the teacher presentation, research, and their own background knowledge of China.
3. Display and review the various types of questioning and thinking skills related to each level of Bloom's Revised Taxonomy and encourage students to craft questions that are in the upper levels for deep inquiry.
4. Students submit initial questions on a form to be reviewed in the next lesson.

Sample Lesson Plan continued

Day 2

1. Display anonymous examples of questions submitted the previous day. Students identify higher-level questions by noting the level of Bloom's Revised Taxonomy each question engages. Students discuss how to rework and support the lower-level questions.

2. Display levels of inquiry (open, guided, structured, confirmation). Students reflect and determine which type of inquiry they are engaged in as a class discussion. Students determine that open inquiry allows for choice in topic, research methods, and product or delivery of findings.

3. Students launch research while you confer with students to guide them in developing higher-level questions and to help them with research.

Day 3

1. Discuss possible options for collecting and displaying information learned through research.

2. Students continue research into their curiosity areas for another full class period.

Day 4

1. Students participate in a gallery walk of final products of their open inquiry about China. Students receive peer feedback through comment sheets left at their desks for constructive feedback, compliments, questions, and accountability.

2. Students complete a reflection form on this learning experience. They evaluate their levels of engagement and achievement, as well as the strengths and weaknesses of this type of inquiry activity for their preferred learning modalities.

Reflection/Assessment

Students will create products for a gallery walk that demonstrate their learning from their higher-level inquiry. Products may include the following examples:

- notes
- presentations or slideshows
- labeled diagrams
- compare-and-contrast charts
- illustrations
- surveys
- timelines
- flip charts

"Teach Me" Checklist

Use this checklist to reflect on the extent to which you use instructional strategies with your underserved gifted students that demonstrate how much you CARE about their learning. Review your results to become more aware of your areas of strength and your areas for growth.

Key:
Beginning: You're aware and want to try.
Developing: You have tried or are trying.
Leading: You are consistently aware, implementing changes, and making others aware.

Connect Learning to Students' Lives	Beginning	Developing	Leading
I connect learning to students' background experiences and make sure that the learning materials represent their cultural backgrounds.			
I give students opportunities to create authentic products for real audiences.			
I give students the opportunity to self-direct their learning and to choose how they demonstrate their learning.			
I help students connect with the future.			

Ability Group Students Flexibly	Beginning	Developing	Leading
I use grouping strategies that focus on students' interests: expert groups, perspectives groups, independent research groups, and so forth.			
I use ability grouping to encourage my students to work in their ZPDs.			
I identify and support students' academic, cognitive, and social needs during group work as needed.			
I guide students' self-reflection in group work.			
I incorporate culturally responsive teaching strategies into group work.			

Respectfully Differentiate for Students	Beginning	Developing	Leading
I modify what happens in my classroom in order to better meet the diverse learning needs of my students.			
I incorporate choice into learning activities, such as through choice boards and RAFTs.			
I scaffold learning by chunking assignments and projects to build students' self-efficacy.			
When evaluating students' work, I consider their effort and how they engaged in the learning process.			

Engage Students in Higher-Level Thinking	Beginning	Developing	Leading
I embed an appropriate level of difficulty into lessons.			
I ask students to think and respond at a higher level: analyzing, evaluating, and creating knowledge.			
I use Socratic seminars.			
I use the Depth and Complexity Framework.			

From *Start Seeing and Serving Underserved Gifted Students: 50 Strategies for Equity and Excellence* by Jennifer A. Ritchotte, Ph.D., Chin-Wen Lee, Ph.D., and Amy K. Graefe, Ph.D., copyright © 2020. This page may be reproduced for individual, classroom, or small group work only. For all other uses, contact Free Spirit Publishing Inc. at freespirit.com/permissions.

4 CHALLENGE ME

> We are all concerned about the future of education. But as I tell my students, you do not enter the future—you create the future. The future is created through hard work.
> —Jaime Escalante

★★★★★

Challenge is a critical aspect of educating underserved gifted learners to the best of your ability. All people—including underserved gifted learners—need to be challenged to grow and reach their full potential. Without challenge, their academic development may slow or even stop. Consider the example of an economically disadvantaged child who was reading two to three years above grade level during his early elementary school years but scored at grade level on a middle school reading assessment because he lacked access to outside-of-school resources that could have cultivated his reading potential. Instead of stagnating, how might this child's aptitude for reading have continued to grow throughout elementary school and into middle school with the proper challenges in place?

It is educators' responsibility to know when students are ready to be challenged and how best to challenge them. Challenge, although necessary for academic and personal growth, may be detrimental to students if it is not thoughtfully embedded into their learning experiences. As chapters 2 and 3 explain, zone of proximal development (ZPD) challenges are best. Students will become frustrated if they lack the requisite knowledge, skills, and support to handle the challenge.

All students need opportunities to experience struggle and to know what it feels like to persevere (with proper support) as opposed to just giving up. Because of the barriers underserved gifted learners face, teachers need to care deeply about their success. But caring is not enough. Teachers need to develop engaging lessons at the appropriate instructional level, masterfully facilitate the learning process, and give students constant encouragement and support to ensure they get the most out of their educational experiences.

Examining the close relationship between *teaching* underserved gifted learners well and *challenging* them is the purpose of this chapter. Sometimes certain students in your classroom will require something significantly more in-depth or more complex than your other students do to meet their intellectual, academic, or affective needs. Many of the strategies in this chapter are best practices for challenging all gifted learners; however, these strategies have been adapted to show how they can be used effectively to challenge underserved gifted learners specifically. Most gifted students, for example, would benefit from delving deeper into a topic of interest and showcasing their learning to an authentic audience. The advanced reader mentioned earlier could have had a successful continued learning trajectory if teachers had supported and challenged his continued learning.

If you use the Multi-Tiered System of Supports (MTSS) model, you are already familiar with the concept of providing intentional guidance with a challenging learning opportunity. MTSS is an approach to educating students that recognizes the need for differing levels of social, emotional, behavioral, and academic supports, dependent on the individual child. The foundational level, or Tier 1 of MTSS, is composed of strategies that benefit every child in your classroom (and will challenge many of them). This level is all about good teaching. Tiers 2 and 3 of MTSS focus on specialized opportunities and support that are necessary only for some students. So, while all your students need challenge, your gifted learners may require specialized challenge to truly grow, and your underserved gifted learners may require even more individualized learning opportunities that take culture, ability, language, disability, and socioeconomic status into consideration. This type of challenge is the focus of this chapter.

> **What I Want You to Know About Me** ★★★
> "I like to be challenged and will always try as hard as the teacher who is teaching me."

As an educator, you should aspire to positively impact your underserved gifted learners' lives, help them realize and cultivate their potential, and make sure they know you are fully committed to their success. Underserved gifted learners should aspire to reach the academic and personal heights they are capable of reaching. That is why we've chosen the acronym ASPIRE to organize the strategies in this chapter. You can help your underserved gifted learners accomplish challenging goals and achieve to their fullest potential when you:

- **Add** challenge thoughtfully.
- **Supply** the support necessary for success.
- **Provide** opportunities for mentorships.
- **Identify** possibilities for independent investigations.
- **Recognize** when acceleration is vital.
- **Embed** curriculum compacting into learning units.

ASPIRE Strategies: Add Challenge Thoughtfully

It is not always easy to know when students are ready for challenge. If you do not take time to assess carefully whether students are prepared for challenge, you may unintentionally expose them to learning experiences that hinder their academic and affective development. You do not want your underserved gifted learners to feel uncomfortable or unsupported in their learning environment. Rather, you want them to feel confident when they take on new challenges and academic risks. That's why it's important to identify students' readiness for challenge. You can do this by using the toolkit strategy on page 106.

> **TOOLKIT STRATEGY**
>
> ## Determining Learner Readiness for Challenge
>
> Conduct informal learner observations. Look for these signs of readiness for challenge:
>
> - The student is passively engaged in learning or is disengaged. (Note: Unfortunately, teachers often see students who are disruptive in class or refuse to participate and automatically label them as behavior problems. These behaviors can be signs of boredom in gifted students. Educators can often address them positively by providing more challenging learning opportunities.)
> - The student learns new material quickly and with minimal effort.
> - The student delves deeper into class topics through posing challenging questions or making connections that demonstrate higher-level thinking.
> - The student demonstrates curiosity beyond class requirements by taking extra initiative in school or at home to learn more about a topic.
> - The student shows persistence and a focus on learning mastery and growth.
> - The student is receptive to constructive feedback and open to receiving additional support.

After you've collected information from your informal observations, have a conversation with the student. Share with your student what you've seen that indicates to you she is ready to be challenged. This can be validating for underserved gifted learners and can build their self-efficacy as they engage in more challenging tasks.

Your student may tell you that she is not ready for additional challenge quite yet. Instead of forcing a challenge, talk to your student about what supports she needs to feel more comfortable taking on a new learning challenge. Make a plan together for challenge with support.

ASPIRE Strategies: Supply the Support Necessary for Success

Challenging underserved gifted learners often requires not only the support strategies presented in chapter 3 (such as scaffolding, preparing mini-lessons, and surveying learning needs), but also even more targeted supports. This is due to potential gaps in learning and gaps in opportunities to cultivate the skills needed to persevere through challenging learning activities. Try using the toolkit strategy "Academic Challenge Support Tips" to encourage your underserved gifted learners when they encounter new academic challenges and to help them achieve success.

TOOLKIT STRATEGY

Academic Challenge Support Tips

PROVIDE ONGOING ENCOURAGEMENT

When your students face new academic challenges, take on the role of their coach and cheerleader. Remind them why you believe they are capable of handling this new challenge: "You have the background knowledge. I've watched you persevere before. I know you have (or can develop) the skills to do this!"

CULTIVATE STUDENTS' INTELLECTUAL IDENTITY

During a challenge, ask your students questions that will help them realize the new knowledge and skills they are acquiring and how they can apply these to future academic challenges: "What are you learning about yourself as a scholar? What are you realizing about the way you learn best and solve problems? How will you apply what you've learned about yourself to future challenges in this class, in other classes, and outside school?"

MAINTAIN A COLLABORATIVE ATTITUDE

Remember that collaboration is not evaluation. During a challenge, it is important to avoid critiquing what students are doing or stepping in and doing it for them. Rather, take on the role of a guide or collaborator throughout the learning process:

› Embed opportunities to practice new skills to help students gain mastery.

› Highlight the most important components of a task and create a plan together for addressing each component.

› Explore possible ways to complete a task together; however, never complete a task for a student.

› Use questioning to facilitate problem-solving. Make sure your questions are open-ended and not leading students to solve problems the way you would solve them.

FOSTER HEALTHY COMMUNICATION

It is important for students to know they can ask for support during a challenging learning task. Make sure you are always looking for signs of frustration and encouraging communication in a safe, proactive way:

› Emotional literacy helps students identify how they are feeling, so they can better understand and manage their reactions during difficult situations. There are many examples of emotional literacy charts available online and in print (Ritchotte, Zaghlawan, and Lee 2017). These charts often contain images of a variety of emotions (such as emojis) with several adjectives that describe the emotions conveyed by each image. You can laminate a version of this chart that you like or create your own age-appropriate version and have your students keep it on their desks or in a more discreet place, like a planner. Your students can mark the emotion they are feeling on the chart with an erasable marker during a challenging task to help you see immediately that they need extra support.

› You may also try temperature readings. Emotions occur on a continuum from calm to intense. Label an image of a thermometer with about five words describing the range of emotions a child might feel throughout the day. You could brainstorm these words as a class. Print a copy of the labeled thermometer for each student, or keep a copy on hand to check in with your students and gauge how they're feeling. Help your students understand that it's important to tell you they need help before they reach their boiling point.

- Even when you are not supporting your students directly during challenging tasks, observe their behavior and check in periodically.
- If students seem frustrated, ease your way into a dialogue about this. Instead of saying, "You really seem frustrated," which might provoke a defensive reaction, try commenting on what you've seen students doing well. Or simply say, "Talk me through what you've been working on."

PROMOTE PERSEVERANCE

Although it may be difficult to watch your students struggle, if they are ready for challenge, you may need to take a back seat while they work through a difficult task. Taking a back seat does not mean abandoning your students. It means giving them the support they need without swooping in and solving problems for them:

- Use a three-times rule. When students are stuck, they need to try to solve the problem three times, using three different approaches.
- Encourage students to see their mistakes as learning opportunities. Point out times when they've made mistakes and gleaned important insights from those mistakes.
- Engage students in a conversation about why they are stuck. Do not allow them to say, "I can't." Through this conversation, they might identify problematic patterns in their thinking and find a way to move forward.
- Celebrate with students when they get unstuck!

ASPIRE Strategies: Provide Opportunities for Mentorships

As we discussed in chapter 3 (page 64), underserved gifted learners may have limited exposure to future career options. For example, immigrant or refugee students' families may still be learning English, and this may restrict the types of jobs they can hold initially. Families living in economically disadvantaged communities may not see the types of careers that they would see in a well-resourced community.

> **REAL-WORLD EXAMPLE**
>
> Mr. Neilsen took three of his students on a field trip outside the small, economically disadvantaged city where they attended high school to visit a larger, more prosperous city. There they attended a theatrical production of August Wilson's play *Fences*. Before this trip, the three students had never left the city they grew up in. One commented that he could not believe people actually had jobs that focused on designing sets and costumes.

Lack of exposure should not limit your students' future job options. Underserved gifted students need opportunities to hear about, read about, and discuss career options from an early age. They also need to see people like them (however they define that) in those roles. You can facilitate your students' exposure to career options by identifying books or movies that have members of underserved populations as main characters in those roles. You can also identify members of the community (or nearby communities) who work in various professions and are willing to talk to your students about their jobs. Your students will gain valuable perspectives from people who share their backgrounds, academic interests, learning experiences, or difficulties in life and may begin to picture themselves in similar professions.

Some of your underserved gifted learners may have intense interest or show advanced ability in a specific topic or field, which might provide the foundation for success in a certain career. It can be beneficial to set up these students with mentors. This type of mentorship is a relationship in which mentors and mentees pursue common interests. For example, a fifth-grade teacher at a Title I elementary school had a small group of economically disadvantaged gifted students who really wanted to start a robotics club. But they had limited knowledge about robotics and didn't know where to start or how to fund a club. The teacher reached out to a local university and high school. One of the university's community outreach centers provided a stipend to purchase three robotics kits for her students, and several of the students from the robotics team at the local high school (many of whom were also from underserved populations) volunteered at the elementary after-school robotics club meetings to mentor the younger students.

As illustrated in the robotics club example, you will probably need partners to help you start a mentoring program. Here are some things to consider as you begin:

› **Learn everything you can about your students.** Whether you partner with another organization or recruit mentors within your school community, you will need to make sure that mentors have interests similar to those of your underserved gifted learners and can provide support and cognitive engagement in those areas. To select mentors successfully, you'll need to know your students well. One way to get to know your students is to survey their academic and nonacademic interests. (See the "Mentorship Questionnaire" toolkit strategy on page 110.)

› **Tap into existing resources.** If you can, use an organization that already provides the type of support you need. For example, if your school already partners with a Big Brothers Big Sisters (BBBS) program, use BBBS volunteers if possible. Or, local high school or college students might enjoy sharing and cultivating interests with younger students. For example, students from a high school drama club may be excited to partner with an elementary after-school program to mentor younger students who are interested in theater. This is also a great way for older students to earn community service hours if these are required at their school.

› **Based on your students' interest surveys, recruit and review mentors in various fields.** Talk with your friends and colleagues to find experts in your community who would be willing to participate in a mentoring program. Many successful professionals are willing to give back to their communities and are honored to be asked to serve in this role.

- **Select your mentors carefully.** The primary purpose of a mentorship program for underserved gifted students is to extend their learning and expand their opportunities through the pursuit of common interests. Common interests alone, however, are not always enough to foster a successful mentor-mentee relationship. Personality and temperament also come into play, so consider these factors when you are choosing mentors.

- **Involve families.** It is important to work respectfully with the families of your underserved gifted learners. Inform them about your plan to begin a mentorship program and explain why you think it would be beneficial for their children. Identify and validate any perceived barriers to the mentorship plan (such as transportation or time commitment outside school) and try to work through these together for the students' benefit. Family members may feel more comfortable with a mentorship program if they have a chance to ask questions, express concerns, and meet potential mentors.

- **Train and support your mentors.** After you select a mentor, hold an initial information session so you can explain the role, share helpful information about the student, and lay out your expectations for both the mentor and the mentee. Your mentors will probably need ongoing support. Hold regular check-ins with the mentor and mentee individually to make sure everything is progressing smoothly and have them both reflect and debrief after they have finished the experience. This final session can help you with future planning.

- **Be mindful of policies on recruiting volunteers to work with students.** It is common for districts to require mentors to undergo a background check before they can meet one-on-one with students. If you are collaborating with another organization that provides mentors, it may have already screened candidates. This screening may be acceptable to your district but find out for sure.

TOOLKIT STRATEGY

Mentorship Questionnaire

To determine which students would benefit from a mentorship relationship and to help you find mentors who share similar interests, you first need to learn as much as you can about students' specific interests. Determine whether these interests are new or have been explored by the student for quite some time, so you can set an appropriate level of challenge with the student's prospective mentor. (For example, you do not want students who are newly interested in a topic to become discouraged because their mentors are misinformed about their preexisting knowledge.) A survey like the reproducible "Mentorship Questionnaire" on pages 133–135 will help you decide what type of support your students may need to fully pursue their interests with their mentors. This questionnaire will give you an idea of what expertise and qualities to look for in potential mentors.

Mentors and mentees will likely engage in a variety of activities together during the agreed-upon time frame. Mentorships may last a month, a semester, an entire school year, or multiple school years. Meetings may occur weekly, biweekly, or monthly. They may happen before school, after school, during lunch, on weekends, or over school breaks. Activities will vary. They may consist of discussion, learning and practicing new skills, conducting research together, taking learning trips outside school, creating small and large products, and so on.

> TOOLKIT STRATEGY
>
> ## Mentorship Evaluation Rubrics
>
> Evaluation is extremely important to any mentorship program. You can use evaluation rubrics with mentors and mentees throughout the mentorship experience to determine how they both feel it is going and to make any needed modifications. (For a reproducible mentor rubric, see page 136. For a reproducible mentee rubric, see page 137.)
>
> The mentor should see the mentor rubric before the activities begin to understand the expectations. As the teacher overseeing the mentorship, you can collect informal information from both the mentor and the student to complete the mentor rubric on your own. Or, you may choose to complete the rubric together with the mentor.
>
> The student may complete the mentee rubric with you or, if comfortable, with the mentor. Discuss with the mentor the need for the student to feel safe expressing feelings about the mentorship experience. There is no room for defensiveness.
>
> The moment the student feels uncomfortable in the mentee-mentor relationship, you will need to step in immediately and determine next steps. These steps may include mediating the relationship between the mentor and mentee to ensure they both have a positive experience. If the mentorship cannot be repaired, you may need to identify a new mentor for the student.

SPOTLIGHT

We decided to use mentorship with some of our students at our elementary school. We selected and taught fourth-grade students to be mentors to a group of first-grade students, who would act as the mentees. We wanted to give the fourth-grade students the opportunity to be of service to someone else, to develop a sense of responsibility and self-awareness, and to have the freedom to be creative. After we read and researched what it takes to start a mentor program, we worked together to design an introductory mentorship program at our school with a specific group of students.

One of the first things we did was discuss with our students what it means to be a mentor and a mentee. We had students think of people in their lives that they looked up to and felt comfortable with. We brainstormed what the words *mentor* and *mentee* mean and how a mentor or mentee can affect others. The goals for this project were for students to understand what it means to be a mentor and a mentee and for them to embrace the challenge of leading younger students in their learning. We knew that we could not start a full-blown mentoring program right away, but we wanted to plant seeds for a future partnership with members of the community.

Students were more excited to come to school on days when they met with their mentees. These days saw a 7 percent increase in attendance. In addition, student behavioral referrals fell by 10 percent throughout the mentorship period. The program gave students leadership opportunities that they might not normally get.

Many students flourished when they felt that they could use their knowledge to help others.

Our mentorship program was geared toward all learners, not just the gifted and talented population. We were surprised when some of our lower-performing students created some very creative projects for their mentees. This made us think that we had not given students enough time to show their creativity in the regular classroom setting. This mentorship activity allowed us to do some talent spotting for students who showed high levels of creativity. Sometimes our bias can affect how we expect students to perform in school.

—*Contributed by Jessica Huggins, interventionist, and Dimitra Collier, elementary school teacher, Price Elementary School, Louisville, Kentucky. Used with permission.*

ASPIRE Strategies: Identify Possibilities for Independent Investigations

Independent investigations, sometimes called independent studies or directed studies, are an instructional strategy teachers can use to challenge their underserved gifted learners. The primary purpose of an independent investigation is to give a student the opportunity to pursue a topic in which the student is intensely interested—and pursue it to a degree that would not be possible in a whole-class setting. This opportunity is important for a couple of reasons:

› First, underserved gifted learners often have interests related to their home lives and past experiences that their classmates do not share and that would not typically be addressed in school. These students may feel as if school is never for learning about what is most important to them. Independent investigations are one way to validate students' interests and keep students engaged.

› Second, underserved gifted learners often have either a wide variety of interests (everything interests them—at least for a while) or they have a single passion, often from an early age (they want to know everything there is to know about a topic). Independent investigations are a way to provide time that's not available in a typical school day and that may not be available at home for students to explore the breadth or depth of a topic to their heart's content. This exploration is a great way to empower underserved gifted learners.

> **REAL-WORLD EXAMPLE**
>
> Chris was a seventh grader. He confused many of his teachers, because he was identified gifted in reading but also received accommodations for a writing disability. In Ms. Russell's advanced language arts class, when she asked Chris to respond to writing prompts or make flash cards for Latin root words, Chris would put his head down on his desk.
>
> Ms. Russell talked to Chris and his parents privately about his disability. She found out that Chris didn't want to be in advanced language arts anymore. He thought he wasn't "smart" enough and was slowing down the class. Ms. Russell decided to collaborate with the special education teacher to give Chris extra support

> during writing assignments. She also wanted to build his confidence in the class to help him see his strengths and understand that he did belong there. She decided to allow Chris to conduct an independent investigation into a topic of his choice and showcase his learning in a way that made him feel confident.
>
> Chris was fascinated by Rube Goldberg machines, complicated machines designed specifically to perform simple tasks in elaborate ways. For his independent investigation, with guidance from Ms. Russell, Chris first researched Rube Goldberg machines and dictated notes through his computer instead of taking written notes. Since Chris loved to draw, next he used his research to design and create a blueprint for a Rube Goldberg machine. With help from Ms. Russell and his parents, he collected random items he could use to build his machine. For the third part of his independent investigation, Chris not only built his Rube Goldberg machine, but also recorded the process on video and narrated the creative problem-solving steps he took to make the machine function as intended. For the final part of his independent investigation, Chris asked for the opportunity to teach the class about Rube Goldberg, show his own video, and bring in the machine to demonstrate how it worked.
>
> At Chris's demonstration, his thirty classmates watched in complete silence as he dropped the marble and it traveled down plastic tubing and knocked down dominoes and various other objects. The students gasped and clapped when finally, a sign rose to the top of the machine. It read: "Do I get an 'A'?" Chris beamed with pride that afternoon and for the rest of the school year. He never again questioned whether he belonged in an advanced language arts class.

Another benefit of independent investigations is that they allow students to learn and practice skills necessary for future learning and success. Chris, for example, learned valuable research skills through the process of investigating how to create a Rube Goldberg machine. He also practiced problem-solving skills and learned perseverance when he couldn't get his machine to work correctly. Independent investigators apply critical-thinking, creative-thinking, and problem-solving skills to learning and understanding. Helping your students learn and practice these skills is one of the most important things you can do as an educator.

You may find that your underserved gifted learners have the passion and desire to pursue an independent investigation but do not have some of the foundational academic skills necessary to complete it successfully. You will need to address this gap so your students can truly enjoy the process of answering their own questions or finding solutions to their own problems. You can often do this while your students are working on their independent investigation, which helps them see more easily the need to address certain learning gaps. Your students may even become very motivated to focus on acquiring missing skills if they know they need these skills to engage more fully in their independent investigation.

For some students, figuring out exactly what they want to learn about might be difficult. You would not necessarily expect students who have had no experience with independent investigations to develop good research questions at first. But with the appropriate degree of support from you, they can certainly learn that skill. Here's how:

1. Start by modeling how you would write a research question for one of your interests. Write a research question, and then think out loud about why it might

not work or might not help you learn exactly what you want to know. Continue thinking out loud about what you would do to modify your research question.

2. Practice developing questions together with your students. In the "Real-World Example" on page 112, Ms. Russell brainstormed research questions with Chris after school. She asked him to tell her everything he was curious about concerning Rube Goldberg and his machines, and she wrote down Chris's thoughts on a piece of paper. Ms. Russell used this list of thoughts to pose possible questions to Chris, then modified them based on his input. For example, she said, "Chris, maybe you want to ask, 'What inspired Rube Goldberg to become an inventor?'"

3. Eventually your students will take over generating research questions (with your feedback). Ms. Russell provided time for Chris to process and pose his own questions. She helped him refine his questions as needed and wrote them down on a piece of paper so he could see and more easily edit them.

4. You can further facilitate this exploratory process by providing readings and resources to help your students determine exactly what they want to learn about through the independent investigation. Chris found several books at the library on Rube Goldberg machines. Ms. Russell also created an online digital binder for him with several additional resources. (For examples of digital binders, visit livebinders.com.) She explained how to identify credible sources and showed Chris how he could add resources to the digital binder at school and home.

Scaffolding may be necessary in other areas too. For example, you may have twice-exceptional students or ELL students who have difficulty taking in information through reading. Find audio recordings or movies to provide some of the information they need. Students need not share the information from their independent investigations in a written format. This is a wonderful opportunity to let your students get creative. Could they present what they've learned through a skit? Could they make a podcast? There are so many possibilities.

Bear in mind that while choice is empowering, too much freedom can be overwhelming to underserved gifted learners, who may need more structure to feel that they can meet or surpass the expectations of an independent investigation. Following are some tips for providing structure. (See also the "Independent Investigation Planning Guide" toolkit strategy on the next page.)

- Work together to create guidelines. These should include elements such as when the project is due, when the student will work on the project during the school day, expectations for a final product, and a potential real-world audience who can provide meaningful feedback on the product.

- Put the due date on an independent investigation calendar and then plan backward to break the project into chunks and create a deadline for completing each chunk. You might say, "To present your independent investigation on this date, you will need to practice it. How many days do you think you will need for that? Before you can practice, you need to have completed . . . ," and so forth.

- Check in with the student regularly. Put check-in dates on the independent investigation calendar. Schedule check-ins slightly before (and possibly also on) the day of each deadline. During check-ins, ask the student to reflect on what is going well, what the next steps in the process are, and where additional support may be needed.

> **TOOLKIT STRATEGY**
>
> ## Independent Investigation Planning Guide
>
> This guide is designed to support students in planning an independent investigation. Walk your students through the following steps and jot down their ideas. (For a reproducible version of this guide, see page 138.) Students can modify their ideas throughout the independent investigation process.
>
> 1. **Explore topics that interest you.** What are your passion areas? What are you excited to spend several weeks learning more about?
> 2. **Learn more about one topic that really interests you.** Read, listen to, and watch informative materials on your topic. Use credible sources, such as reference books, government or professional organizations' websites, and documentaries and TED Talks.
> 3. **Generate questions or problems.** Avoid thin questions or problems that can be answered or solved quickly and easily.
> 4. **Create an investigation plan to answer questions or solve problems.** Will you apply quantitative methods (analyzing numerical data, such as survey responses) or qualitative methods (such as telling a story with words)? Or will you use both? What's your timeline for completion?
> 5. **Select an authentic audience for your investigation.** Who will benefit most from (or be most interested in) your investigation findings?
> 6. **Execute the investigation plan.** What steps will you take to carry out your investigation plan?
> 7. **Analyze and interpret data.** How will you make sense of the information you collected?
> 8. **Ask, "So what?"** What information do you hope to be able to share with your audience through this independent investigation?
> 9. **Prepare for a presentation or product.** How will you make your presentation or product interactive? How will you ensure it conveys the full scope of your independent investigation? Think outside the box! Try something other than a slide presentation or a poster.
> 10. **Reflect.** How will you consider what you have learned not only about your interest arewa, but also about yourself as a scholar? How will you apply what you learned from this independent investigation to future experiences both in school and outside school?

Sometimes a student finishes an independent investigation quickly but creates a low-quality final product. To prevent this, provide a student-friendly rubric that explains exactly what the expectations are for the final product. The rubric needs to be as specific to the product as possible. For example, a skit would certainly have at least some different expectations than a podcast would.

Another strategy to improve the quality of products is to provide exemplars when possible. Exemplars are high-quality examples of a certain type of completed product. You may not have any of these as you begin using independent investigations, but as your students complete high-quality examples, most will be honored to let you keep a copy to share with future students. You could also create your own exemplars, but it's often more powerful for students to see what other students have created. If you do share exemplars, it's important to tell your students that these are certainly not the only way to complete independent investigations. Each exemplar is just one way, and it's designed to help students get started—not dictate exactly what they should do.

Independent investigations offer a great opportunity for students to develop skills such as perseverance, self-monitoring, and self-evaluation. Remember Chris? His independent investigation gave him the opportunity to develop perseverance, and he experienced the satisfaction that comes with seeing a project through to completion. For some students, it may be necessary to start with short-term independent investigations with somewhat simpler final products. This modification can help students learn the importance of following through with commitments—without the frustration of having to stick with investigations long after they've lost interest.

Following are some additional considerations to keep in mind as your underserved gifted learners embark on independent investigations:

- While there are forms of independent investigation that would probably benefit all your students (such as Genius Hour, a set time during the school day devoted to student-led inquiry), you will likely still need to modify these to meet the unique interests and needs of your underserved gifted learners. Consider a small group of students from an economically disadvantaged rural school district who received scholarships to attend their first university-based summer program for high-ability learners. In one of their classes, they were challenged to create a blueprint for something they would like to see built in the future. They decided to work together on their blueprint, but they quickly felt overwhelmed by the open-endedness of the task. Their teacher sat down with them and asked what they would love to see built in their neighborhood that people could really benefit from and enjoy. One of the students said, "A park with a new basketball court and swings, where kids can meet up after school, that has a place where older people can walk their dogs. I think lots of people would really like that." All the students in the group got excited about that. They immediately began brainstorming design ideas for a community park that was personally meaningful to them. (Contributed by Lisa Charles and Margie Lacy, teachers at Bowen Elementary, Louisville, Kentucky. Used with permission.)

- Independent investigations pair nicely with curriculum compacting. They could be one of the work options provided when students successfully demonstrate mastery of a topic through pretesting and are able to compact out of class instructional time and assignments, thereby freeing up time for them to work on something else. (See page 130 for more information about compacting.)

- It's important to include a final reflection that asks not only about students' perceptions of the independent investigation process and their final products, but also about their growth in areas such as effort, perseverance, and so on. See the "Independent Investigation Self-Evaluation" toolkit strategy that follows. This reflection helps set the stage for future independent investigations and can be a great resource for goal setting.

> **TOOLKIT STRATEGY**
>
> ### Independent Investigation Self-Evaluation
> Self-evaluation is always important for student growth. Your students can use a rubric composed of the steps in the planning guide to evaluate the work they do during an independent investigation. First, they can identify whether they think they did a good job at each step or need to grow in that area. Then they can jot down notes about their performance as they reflect on it. (For a reproducible version of this rubric, see page 139.)

Young Chautauqua as a Strategy to Challenge Underserved Gifted Learners

Young Chautauqua (YC) is one strategy teachers can use to challenge underserved gifted learners. YC is based on the Chautauqua education movement that began in 1874. Originally, teachers came together at Chautauqua Lake in western New York to learn. The camplike gathering grew so popular that similar assemblies sprang up across the United States, and the programming expanded to include general education, recreation, and entertainment. Soon families from all around were coming together to listen to speakers and engage in conversations about issues of the day.

The original "mother Chautauqua" still thrives in New York. The nationwide "daughter Chautauquas" do not—but since 1993, the Federation of State Humanities Councils has continued the tradition in a new format called Young Chautauqua. Today, students who participate in YC bring history to life by impersonating historical figures and then answering questions both in and out of character. This requires students to conduct in-depth research, create a monologue, and then present the figure to the public.

The process for a YC scholar is as follows:

1. The school provides a teacher and space for practices.

2. The YC director provides an overview for all participants and helps teachers become familiar with YC and all the available resources.

3. Teachers and librarians help students identify historical figures they can be passionate about and start learning about these figures through short biographies, book-length biographies, and primary sources.

4. Students take notes on why people should remember their chosen figures. What is the most important thing the figure accomplished that had a positive impact on society? What hardships did the figure face, and how did the figure overcome them? In what context did the figure live? What important people might the figure have known while alive?

5. Students then write a monologue that will be three to five minutes long. If writing is a problem for the YC scholar, allow alternative ways to prepare the talk.

6. Adult Chautauqua scholars demonstrate what it means to embody a historical figure so that students can experience what the end result of their projects might look like (exemplars).

7. Coaches help students find costumes. Thrift shops, museums, antique shops, and friends' and families' closets all offer great potential for costume development.

8. Students present to various audiences and get feedback on their presentations. Coaches who can critique students in a positive way are invaluable. Peers can be trained to give input too.

9. The final presentation consists of a performance in character followed by a question-and-answer period in character. The presenter then steps out of character and answers questions as the scholar.

SPOTLIGHT

In Colorado, the YC program is a family, school, and community affair. Family members love to see their students engaged in and enjoying history. They are invited to all events along with their scholars, and families are often involved in the research and presentation preparation process, learning along with their children. Everyone in the school benefits, as student scholars often present their historical figures to classrooms in all grade levels and to whole-school assemblies. Additionally, the community often invites the scholars to practice by presenting to service clubs, churches, and museums and at other appropriate venues. Local newspapers often cover these and other YC events. Families like to see their scholars perform at these events and receive recognition in the paper.

Teachers enjoy YC because it offers a chance to begin a creative program with support from the Humanities Councils, including funding; donations from the community; access to professional scholars who model the process for YC students; and coaching from volunteers. For example, Colorado Humanities has created YC handbooks for teachers. This organization has also worked with teachers to create thirty-three bilingual biographies of Colorado historical figures. Students also have the opportunity to work with a professional researcher, who teaches them research skills and guides their overall research efforts.

A whole grade level, a whole class, a small group, or an individual student may participate in YC. Some educators have used YC very successfully to provide targeted support to specific underserved gifted learners who desire and are ready for additional challenge. YC can be adapted easily to fit students' needs, such as by differentiating the amount of research support provided and by carefully choosing the authentic audiences to whom students present.

YC can be used to provide additional challenge in any content area. YC teaches students to read for understanding, to research, to answer questions, to create an interesting and historically accurate figure, and to write a monologue. Students learn public speaking skills beyond the basics. They ask themselves, "What does a good opening and closing look like? What are good questions someone might ask? What is the most effective way to share information about my figure's historical context?" Additionally, and maybe most importantly for underserved gifted learners, YC scholars have the opportunity to identify positive contributions their figures have made to society and to connect with their figures by identifying traits they admire and want to nurture in their own lives.

YC engages students in high levels of creativity through requiring them to dress up and challenging them to actually "become" their historical figures. Teachers may limit historical figures to those the course content already includes or expand the options to include figures that students would not otherwise have the opportunity to learn about. Students may also choose their own figures. Many excellent role models are available to help students learn about and take pride in their cultures.

Many students, including underserved gifted learners, who have grown up participating in YC praise what they learned in this program and how they use it in their adult lives. Some YC scholars have even grown up to become adult scholars who travel and present their characters.

Imagine Eduardo, whose family spoke only Spanish. Eduardo's teacher didn't think he could read. For his YC figure, he chose poet, boxer, and political activist Rodolfo "Corky" Gonzales (1928–2005) because his dad had once been involved with Gonzales. He took home the Colorado Humanities bilingual biography about Gonzales to read with his father. When Eduardo was chosen to present his character at Centennial Village Museum, his whole family came to watch. His father was so moved that he cried. He was so proud of his son's academic achievement.

José, another participant, recently called the Young Chautauqua director to say that he was now the educational journalist at a prominent newspaper. He said, "All the things I learned in Young Chautauqua are the skills that help me do my job." José was once a shy student who chose Cesar Chavez (1927–1993) as his YC historical figure. His shyness became a strength when he portrayed Chavez during his hunger strike. José was chosen from several hundred YC scholars to present his character in a cameo role at the Big Tent Chautauqua before an audience of eight hundred people.

Binti, a high school–age girl who had come to the United States as a refugee from East Africa, chose Dr. Martin Luther King Jr. as her YC figure. She spoke so eloquently that if you closed your eyes, you would believe that you were listening to King. She also was chosen to present her character in a cameo role to a large audience at an evening tent Chautauqua.

—*Young Chautauqua information and Spotlight contributed by Dr. Thelma Bear Edgerton, Young Chautauqua director and former district gifted-education coordinator for Greeley-Evans Schools, Colorado. Used with permission.*

TOOLKIT STRATEGY

Young Chautauqua Presentation Rubric

Here is a rubric you can use in evaluating YC scholars:

1. **Research and content (1–10 points):** Has the student done solid research or just the minimum? Does the student understand the figure's historical context? Does the student know the most important events in the figure's life?

2. **Presentation (1–10 points):** Evaluate the student on eye contact, body language, and appropriate gestures or movements. Is the student's speech clear and easy to hear? Does the student have a good opening and closing? Is the presentation well organized?

> 3. **Question and answer (1-5 points):** How does the student handle the question-and-answer session? Are the student's answers knowledgeable? Is the information accurate? Does the student use questions to give more information about the figure and historical context, or are the answers just a few words?
>
> *—Contributed by Dr. Thelma Bear Edgerton, Young Chautauqua director and former district gifted-education coordinator for Greeley-Evans Schools, Colorado. Used with permission.*

Infusing Challenge into Regional Programming for Economically Disadvantaged Rural Schools

Rural school students experience education differently from urban students. According to a report of the Rural School and Community Trust, nearly half of all rural students come from low-income families (Showalter et al. 2017). In contrast to the abundance of school choice that students in more urban areas often have, rural students instead have one option—and in many cases, only one building—in which to complete their entire preK–12 education. This results in a familiarity among teachers and students, who are often together for multiple grades in primary school, or who see one another constantly because there's only one math or science teacher covering all of middle school and high school. This can be both an advantage and a disadvantage. It can be an advantage because relationships among educators, students, and their families have the potential to be more personal. However, it can be a disadvantage if educators hold onto inaccurate assumptions about achievement, ability, and capability based on past interactions and experiences with students. Rural teachers face high expectations for classroom differentiation, because they must maintain multiple grade levels of instruction and grading each day. The opportunity to differentiate by offering separate "honors" or "advanced" classes is not feasible in schools where one math teacher struggles to address each grade level once per day.

What, then, can educators do for rural gifted students? In a rural area, there may be only three gifted-identified students total in the K–6 population. These students may come from economically disadvantaged homes and schools. How do schools program effectively for gifted students when having intellectual peers means engaging with students in neighboring school districts that are miles apart and spread out over multiple counties?

One possible solution to this dilemma is to approach programming, differentiation, and challenge from a regional level. Regional programming offers a way for geographically isolated students to connect on a personal level. Technology allows people to interact with anyone, anywhere in the world. But remote interactions aren't the same as in-person interactions. The personal connection gained by students when they spend time with like-minded and like-ability peers is invaluable. Providing regional gifted programming at low cost to the school is an effective method for reaching students from economically disadvantaged backgrounds. It is also an effective method for helping rural gifted students achieve their potential and see how their intellectual gifts may benefit their future community, wherever that may be.

SPOTLIGHT

In Colorado, gifted education is organized into eleven regions, with a gifted regional consultant liaising from the state level to each region's local gifted coordinators. The Northeast and East Central regions of Colorado have been offering regional events in partnership since 2009. These events provide meaningful and challenging enrichment, student interaction with like-minded peers, and opportunities for parents to learn from national speakers on varying gifted-education topics. These events are offered during normal school hours so students can attend using school transportation. The cost includes lunch and/or dinner to minimize attendance barriers faced by economically disadvantaged students.

At the elementary level, the regional events are called "Ultimate Celebration," and each year the students celebrate a specific topic. Recent events have included "Celebrating Waves," which covered a variety of sound waves, ocean waves, and electric currents; and "Celebrating Creativity," which allowed students a chance to look at and re-create Georgia O'Keefe paintings through chalk, participate in African drumming, and work with Shakespearean plots. The spring 2018 offering was "Celebrating Space Exploration," and students engaged with the Challenger Learning Center of Colorado in making and launching rockets, touring a portable planetarium, and participating in an interactive workshop on living in space.

At the secondary level, each year students are invited to two events. The first is a one-day event called "Ultimate Summit," and the second is a three-day event at the end of the school year called "Ultimate Scavenger Hunt." Both events are held "in search of" a concept or big idea. At this level, the programming expands to engage students in thinking about large-scale problems such as world economies and trading, varying thinking styles including habits of mind and creative problem-solving, and future career choices available to them. Themes have included "In Search of Excellence," which challenged students to examine what excellence really means versus achievement or perfection; and "In Search of Creativity," which asked students to examine their own levels of creativity, expand their definitions, and try new avenues of creative engagement. Programming at this level is evenly split between social and emotional education and intellectual pursuits.

In all regional events, educators forge partnerships with outside organizations (such as the Challenger Learning Center mentioned previously). Students register in advance, and schools pay a registration fee to assist with covering costs for the day. At these events, students become acquainted with their peers from other schools and often walk away feeling satisfied with the social interactions as well as the learning. Presenters comment back to the gifted coordinators about how the discussions are often surprisingly high-level, spirited, and engaging. Each event culminates in the evening with a presentation for parents, often a nationally known speaker who offers parents valuable information about gifted students, social and emotional traits, and parenting this population.

>—*Rural schools information and Spotlight contributed by Paula McGuire, gifted-education regional consultant, Northeast Region of Colorado; and Jodi Church, gifted-education regional consultant, East Central Region of Colorado. Used with permission.*

ASPIRE Strategies: Recognize When Acceleration Is Vital

The purpose of academic acceleration is to challenge students appropriately by moving them through academic material or through the academic system faster than other students of the same age. *Acceleration* is a word that sometimes causes concern among parents and educators. First, rest assured that there is much research to support the benefits of acceleration that's implemented thoughtfully and collaboratively. Research on acceleration has consistently demonstrated academic gains for students, improved self-esteem and self-concept, and positive post-school outcomes (Assouline, Colangelo, and VanTassel-Baska 2015; Colangelo, Assouline, and Gross 2004). Academic acceleration has also been found to meet the need for challenge of underserved gifted learners (Lee, Olszewski-Kubilius, and Peternel 2010). While the benefits of acceleration are similar for all gifted students, acceleration options often are not available for underserved gifted learners. For example, a study on accelerated learning among Oregon public high school students showed that schools with a higher percentage of economically disadvantaged students tended to have lower participation in accelerated learning options, such as dual credit and Advanced Placement courses. Further, economically disadvantaged students were less likely to participate in accelerated learning compared to non–economically disadvantaged students (Regional Education Laboratory (REL) Northwest 2018). With this in mind, educators need to make sure they are not only informed about the many types of acceleration, but also are making efforts to expand access to accelerated learning for historically underserved gifted learners.

One of the most comprehensive resources on acceleration is the report *A Nation Deceived: How Schools Hold Back America's Brightest Students* edited by Drs. Nicholas Colangelo, Susan Assouline, and Miraca Gross, published in 2004. In 2015, Assouline, Colangelo, and Joyce VanTassel-Baska published a follow-up to this report titled *A Nation Empowered: Evidence Trumps the Excuses Holding Back America's Brightest Students*. These reports not only showcase extensive and rigorous research on the benefits of acceleration, they also help educators make informed decisions about acceleration based on what is best for their individual students.

Many types of acceleration can be used to meet various educational goals. The Acceleration Institute has identified twenty types of acceleration. Our discussion is limited to the types we believe would be most beneficial to underserved gifted learners and most practical to use. At a basic level, academic acceleration can be broken down into content acceleration, whole-grade acceleration, and a blending of these approaches for high schoolers in the form of Advanced Placement classes, International Baccalaureate classes, and concurrent or dual enrollment. These types of acceleration have similar goals but different considerations for implementation.

Content Acceleration

Content acceleration is focused on providing the appropriate level of challenge in a particular content area. It actually encompasses some of the other topics addressed in this book, such as differentiation and curriculum compacting. Most types of acceleration are cost-neutral or low-cost in financial terms. Content acceleration tends to be not only inexpensive, but also low-cost in terms of risks to students.

Although content acceleration is considered low risk, if it is not implemented thoughtfully, it may affect students negatively. For example, suppose you are a seventh-grade teacher, and you have a gifted ELL student named Mari in your classroom. You recognize that Mari can understand and apply mathematical concepts much more quickly than other students in your class can. You are certain that she could easily tackle algebra next year. This would provide her with additional challenge and the opportunity to have conversations with other students who have similar mathematical ability—both of which could be validating and cognitively engaging for her. However, algebra is not offered in your middle school, so Mari would have to go to the high school three mornings a week. The district would provide transportation, and luckily Mari's middle school schedule could be arranged so that she would miss only her math period at the middle school. Still, you know that this decision will have to be made thoughtfully. You don't want to set her up for failure by putting her in a situation that diminishes her self-confidence or her love of mathematics.

You make a list of potential concerns:

> From day one, you have worked diligently to get to know Mari. Still, it took three months until she felt comfortable enough to share her thoughts in class. Would Mari's algebra teacher next year at the high school have the time and inclination to invest this much effort in developing a relationship with her? If not, would Mari ever feel comfortable enough to ask questions or engage in discussions?

> Sometimes academic English is an obstacle for Mari. Right now, she is in math class with her cousin Alvin, who periodically translates information for her into Spanish. First, would Mari's teacher next year understand that her need for English support doesn't negate her high capability in math? Second, would the high school be able and willing to provide language support so Mari could succeed in algebra?

> Would Mari's family be comfortable with her taking classes at the high school while her same-age cousin is taking eighth-grade math at the middle school? What is the most respectful way to share the potential benefits of math acceleration for Mari with her family?

> You recognize that if Mari skips eighth-grade math, she may have some gaps in her learning. You're certain that if next year's teacher would take a few extra minutes with Mari upon recognizing that she has missed instruction in a particular area, Mari would pick up those concepts quickly and be able to move on with learning algebra. Would her algebra teacher next year be able to recognize such gaps and be willing to address them?

Your list of concerns suggest that you need to discuss the possibility of math acceleration for Mari with all the key players in this decision. The discussion should include her parents (or important family members), administrators at both schools, her math teacher from this year, the algebra teacher Mari would have next year, and Mari herself. Mari needs to understand the potential benefits and drawbacks of the proposal, be able to share her concerns, and be involved in the problem-solving.

If you are considering content acceleration for your underserved gifted students, the toolkit strategy on page 124 can help you understand your options. See pages 140–144 at the end of this chapter to see a sample curriculum unit for an elementary accelerated math class incorporating social justice and real-world applications. You can also find this sample curriculum unit and other lesson plans in the digital content. See page 180 for download instructions.

TOOLKIT STRATEGY

Choosing Content Acceleration Options Thoughtfully

Type of Content Acceleration	Definition	Considerations
Differentiation	Teachers modify instruction and instructional materials to meet acceleration needs of individual students or small groups.	Appropriate differentiation requires an understanding of students' characteristics and content standards. If you want to differentiate instruction, you may need to differentiate assessments as well.
Curriculum compacting	Teachers eliminate curriculum (based on preassessments) to let students move through it quicker. Students use the extra time for extension or enrichment activities.	If you're new to compacting, start small. Try it with a small group of students instead of a whole class. Collaborate with colleagues who also want to use compacting. You may need support to get the process going.
Telescoping	Teachers provide instruction at a much quicker pace than normal to accelerate students one grade level in a specific content area. For example, students may complete Algebra I and Algebra II in one year instead of two years.	This is a great option for students who may not know the material initially (so they would not necessarily pass a pretest) but who pick it up quickly.
Self-paced instruction	Students move through a unit or a course at their own pace. Some self-paced courses have final due dates; some are open-ended. They are often offered in an online format.	This option offers lots of flexibility for students, but if students are not self-directed learners, they may struggle to complete the unit or course successfully. Teachers may require that students complete one unit or lesson before receiving the next (continuous progress). This allows them to track how students are progressing.
Advanced Placement (AP)	AP courses were designed to help students prepare for college. Students can choose to take AP courses only in specific content areas. These are college-level courses, and students can actually receive college credit (or be exempted from certain classes) from many colleges by passing a year-end exam.	This is a great way to accelerate in individual content areas based on strength and/or interest at the secondary level. In certain instances, it would also be appropriate for a middle school student to take an AP course at a high school.

Type of Content Acceleration	Definition	Considerations
Dual enrollment	Students take courses at a high school, taught by high school teachers who have met the criteria to be adjunct college professors. Students receive credit at both institutions.	Dual enrollment is often a great way for students to experience their first college course because it is taught by a secondary teacher who typically already knows the students. Successful completion of the course earns credit from the college or university with which the teacher is associated.
Concurrent enrollment	Middle school students take classes at both the middle school and the high school, or high school students take classes at both the high school and a college. Sometimes these courses are offered online.	Some districts will pay at least a portion of concurrent enrollment costs. This is a nice option for students who have completed (or will complete) the coursework needed to graduate early but who do not want to do this. It's also a great option for students who have a passion for a content area and have exhausted all class options in that area at either the middle school or high school.
Credit by examination	Students receive high school or college credit for a course by demonstrating mastery (for example, taking and passing an exam) without having to take the course.	For students who have achieved a great deal of knowledge about a specific topic or content area, this is a great way to validate their learning while allowing them to accelerate to an appropriately challenging course. Additionally, when students can obtain college credit through examination only, this often decreases the number of coursework hours required of them for graduation.

Whole-Grade Acceleration

Like content acceleration, whole-grade acceleration can be quite beneficial—but it must be approached more cautiously. The decision to advance a student an entire academic year needs to be well thought out because it cannot be reversed easily. When approached in a comprehensive and thoughtful manner, the research overwhelmingly supports that whole-grade acceleration offers positive, long-term academic and social benefits for most students (Assouline, Colangelo, and VanTassel-Baska 2015). While research on the benefits of whole-grade acceleration specifically for underrepresented gifted students is limited at this time, it should not be eliminated as a potential acceleration option. Just as with all other students, whole-grade acceleration for gifted students from underrepresented populations requires an in-depth analysis of the potential benefits and drawbacks for a particular individual before a decision can be made.

Whole-grade acceleration is moving a student at least one grade level beyond where they would typically be at their current age. For example, a student who should be in second grade based on age is accelerated to third grade based on evidence of need for additional challenge. Early entrance to kindergarten is another example of whole-grade acceleration. The Iowa Acceleration Scale (IAS) is a reliable tool that educators and parents often use to determine if whole-grade acceleration is appropriate for a particular child. For students in kindergarten through eighth grade, a systematic procedure is employed by the school to guide whole-grade acceleration decisions. After careful evaluation of school factors, family factors, and individual factors, educators can make thoughtful recommendations on whether a child should skip a grade. Specifically, educators gather general student and family information; the child's school history; critical items to consider for whole-grade acceleration (for example, would the child be accelerated into a class with a sibling?); student ability, aptitude, and achievement information; additional school and academic factors (for example, would the child have to move to a different building?); developmental factors; interpersonal skills; attitude (student and family); and support (family). Each of the subscales are scored and added together to calculate a cumulative score, which can then be used to determine how good a candidate the child is for whole-grade acceleration.

Lisa Turk, a mother of a gifted child who underwent this process, remarked, "It was so interesting to see how the grade-skipping process worked—how the testing was designed to meet the needs of the whole child. They looked at the social and emotional needs, parental and teacher support, as well as academic needs. The research regarding the fact that most students who have been accelerated see it as a positive experience was very gratifying. I feel the IAS is a very beneficial test. I like that it measures so many things, including academic ability, developmental factors, interpersonal skills, and attitude and support."

At the secondary level (grades nine through twelve), it is less likely for a student to be accelerated a whole grade (from ninth grade to tenth grade, for example). At this level it is much more common for a student's acceleration needs to be met through programs such as Advanced Placement classes, International Baccalaureate classes, or concurrent or dual enrollment options. If you are considering whole-grade acceleration for your underserved gifted students, the following toolkit strategy can help you understand your options.

TOOLKIT STRATEGY

Choosing Whole-Grade Acceleration Options Thoughtfully

Type of Whole-Grade Acceleration	Definition	Considerations
Early entrance into kindergarten or first grade	Student begins kindergarten or first grade a year early.	Many districts have specific assessment requirements that must be met for a child to enter school early. These include examining not only academic readiness but also affective readiness.

Type of Whole-Grade Acceleration	Definition	Considerations
Whole-grade acceleration	Student moves at least one grade level beyond where they would typically be at their current age.	Use caution with this type of acceleration. While research indicates that this is beneficial when implemented well, be sure to use the available resources (such as the IAS) to help in decision-making.
International Baccalaureate (IB) classes	IB is an international program that emphasizes critical and creative thinking and provides college-level coursework throughout high school. Students may earn college credit (or be exempted from certain courses) from many universities by passing year-end exams. IB elementary and middle schools focus on critical and creative thinking.	This isn't whole-grade acceleration in the sense that students taking these courses will finish high school quicker. Rather, all courses in this program are accelerated. Students who successfully complete this program earn an internationally recognized IB diploma.
Early College High School (ECHS)	Students have the opportunity to complete an associate's degree by the time they graduate from high school by taking a combination of high school and junior college classes at their own high school.	This option is usually designed to provide academic and affective support to students considered less likely to attend college. ECHS courses are often taught by professors who are content specialists rather than by individuals with teacher training.
Technical education program completed while in high school	Students trade some of their high school time to take courses at a community college technical education program. By the time they graduate from high school, they can also have a certificate from the community college (for example, in automotive collision repair or as a nurse's aide).	This option allows students graduating from high school to be immediately marketable. Some students may take this as a first step toward a higher degree in the same or a similar field (for example, moving from a nurse's aide certificate to a more advanced nursing degree). Some high schools help pay for students to take these classes.
Early entrance to college	Students complete the necessary credits and graduate early from high school or leave high school without completing all requirements to begin college.	Depending on the school situation and personal situation of the student, either option can be a beneficial means of acceleration. However, this is best implemented with the support and guidance of adults (such as parents and school counselors) who know the student well.

AP, IB, and Concurrent or Dual Enrollment and Underserved Gifted Learners

Underserved gifted learners are typically not well represented in accelerated programming such as AP, IB, and concurrent or dual enrollment in high school. This is often due to one of the following factors (or a combination of them):

> Underserved gifted learners may still be developing the academic skills necessary to be successful on their own. For example, students who are still learning academic English, either because English is not their first language or because they have not had much exposure to academic language outside the classroom, may struggle initially with understanding concepts and with communicating their ideas clearly.

> If language barriers or lack of enrichment or extension experiences outside the classroom have kept underserved gifted learners from participating (and being successful) in academically challenging situations in the past, they may lack confidence in their ability to succeed in accelerated courses, and may therefore choose not to risk "failing" at them.

> Implicit bias in educators may affect which students they encourage or even allow to participate in accelerated courses. Teachers and administrators sometimes subconsciously determine that certain students will not succeed in advanced classes—without fully considering the strengths of individual learners. It is often ELL students, economically disadvantaged students, 2e students, and students from cultures other than the dominant culture of a particular school whom educators inaccurately perceive as unable to be successful in accelerated courses.

However, if students have the ability and the desire to participate—especially in situations where teachers and counselors can provide extra support, such as AP or IB courses at the student's home school—it's important to encourage and to assist them. This may mean the teacher is providing extra study sessions for this group of students or scaffolding material so that they can access it better. Your underserved gifted learners can still process at high levels of critical and creative thinking even if they need modifications in the way they receive the information from you (for example, providing notes ahead of time so they can familiarize themselves with the upcoming concepts and feel comfortable participating in discussion) or in the way they share what they have learned while they are building their academic skills to full capacity (for example, providing the opportunity to synthesize what they have learned verbally rather than being required to write an essay). Underserved gifted learners actually need these opportunities to develop toward their full potential.

It's also important to make sure that school staff members have ongoing training in how to recognize and support underserved gifted learners. Otherwise, you may be setting up these students for failure by encouraging them to challenge themselves in a setting where their teachers don't provide the support they need to succeed. This could end up being a situation that reinforces the inaccurate notion (in teachers and students) that underserved gifted learners are incapable of performing at high levels in accelerated courses.

Not only do many of these types of acceleration for high school students offer ways to provide appropriate intellectual challenge for underserved gifted learners, but they also give students the opportunity to earn college credits at a bargain rate. This may be really important for economically disadvantaged underserved gifted learners.

SPOTLIGHT

Greeley Central High School was a culturally, linguistically, and economically diverse school. However, the school's diversity was not fully reflected in the students enrolling in honors and AP classes. Figuring out how to make these classes more representative of the student body (where a majority of students were Latinx and/or economically disadvantaged) became a priority for educators in the building. With support from the building and district administrators, and under the leadership of the AP coordinator, the school applied for and received a Colorado Legacy Foundation Grant. The purpose of this grant was to help schools build a pipeline into AP courses by making honors and AP classes more accessible to students from culturally and linguistically diverse (CLD) backgrounds and economically disadvantaged households and by fostering a school culture where all students might better succeed in rigorous courses.

Over a three-year period, Greeley Central worked to remove some of the barriers that often keep underrepresented gifted learners from participating in advanced coursework. For example, with guidance and support from project leaders of the grant, educators decided that anyone who was motivated to do so could register for an honors or AP course and no longer needed a teacher recommendation or a certain grade point average. They also eliminated summer homework that had been required to be completed by the first day of these classes in the fall. Additionally, the AP coordinator and the gifted-education specialist visited classrooms prior to registration each spring to make sure that all students in the building had the opportunity to hear about honors and AP classes and ask questions. They also presented information about these courses to parents and incoming students at freshman orientation. Further, the AP coordinator organized an AP informational night for families during parent-teacher conferences.

Underrepresented students in the AP courses received targeted support in several ways. First, the AP program coordinated with the Advancement Via Individual Determination (AVID) program to help students develop the skills that they would need to be successful in AP classes. Second, AP teachers provided regular weekend and after-school study sessions (with food) for all students in the program. Finally, the AP coordinator and gifted-education specialist provided additional one-on-one support to students as needed. In addition to the support for students, Greeley Central AP teachers also received training in increasing the rigor in their AP classes and in working with populations of students traditionally underrepresented in advanced coursework. This training included how to move beyond the traditional way in which AP classes are typically instructed to better meet the needs of their diverse learners. The grant also funded up-to-date teaching materials for some classrooms.

All students who took AP courses were strongly encouraged to also take the AP exam at the end of the school year. Half the exam fees were paid for students taking AP language arts, science, or mathematics exams, and students receiving free or reduced lunches had all their AP exam fees paid in all content areas. Additionally, to recognize and validate the extra work and effort necessary for AP success, both the teacher and student received a one-hundred-dollar stipend when the student passed an AP exam in language arts, science, or mathematics.

Over the three years of the grant, participation by Latinx gifted students, gifted students whose home language was Spanish, and economically disadvantaged gifted students increased significantly. And contrary to what was expected based on the national data available, both Latinx gifted students and gifted students whose home language was Spanish were just as likely to pass their AP exams as white gifted students. Further, gifted Latinx students passed their AP exams at a higher rate than gifted white male students.

Although the grant funding ended, educators at the school, with guidance from the AP coordinator and support from administration, continued working to find ways to support underserved populations with rigorous coursework and hosted its first three-day AP Bootcamp in summer 2019. This was an opportunity for students, free of charge and prior to the beginning of the school year, to receive targeted support in acquiring and enhancing foundational academic and organizational skills needed to be successful in this academic setting.

—*Contributed by Steve Burch, Greeley Central High School AP coordinator, and Amy Graefe, former Greeley Central High School gifted education specialist, Colorado. Used with permission.*

ASPIRE Strategies: Embed Curriculum Compacting into Learning Units

Curriculum compacting is a strategy that educators can use in the classroom for underserved gifted learners who have already mastered the material about to be taught. This strategy is often considered a form of content acceleration (see page 122) and is an easy, low-cost way to challenge students and encourage continuous progress in their learning. When teachers use curriculum compacting, they eliminate work their students have already mastered. Curriculum compacting provides an opportunity for underserved gifted students to demonstrate their domain-specific strengths that might otherwise go unnoticed. Retention of students from CLD backgrounds in gifted programming is a well-documented issue (Ford, Grantham, and Whiting 2008). Helping CLD students keep their achievement at high levels is one way to help them stay engaged in learning. Educators can use curriculum compacting often to ensure underserved gifted learners have opportunities to embrace appropriately challenging learning on a regular basis.

To understand why compacting is important, imagine being asked to write out the letters of the alphabet over and over again. Wouldn't you expect that after showing someone you could do it once, you could move on to more challenging material? How might having to repeatedly do something you have already mastered affect your level of engagement in and attitude toward school? You might start to shut down and think that your learning doesn't matter to anyone. If your teachers don't care, why should you care? Thoughts like these can negatively shape a gifted learner's educational trajectory. For underserved gifted learners, thoughts like these could completely derail any aspirations cultivated up until that point. A gifted student from an underserved population who had a supportive teacher the year before, engaged in challenging learning, and developed a strong academic identity might stop caring about learning, lose the spark that was ignited the year before, and underachieve.

To use curriculum compacting in your classroom, see the following toolkit strategy, "Curriculum Compacting Steps."

> TOOLKIT STRATEGY
>
> ## Curriculum Compacting Steps
>
> 1. Pretest your students on the skills and concepts in an upcoming unit or chapter. If it is a short chapter, you can consider combining it with another one. You want to make sure that there is going to be enough material taught to make it worth your time to compact the curriculum, but you don't want so much material that your pretest is really long.
>
> 2. Determine which of your students have at least 80 percent mastery of the skills and concepts assessed on the pretest. (Never require 100 percent mastery.)
>
> 3. For the students who demonstrate at least 80 percent mastery, create a contract that shows them what they have already mastered and what they still need to learn. When you are teaching something they already know, they will not need to sit with the class for instruction. However, when you are teaching something they don't already know, they will be required to sit with the class and participate in discussion and homework just like everyone else. (They are always welcome to join the class for lessons if they would like to do so—even if the contract shows they have already mastered the material.)
>
> 4. Because these students will have the option to work independently or with a small group of other students who have also mastered the material while you are teaching the rest of the class, the contract should include a list of acceptable ways that students can spend this time. You may decide to offer options personalized to the strengths and interests of underserved gifted learners in your class. (Your students may have some great ideas for this list.) Add these to the contract and work collaboratively with your students to determine which option(s) they will choose.
>
> 5. Make sure that you also include guidelines for how students are to work and how often you will meet with them to check in and provide any needed support. The contract might say, "I understand that when you are teaching the rest of the class, I will not interrupt with questions about my contract activities" and, "I understand that I will have the opportunity to meet with you the last fifteen minutes of every class." You and the students who will be using the contract can design these guidelines collaboratively.

There are various philosophies about how students should spend their contract time when curriculum is being compacted. Some teachers offer extension or acceleration options in the compacted subject; some offer enrichment opportunities in the subject; some offer general enrichment opportunities (not necessarily in the subject); some include a combination of all three. You can determine what works best for you based on your personal philosophy and your school's and district's philosophies. But it is critical that you do offer enrichment and/or acceleration options when a student has compacted out of material, even if you start small and add options as you and your students become more comfortable with the process. Research shows that providing enrichment and accelerated learning options as early and often as possible in an underserved gifted student's schooling is vital to developing a strong academic identity and achieving to potential (Olszewski-Kubilius et al. 2017).

If the pretest is comprehensive enough and the student scores well overall (not just on certain portions), some teachers record the score the student receives on the pretest as the final score for the unit. Students can then choose to take the final assessment to bring up the grade if they want to do that. These teachers ask, "Why make them continue to prove to me that they already know something?" Other teachers require that these students take the final assessment, and the score they get on that is the score that goes in the grade book. These teachers believe that this approach helps make students responsible for determining whether they want to join the whole group for instruction at any point. And it provides another layer of documentation that the students do know the material and that curriculum compacting isn't "hurting" them. Both options are fine. Just as with the contract choices, you need to decide what fits best with your philosophy and your school's philosophy.

Chapter Summary

Providing challenges along with the necessary support and guidance is essential for underserved gifted learners to ASPIRE to excellence. As educators, we can **A**dd challenge thoughtfully, **S**upply the support necessary for success, **P**rovide opportunities for mentorships, **I**dentify possibilities for independent investigations, **R**ecognize when acceleration is vital, and **E**mbed curriculum compacting into learning units. Although challenging learning opportunities are often available at many schools, underserved gifted students need equitable access to those learning opportunities. The strategies in this chapter are intended not only to help you identify ways to thoughtfully challenge your underserved gifted students, but also to help you remove barriers that often prevent underserved gifted learners from participating and succeeding in such activities. To reflect on your progress in using these strategies, fill out the reproducible "'Challenge Me' Checklist" on pages 145–146.

Mentorship Questionnaire

1. What are your top three areas of **academic interest**? (Write "1" next to your most favorite, "2" next to your second favorite, and "3" next to your third favorite.)

Language arts:	**Social studies:**
____ literature	____ history
____ languages	____ economics
____ writing	____ religion
____ other: _____	____ geography
	____ philosophy
	____ cultures
	____ other: _____
Arts:	**Science and mathematics:**
____ painting	____ chemistry
____ drawing	____ engineering
____ photography	____ biology
____ ceramics	____ geology
____ architecture	____ astronomy
____ dance	____ technology
____ film	____ mathematics
____ music	____ physics
____ theater	____ robotics
____ other: _____	____ other: _____

2. Why are you interested in learning more about these areas?

   _____
   _____
   _____
   _____

3. What do you already know about these areas and what would you like to learn more about?

   _____
   _____
   _____
   _____

From *Start Seeing and Serving Underserved Gifted Students: 50 Strategies for Equity and Excellence* by Jennifer A. Ritchotte, Ph.D., Chin-Wen Lee, Ph.D., and Amy K. Graefe, Ph.D., copyright © 2020. This page may be reproduced for individual, classroom, or small group work only. For all other uses, contact Free Spirit Publishing Inc. at freespirit.com/permissions.

Mentorship Questionnaire continued

4. What are your **special interests or talents** and related things you like to do when you're not in school?

5. What do you enjoy most about these interests and activities?

6. Is there anything about them that you would like to explore further? Please explain.

7. What are your **career interests** right now?

8. What knowledge or skills do you think you will need to pursue your interests successfully? (for example, more knowledge about your interest area, study skills, research skills, career-planning skills, time-management skills)?

Mentorship Questionnaire continued

9. What do you want your mentor to know about you?

   _____
   _____
   _____
   _____

10. What characteristics or qualities would you like your mentor to have?

    _____
    _____
    _____
    _____

11. Describe a project or types of activities you would like to work on with your mentor.

    _____
    _____
    _____
    _____

12. Is there anything else that you feel is important for your teacher and mentor to know about you?

    _____
    _____
    _____
    _____

Mentorship Evaluation Rubric 1: For the Mentor

Evaluation Areas	Let's work on this.	This is good, but it could be better.	This is going great!
The mentorship activities are engaging for the mentee.	The mentee is not engaged in activities.	The mentee is somewhat engaged in activities.	The mentee is excited and fully engaged in activities.
Activities align with the mentee's passion.	The activities are not well aligned with the student's content-area passion.	The activities are mostly aligned with the student's content-area passion.	The activities are focused on the student's content-area passion.
The activities are clearly explained to the mentee.	The mentor cannot clearly explain the mentorship activities.	The mentor can explain the mentorship activities.	The mentor has obviously prepared for the activities and can clearly explain them.
The mentorship activities are appropriately challenging for the mentee.	The activities are too difficult or too easy for the mentee.	The activities are a good fit for the mentee. The mentee feels a little bit challenged.	The activities are definitely challenging, but the mentee is handling them well with the mentor's support.
The time commitment is ideal for both the mentee and mentor.	There are too many or not enough meetings. The mentee, the mentor, or both are not as committed as they should be.	The time commitment is working well for both the mentor and the mentee so far, but it may need to be adjusted in the future.	The time commitment is perfect. The mentor and mentee both look forward to getting together and are committed to the mentorship.
A high-quality product is produced (when applicable).	No culminating product was created.	The mentee and mentor created a product together, but the mentee was given limited autonomy in the process and/or the product was of lower quality than hoped for.	The mentee and mentor created a high-quality product together. The mentee not only chose the type of product, but also made choices during the planning and implementation processes.

From *Start Seeing and Serving Underserved Gifted Students: 50 Strategies for Equity and Excellence* by Jennifer A. Ritchotte, Ph.D., Chin-Wen Lee, Ph.D., and Amy K. Graefe, Ph.D., copyright © 2020. This page may be reproduced for individual, classroom, or small group work only. For all other uses, contact Free Spirit Publishing Inc. at freespirit.com/permissions.

Mentorship Evaluation Rubric 2: For the Mentee

Evaluation Areas	Let's work on this.	This is good, but it could be better.	This is going great!
The mentorship activities are engaging.	I am not engaged in any of the mentorship activities.	I am somewhat engaged in the mentorship activities.	I am excited and fully engaged in the mentorship activities.
The activities are aligned with your passions.	The mentorship activities are not at all related to my passion areas.	Most of the mentorship activities are related to my passion areas.	The mentorship activities are completely focused on my passion areas.
The activities are clearly explained to you by your mentor.	The mentorship activities are pretty confusing and not well explained by my mentor.	The mentorship activities are explained and seem clear.	I know my mentor has really prepared these activities. They are explained really well.
The activities are just the right amount of challenge for you.	The mentorship activities are either too hard or too easy for me.	Most of the mentorship activities are a good fit for me as a learner. I feel a little bit challenged.	The mentorship activities are definitely challenging, but my mentor gives me enough support to complete them successfully.
The amount of time you spend together is perfect for both you and your mentor.	There are too many or not enough meetings. I don't feel very committed to this, and/or my mentor doesn't feel very committed.	The amount of time we spend together is good for both of us for now. It might need to be adjusted in the future.	The amount of time we spend together is perfect. I look forward to getting together with my mentor and feel that we both are really committed to this mentorship.
You created a product you are proud of with your mentor (when applicable).	My mentor and I did not create a product.	My mentor and I created a product, but I didn't have a whole lot of input in the process (choosing it, planning it, creating it), or it didn't turn out as well as I'd hoped it would.	My mentor and I created an awesome product! We collaborated on all the parts. My mentor listened to me and let me make choices throughout the process.

Used with permission from Jessica Huggins, interventionist, and Dimitra Collier, elementary school teacher, Price Elementary School, Louisville, Kentucky.
From *Start Seeing and Serving Underserved Gifted Students: 50 Strategies for Equity and Excellence* by Jennifer A. Ritchotte, Ph.D., Chin-Wen Lee, Ph.D., and Amy K. Graefe, Ph.D., copyright © 2020. This page may be reproduced for individual, classroom, or small group work only. For all other uses, contact Free Spirit Publishing Inc. at freespirit.com/permissions.

Independent Investigation Planning Guide

Steps	Tips	Ideas
1. Explore topics that interest you.	What are your passion areas? What are you excited to spend several weeks learning more about?	
2. Learn more about one topic that really interests you.	Read, listen to, and watch informative materials on your topic. Use credible sources, such as reference books, government or professional organizations' websites, and documentaries and TED Talks.	
3. Generate questions or problems.	Avoid thin questions or problems that can be answered or solved quickly and easily.	
4. Create an investigation plan to answer questions or solve problems.	Will you apply quantitative methods (analyzing numerical data, such as survey responses) or qualitative methods (such as telling a story with words)? Or will you use both? What's your timeline for completion?	
5. Select an authentic audience for your investigation.	Who will benefit most from your investigation findings?	
6. Execute the investigation plan.	What steps will you take to carry out your investigation plan?	
7. Analyze and interpret data.	How will you make sense of the information you collected?	
8. Ask, "So what?"	What information do you hope to be able to share with your audience through this independent investigation?	
9. Prepare for a presentation or product.	How will you make your presentation or product interactive? How will you ensure it conveys the full scope of your independent investigation? Think outside the box! Try something other than a slide presentation or a poster.	
10. Reflect.	How will you consider what you have learned not only about your interest area, but also about yourself as a scholar? How will you apply what you learned from this independent investigation to future experiences both in school and outside school?	

From *Start Seeing and Serving Underserved Gifted Students: 50 Strategies for Equity and Excellence* by Jennifer A. Ritchotte, Ph.D., Chin-Wen Lee, Ph.D., and Amy K. Graefe, Ph.D., copyright © 2020. This page may be reproduced for individual, classroom, or small group work only. For all other uses, contact Free Spirit Publishing Inc. at freespirit.com/permissions.

Independent Investigation Self-Evaluation Rubric

Steps	Performance		Reflection
	I did a good job.	I need to improve.	
1. Exploring and narrowing down topics that interest me			
2. Learning more about one topic that really interests me			
3. Generating questions or problems			
4. Creating an investigation plan to answer my questions or to solve my problems			
5. Selecting an authentic audience for my investigation			
6. Executing my investigation plan			
7. Analyzing and interpreting data			
8. Asking, "So what?"			
9. Preparing for and creating a presentation or product			
10. Reflecting			

From *Start Seeing and Serving Underserved Gifted Students: 50 Strategies for Equity and Excellence* by Jennifer A. Ritchotte, Ph.D., Chin-Wen Lee, Ph.D., and Amy K. Graefe, Ph.D., copyright © 2020. This page may be reproduced for individual, classroom, or small group work only. For all other uses, contact Free Spirit Publishing Inc. at freespirit.com/permissions.

Sample Curriculum Unit: Not Just Math

Overview and Objectives

The unit includes acceleration through math concepts. Fourth-grade students will be moved forward to the fifth-grade standard of volume. Students will move through this unit based on preassessment and formative assessment data. If students show mastery on material, they will be moved through the material more quickly. So, pacing and acceleration are both present. Toward the end of the unit, students apply their knowledge of these concepts to project-based learning that addresses real-world social justice issues. This unit addresses many diverse learning needs.

- Students will create a 3-D model of a refugee camp shelter, using appropriate units for dimensions and the perimeter, area, and volume measurements.
- Students will identify and explain other necessities that refugees need in their shelter and describe how they will incorporate these needs.
- Students will explain and justify their models through a multimedia presentation and communicate their project to the class.

NAGC Gifted Programming Standards

<u>Standard 3: Curriculum Planning and Instruction</u>

3.1. Curriculum Planning. Students with gifts and talents demonstrate growth commensurate with aptitude during the school year.

> 3.1.5. Educators use a balanced assessment system, including preassessment and formative assessment, to identify students' needs, develop differentiated education plans, and adjust plans based on continual progress monitoring.
>
> 3.1.7. Educators use information and technologies, including assistive technologies, to individualize for students with gifts and talents, including those who are twice-exceptional.

3.4. Instructional Strategies. Students with gifts and talents become independent investigators.

> 3.4.3. Educators use problem-solving model strategies to meet the needs of students with gifts and talents.

3.5. Culturally Relevant Curriculum. Students with gifts and talents develop knowledge and skills for living and being productive in a multicultural, diverse, and global society.

> 3.5.3. Educators use curriculum for deep explorations of cultures, languages, and social issues related to diversity.

Materials/Resources Needed

- Fifth-grade math curriculum materials (EngageNY, Math Modules 3 and 5—engageny.org/resource/grade-5-mathematics)
- Scholastic Storyworks (storyworks.scholastic.com)
- Tinkercad (tinkercad.com)

Sequence of Learning

1. *Lesson 1: Perimeter, Area, Volume Preassessment (To gauge students' levels of understanding)*
   Based on EngageNY: Module 3, Topic A, Lesson 1 (Area and Perimeter): Using grid paper, students will begin by drawing rectangles and labeling their dimensions. Students will construct their own understanding of the formulas $P = 2 \times (l + w)$ and $A = l \times w$ and then apply these formulas to squares and rectangles. After this mini-lesson introduction, students will transition through math stations that incorporate the use of area and perimeter: technology, math in partners, independent math, and small group with the teacher.

Sample Curriculum Unit: Not Just Math continued

2. *Lesson 2: Area and Perimeter Continued*
   Students will apply their understanding of area and perimeter to real-world word problems. Students will use their grid paper to draw dimensions and then determine the area and perimeter of a square or rectangle. Students check for reasonableness based on what they have learned about perimeter and area. After this mini-lesson, students will transition through math stations that incorporate the use of area and perimeter. Students will then complete an area and perimeter teacher-created exit slip to check for understanding. If students still struggle with this concept, they will be pulled during stations the following day, during small-group instruction with the teacher, to address any misconceptions. Groups change daily based on the needs of the students identified through daily formative assessments and reflections.

3. *Lesson 3: Volume*
   Based on EngageNY: Module 5, Topic A, Lesson 1: Students will use grid paper and cubes to connect their area and perimeter understanding with the new concept of volume. Students build 3-D rectangular prisms based on given dimensions. Students then construct their understanding of the connections among area, perimeter, and volume. Students build the 3-D figures, determine the dimensions, and begin developing the formula $V = l \times w \times h$. After this mini-lesson introduction, students will transition through math stations that incorporate the basic understanding of volume and extensions into the more abstract use of the formula. Each station includes an enrichment option that requires the student to use critical and analytical thinking or accelerates them through the standard more quickly.

4. *Lesson 4: Volume Continued*
   Based on EngageNY: Module 5, Topic A, Lesson 3: Students will build on their understanding from the previous lesson to calculate the volume of rectangular prisms by reasoning about the size and number of layers in the prism. Students who still need a concrete example continue to use cubes or draw cubes to help calculate the volume, but students who grasp the concept quickly should be accelerated to use the formula for volume. Students will then transition through math stations. Students complete the short volume exit slip included in the EngageNY lesson and write a short self-reflection on the back.

5. *Lesson 5: Volume Continued*
   Based on EngageNY: Module 5, Topic B, Lesson 4: Students will begin to apply the formula using multiplication to solve for volume. Students will connect their previous understanding of filling the rectangular prism with cubes to calculate the dimensions of the rectangular prism. Students solve for volume using $V = l \times w \times h$ or $V = B \times h$ (connecting volume to the area of the rectangular prism's base). Students will then transition through math stations. Groups will be based on the data from yesterday's formative assessment.

6. *Lesson 6: Volume Continued*
   Based on EngageNY: Module 5, Topic B, Lesson 5: This lesson will be the final lesson that focuses solely on volume. Only complete the warm-up and guided problems in this lesson, not the student independent pages. All students should be using multiplication with the formulas $V = l \times w \times h$ or $V = B \times h$ to solve for a rectangular prism's volume. Today will be the last day of the workshop model and direct math instruction in the unit. After today's lesson, students will apply their understanding to a project-based, real-world learning experience.

Sample Curriculum Unit: Not Just Math continued

7. *Lesson 7: ELA and Real-World Connection*
   Prior to reading, build background knowledge by discussing the meaning of the word *refugee* and connections students might have with the topic. Students are broken into groups and either read "Out of the Shattered Land" or "Escape from War" from Scholastic Storyworks. Any text that exposes students to the experiences of refugees could be used in place of these texts. Students annotate the text as they read using sticky notes in places where they would like to add comments, ask questions, or highlight information that they find important. As a class, students discuss the living conditions in the countries that many refugees have escaped. Then discuss refugee camp conditions, where many of these people go after they flee their home country. Sticky notes from their text will serve as the exit slip for this lesson.

8. *Lesson 8: ELA and Real-World Connection Continued*
   Discuss yesterday's lesson and what students learned about refugees and refugee camps. Students will then research the UN Refugee Agency Emergency Handbook (emergency.unhcr.org) minimum and maximum dimensions for refugee camps and record their research in their notebook. As a class, students discuss to connect their previous learning of area, perimeter, and volume to their research from today.

9. *Lesson 9: Designing and Measuring*
   Prior to this activity, students may need a reminder on using dot paper to draw 3-D figures. Students are broken into groups of three to further their refugee camp volume, area, and perimeter learning. Students will be given the task to design a 3-D rectangular prism model of one of the living areas for individual refugees and/or families of refugees. Students will draw their design on dotted paper, label their dimensions, and explain who and what the building would be used for in a refugee camp.

10. *Lesson 10: Designing and Measuring Continued*
    Students will create a digital 3-D model of their refugee camp using Tinkercad. Students may need a quick lesson on scaling and ratios to correctly create their 3-D model. After students create their digital 3-D model, they will save it to use in their presentation.

11. *Lesson 11: Designing and Measuring Continued*
    Students then research the average household size in the United States and the number of people who live in those homes. Students design and measure 3-D rectangular prism models of the average home based on the dimensions found in their research. Students will draw their designs, label their dimensions, and explain how many people would live in the building, making sure to compare individual areas with individual areas and family areas with family areas. As a class, students will discuss similarities and differences between the size of the refugee camps and that of an average family home in the United States.

12. *Lesson 12: Designing and Measuring Continued*
    Students will create a digital 3-D model of the average home in the United States using Tinkercad. After students create their digital 3-D model, they will save it to use in their presentation. Students then self-reflect on the progress of their designs and their understanding of the connection to the math concept of volume.

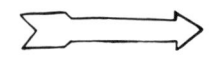

Used with permission from Christina Mudd, fifth-grade teacher, Greenwood Elementary, Louisville, Kentucky. She is involved in local refugee ministries. From *Start Seeing and Serving Underserved Gifted Students: 50 Strategies for Equity and Excellence* by Jennifer A. Ritchotte, Ph.D., Chin-Wen Lee, Ph.D., and Amy K. Graefe, Ph.D., copyright © 2020. This page may be reproduced for individual, classroom, or small group work only. For all other uses, contact Free Spirit Publishing Inc. at freespirit.com/permissions.

Sample Curriculum Unit: Not Just Math continued

13. *Lesson 13: How Can We Improve the Living Conditions of Refugees Across the World?*
    During this lesson students will focus on the disparities in refugee camps. Students will have a better understanding of just how small living conditions are from researching, designing, and building examples. Then students compare the camps to the way many people in the United States live. Teacher will pose the problem and guiding question: *How can we improve the living conditions of refugees across the world?* As a class, students will brainstorm ideas and research ways to build affordable housing to meet the needs of refugees. Students will continue researching what they consider to be acceptable dimensions of a building for an individual and for a family. Students will also research the other needs of refugees but will focus on designing an affordable space for refugees to live.

14. *Lesson 14: Designing and Measuring Continued*
    Students will draw their designs for their new affordable housing with the new dimensions, including appropriate units. Students will work together to include a written explanation of how they came upon their new dimensions, including their comparisons of refugee camps and average homes. Students will justify their new dimensions to prove why they make sense for the number of people who will be living in them, citing their research.

15. *Lesson 15: Designing and Measuring Continued*
    Students will create a digital 3-D model of their new affordable housing using Tinkercad. After students create their digital 3-D model, they will save it to use in their presentation.

16. *Lesson 16: Presentation Preparation*
    Students will create a presentation of their choice to show their refugee camp model, average US home model, and their new design, including the dimensions and how they used the formulas for perimeter, area, and volume. Students will explain what they learned about refugee camps through their texts and research. They will justify their reasoning for building their new spaces by citing texts and research. Students will do a gallery walk of all the projects to provide feedback to each group. They will use this feedback to improve their presentation in the next lesson.

17. *Lesson 17: Presentation Preparation Continued*
    Students will use their feedback from yesterday's gallery walk to make changes to their presentations. They will use the teacher-created rubric as they finish their presentation to check if they have met the criteria for the presentation.

18. *Lesson 18: Presentation to Authentic Audience*
    Students will present their projects to the class, administration, and any community members who may have connections to the real-world content of the project. Students will focus on their presentation skills and will be scored using the teacher-created rubric.

19. *Lesson 19: Post-Assessment*
    In addition to the presentation as a performance assessment, students will complete a teacher-created post-assessment with questions that require the student to solve for the perimeter, area, and volume of rectangles and rectangular prisms in real-world word problems, using the formulas developed throughout the unit.

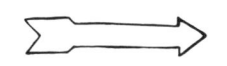

Used with permission from Christina Mudd, fifth-grade teacher, Greenwood Elementary, Louisville, Kentucky. She is involved in local refugee ministries.
From *Start Seeing and Serving Underserved Gifted Students: 50 Strategies for Equity and Excellence* by Jennifer A. Ritchotte, Ph.D., Chin-Wen Lee, Ph.D., and Amy K. Graefe, Ph.D., copyright © 2020. This page may be reproduced for individual, classroom, or small group work only.
For all other uses, contact Free Spirit Publishing Inc. at freespirit.com/permissions.

Sample Curriculum Unit: Not Just Math continued

Reflection/Assessment
Reflection and assessment are embedded in the daily lessons.

Refugee Camp Shelters (Perimeter, Area, and Volume) Project Presentation Rubrics

Student Learning Outcomes	Below Mastery	Approaching Mastery	Meeting Mastery	Exceeding Mastery
Students create a 3-D model of a refugee camp shelter, using appropriate units for dimensions and the perimeter, area, and volume measurements.	Project includes a model of student's proposed new shelter for refugee camp shelters. Project provides dimensions and includes two measurements of perimeter, area, and volume of each structure.	Project includes two or three models: (1) current refugee camp shelter, (2) average US home, (3) proposed new shelter for refugee camp shelters. Project provides dimensions and includes measurements for perimeter, area, and volume of each structure.	Project includes three models: (1) current refugee camp shelter, (2) average US home, (3) proposed new shelter for refugee camp shelters. Project provides dimensions in appropriate units and includes correctly measured perimeter, area, and volume of each structure. May include minor errors.	Project includes three detailed models: (1) current refugee camp shelter, (2) average US home, (3) proposed new shelter for refugee camp shelters. Project provides dimensions in appropriate units and includes correctly measured perimeter, area, and volume of each structure.
Students identify and explain other necessities that refugees need in their shelter and describe how they will incorporate these needs.	Project includes one need for inside the shelter and explains how student will incorporate this need in the shelter.	Project includes at least three needs for inside the shelter and explains how student will incorporate these needs in the shelter.	Project includes at least five needs in detail for inside and outside the shelter and explains in detail how student will incorporate these needs in the shelter and its community.	Project includes at least five needs in detail for inside and outside the shelter and explains how student will incorporate these needs in the shelter and its community. Project includes how these needs will be met affordably.
Students explain and justify their models through a multimedia presentation and communicate their project to the class.	Presentation includes an explanation that justifies the chosen dimensions for the new model.	Presentation includes an explanation that justifies the chosen dimensions for the new model. Presentation includes an explanation that justifies the needs for inside the refugee shelter.	Presentation includes a detailed explanation that justifies the chosen dimensions for the new model. Presentation includes a detailed explanation that justifies the needs for inside the refugee shelter. May include minor errors.	Presentation includes a detailed explanation that justifies the chosen dimensions for the new model. Presentation includes a detailed explanation that justifies the needs for inside the refugee shelter.

Used with permission from Christina Mudd, fifth-grade teacher, Greenwood Elementary, Louisville, Kentucky. She is involved in local refugee ministries.
From *Start Seeing and Serving Underserved Gifted Students: 50 Strategies for Equity and Excellence* by Jennifer A. Ritchotte, Ph.D., Chin-Wen Lee, Ph.D., and Amy K. Graefe, Ph.D., copyright © 2020. This page may be reproduced for individual, classroom, or small group work only.
For all other uses, contact Free Spirit Publishing Inc. at freespirit.com/permissions.

"Challenge Me" Checklist

Use this checklist to reflect on the extent to which you challenge your underserved gifted students and support them in aspiring to reach their fullest potential. Review your results to become more aware of your areas of strength and your areas for growth.

Key:
Beginning: You're aware and want to try.
Developing: You have tried or are trying.
Leading: You are consistently aware, implementing changes, and making others aware.

Add Challenge Thoughtfully	Beginning	Developing	Leading
I use varied ways to identify students' readiness for challenge.			
I initiate conversations with students to discuss the possibility of engaging in more challenging tasks.			
I help students feel more comfortable with additional challenge by providing supports.			

Supply the Support Necessary for Success	Beginning	Developing	Leading
I provide ongoing encouragement.			
I cultivate students' intellectual identities.			
I maintain a collaborative attitude.			
I foster healthy communication with students.			
I promote students' perseverance.			

Provide Opportunities for Mentorships	Beginning	Developing	Leading
I discuss career options with my students.			
I identify role models in books or movies for my students.			
I find community members and role models with whom my students can personally identify.			
I understand my students' academic and nonacademic interests.			
I understand the need for a mentoring program.			
I partner with like-minded people to start a mentorship program.			
I involve families in mentorship program development.			
I have a plan to oversee and evaluate mentorship activities.			

From *Start Seeing and Serving Underserved Gifted Students: 50 Strategies for Equity and Excellence* by Jennifer A. Ritchotte, Ph.D., Chin-Wen Lee, Ph.D., and Amy K. Graefe, Ph.D., copyright © 2020. This page may be reproduced for individual, classroom, or small group work only. For all other uses, contact Free Spirit Publishing Inc. at freespirit.com/permissions.

"Challenge Me" Checklist continued

Identify Possibilities for Independent Investigations	Beginning	Developing	Leading
I provide scaffolding for students to conduct their independent investigations.			
I provide guidelines to help structure the independent investigation experience.			
I facilitate backward planning for independent investigations.			
I have a system in place to help students monitor their independent investigation progress.			
I facilitate student reflection during the independent investigation process.			

Recognize When Acceleration Is Vital	Beginning	Developing	Leading
I understand the two basic types of acceleration: content acceleration (which might also include AP courses) and whole-grade acceleration (which might also include an IB program).			
I know how to thoughtfully choose content acceleration options.			
I know how to thoughtfully choose whole-grade acceleration options.			

Embed Curriculum Compacting into Learning Units	Beginning	Developing	Leading
I pretest my students on the skills and concepts in an upcoming unit or chapter.			
I communicate with students about what they have already mastered and what they still need to learn based on pretest data.			
I provide ideas for appropriate learning activities that students can work on while I'm teaching the material they have already mastered.			
I provide guidelines for students' learning contract time.			

From *Start Seeing and Serving Underserved Gifted Students: 50 Strategies for Equity and Excellence* by Jennifer A. Ritchotte, Ph.D., Chin-Wen Lee, Ph.D., and Amy K. Graefe, Ph.D., copyright © 2020. This page may be reproduced for individual, classroom, or small group work only. For all other uses, contact Free Spirit Publishing Inc. at freespirit.com/permissions.

ADVOCATE FOR ME 5

Let us remember: one book, one pen, one child, and one teacher can change the world.
—Malala Yousafzai

★★★★

Alex never expected to graduate from high school. Neither of his parents was a high school graduate, and his home life was difficult. By the time he was sixteen years old, he had run away from home and was living in poverty with his nineteen-year-old sister in a run-down apartment on the outskirts of town. He wasn't able to play sports or participate in extracurricular activities, because he had to work to help his sister with bills and pay for his own day-to-day living expenses.

Alex assumed he would end up dropping out of school to work full time and would often mention this in passing, but several of his teachers and his school guidance counselor refused to let him take this path. They could see that Alex had great potential. Despite working every day after school, Alex kept up with his schoolwork almost effortlessly and demonstrated a natural aptitude for his science and math classes. Alex's chemistry teacher, in particular, checked in with him every day and talked to his guidance counselor about colleges where he might be eligible for enough financial support to continue his education. With help from his chemistry teacher and his guidance counselor, Alex applied to an engineering program at a state university. He was accepted, and he received enough financial aid to cover his tuition and live on campus while he earned a bachelor's degree in chemical engineering.

Like Alex, underserved gifted students may not realize what their futures can be, or they may not believe there is any possible way to achieve their dreams. Alex, for example, assumed that he could never afford college and that his only option was to leave high school early and get a full-time job. Had his chemistry teacher and guidance counselor not recognized his ability, his struggles, and his resignation—and advocated for his future and acted as champions on his behalf—his life trajectory would have been much different. With his parents out of the picture and his older sister just trying to survive, to develop his potential, Alex needed caring adults who believed in his future and were committed to his success.

Underserved gifted students are the seeds of society's future. It's up to educators like you to cultivate and nurture them. Failure to do so often results in a tragic loss of human capital and "widens painful gaps in income, frustrates efforts to spur upward mobility, contributes to civic decay and political division, and worsens the inequalities that plague so many elements of our society" (Finn and Northern 2018). Without efforts to advocate meaningfully on behalf of underserved gifted students, society risks losing future creators, innovators, leaders, and teachers who reflect its own diverse makeup.

Although you have reached the last chapter of this book, you are just beginning your journey as an advocate for underserved gifted learners. It's time to take action. The next step is to use the information you have learned thus far to make a positive impact on the lives of underserved gifted learners like Alex. As you begin, please consider the following questions:

- Which strategies in this book are most practical for you and have the greatest potential to help your students?
- How will you adjust your current teaching practices based on the new knowledge you've acquired?
- How will you educate others about the needs of underserved gifted learners?

It is time to apply what you know about seeing, understanding, teaching, and challenging underserved gifted learners to your classroom, your school, and your students' lives. You have the capacity to be an agent of change and an advocate for your students. In this chapter, you will determine your professional learning priorities for supporting underserved gifted learners, identify opportunities to educate others about this topic, and create an action plan that you can begin using today.

What Does It Mean to Be an Advocate?

Advocacy can take many forms. Arranging a meeting with a state legislator to share concerns that student needs are not being met in Title I schools is, of course, advocacy. However, talking to colleagues about a student who you feel needs extra support is also advocacy. There are two primary types of advocacy (Ridnouer 2011):

- advocacy that promotes the interests of another person
- advocacy that promotes a cause

Neither type of advocacy is superior to the other type. The educator who speaks to a state legislator about needs of students in Title I schools (promoting a cause) and the teacher who reaches out to colleagues to gain support for a student (promoting another person's interests) are both engaging in meaningful advocacy efforts.

You may find yourself engaged in both types of advocacy. Or, you may decide that your efforts are best spent effecting change at either the micro level (classroom or school) or the macro level (district, state, nation, or world). Wherever you focus your advocacy efforts, so long as you are committed to helping underserved gifted learners succeed and you take steps to accomplish this goal, you are making a positive impact on your students' lives. Just remember that advocacy is an ongoing, evolving process. Your advocacy focus may change over time even as your commitment to learner empowerment remains constant. To understand how one teacher's commitment and effort on behalf of underserved gifted students at a school level can positively affect individual students on a micro level, consider the following story.

A "gifted" label in a student's school record is no guarantee of appropriate programming, instruction, or support. What is more: students from underserved populations may never get the opportunity to be labeled as gifted, so they never receive the services they need to achieve their full potential. A school-based gifted and talented coordinator can help address these issues, yet it can be difficult to convince school administration to carve out funding and space for a full-time gifted and talented specialist.

Kelly Ann Stiles was a high school English teacher with a master's degree in gifted and talented education. She developed a position as a teacher on special assignment (TOSA) through careful research and planning plus clear communication of goals to her administration. First, she identified areas for growth in the school's current gifted-identification and gifted-programming practices. Then she created a three-column chart with short-term, medium-term, and long-term goals for a gifted and talented coordinator position, which were tied to school and district plans. Next, she developed a potential job description for herself that outlined her main tasks. She succeeded in establishing this position at her high school.

At first, Stiles's administrators referred to her position as "the great experiment." But they soon began to see its value. As a result of her efforts, within a few weeks the school had received two grants for gifted and talented funding, nearly a dozen teachers were engaged in gifted-education professional learning outside the school day, and students who might otherwise have fallen through the cracks were receiving one-on-one support. Stiles used her new position to advocate for underserved gifted students at her school. For example, to help reduce teacher bias in the gifted-nomination process, the school began using PSAT and SAT test scores as screening tools. The school extended an open-door enrollment policy for honors and AP courses, and teachers began planning appropriate supports to help students from underserved populations excel.

The changing climate in the school led to high-ability and high-achieving students from underrepresented groups being recognized for their academic and social contributions beyond the traditional parameters of GPA rank. District officials also began to show interest in the momentum of the school. Stiles pointed out that through the district's policies, underrepresented gifted students who had limited opportunities to learn also had limited opportunities to be recognized for their academic achievements. To address these equity concerns, district officials offered support in changing policies on how student achievements (such as class rank and valedictorian) were recognized and promoted. In turn, this strengthened the school's and the district's culture of valuing diverse individuals, ideas, and products.

Upon reflection, Stiles felt confident that the shift in her school and district was due to a collaborative effort. She said, "The most important advice I got when I stepped into this position is that people around me need to understand that we are making changes together. It's not about what's being done *to* you; it's about what's being done *with* you." She added, "It's easy for teachers to see keeping track of gifted students' progress, extra meetings, and professional development as more bureaucratic hoops to jump through, but when they see growth and engagement in their gifted students, especially their underserved gifted students, they will hopefully also see the important role they are playing in providing the education that their students deserve."

> **TOOLKIT STRATEGY**
>
> ## Your Past, Present, and Future Advocacy
> Take a moment to reflect on how you have advocated for underserved gifted learners in the past, how you advocate for them presently, and how you hope to advocate for them in the near future. See page 163 for a reproducible form on which you can write your reflections.

SPOTLIGHT ▶

Educators and leaders from across the country came together to advocate for twice-exceptional learners on a macro scale. Their story of advocacy is shared here.

Becoming aware of the unique needs of twice-exceptional (2e) learners has been a long process for educators across the country. A lot of work has been done to recognize and respond to those learning needs over the last fifty years. However, before 2012, educators had no unified way to bring together the research and thinking on best practices. Most importantly, they had no consistent definition to guide support for 2e learners.

It was clear educators needed a shared understanding and common language for 2e. This idea was brought forward in 2012 at a National Association for Gifted Children (NAGC) conference by several members of the Special Populations Network, the Assessments of Giftedness Special Interest Group (SIG), and the 2e SIG. These members recognized that the best way to advocate for 2e learners was to bring together important stakeholders from multiple educational programs and settings, such as general education, special education, gifted education, K-12 education, higher education, private schools, private clinical practice, and family advocacy. A definition created by this stakeholder group would be powerful.

The initial planning group reached out to the Individuals with Disabilities Education Act (IDEA) Partnership for support in engaging stakeholders and establishing the National Twice-Exceptional Community of Practice (2e CoP). The IDEA Partnership provided a facilitator, and the planning group developed an agenda for the first full-day meeting of the 2e CoP. In November 2013, stakeholders from twenty-four national, state, and local organizations with knowledge and understanding about 2e attended the 2e CoP Summit at the NAGC National Convention in Indianapolis.

The 2e CoP Summit resulted in a priority to develop a national definition of 2e. The 2e CoP first agreed on an understanding, based on research and experience, of what 2e is and is not and what 2e learners need to succeed in school. The 2e CoP agreed that a national definition should include a focus on identification, intervention, and social and emotional health.

The 2e CoP met regularly to discuss and refine the definition. All members gave input and finalized the definition after several months of discussions and revisions using a consensus approach. This definition seeks to provide a unifying understanding and a response to the needs of 2e learners. You can read the definition on page 12 in chapter 1.

Having a national definition is just the beginning of the collaborative advocacy work that's needed to support the success of 2e students across the United States. With this consistent definition, the development of materials, resources, and products to improve policy and practice related to 2e students will be better aligned.

—*Contributed by Daphne Pereles, educational consultant, and Lois Baldwin, educational consultant. Adapted from Baldwin, Lois, Susan Baum, Daphne Pereles, and Claire Hughes. 2015. "Twice-Exceptional Learners: The Journey Toward a Shared Vision." Gifted Child Today 38 (4): 206–214. Used with permission.*

Determining Your Main Focus Areas for Advocacy

Just as the members of 2e CoP determined that educators needed a unified understanding of twice-exceptionality, all advocacy begins with a clear and meaningful goal. Your advocacy goal should answer this question: *If my advocacy efforts are successful, how will they positively affect my underserved gifted learners' lives?*

Although you have probably noted toolkit strategies throughout this book that you'd like to try, it may be overwhelming to decide which ones you'd like to try first. To zero in on a starting point, identify your advocacy goal based on the knowledge you've acquired from this book and your current role in students' lives. We've developed the Advocacy Focus Finder (see the toolkit strategy on page 152) to help you identify your priorities in terms of your personal growth, professional growth, and the needs of your school, district, or state. The options provided are the major topics of chapters 1 through 4: seeing, understanding, teaching, and challenging underserved gifted learners.

Your personal growth may or may not be separate from your professional growth. Your personal growth is often influenced by all types of experiences, including those you've had in current and past professional positions. Ask yourself this question when you consider a focus for your personal growth: *Based on who I am as a person and what I believe, what do I value most as personal learning priorities?*

Your professional growth is focused on your current career. If you're a teacher, your professional growth will be specific to your classroom and students. It is highly connected to and informed by what you value personally and by past job experiences. Ask yourself this question when you consider a focus for your professional growth: *Based on my current professional position, what do I value most as professional learning priorities?*

The needs of your school, district, or state are just that. Informally or formally, you have surveyed areas related to the education of underserved gifted students that your school, your district, or your state needs to improve on. Ask yourself this question when you consider a focus for macro-level advocacy: *Based on what I have observed formally or informally, what are the most pressing professional learning needs of my school, district, or state?*

> **TOOLKIT STRATEGY**
>
> ## Advocacy Focus Finder
>
> You may recall that the checklists at the end of each chapter so far—the "'See Me' Checklist," "'Understand Me' Checklist," "'Teach Me' Checklist," and "'Challenge Me' Checklist"—asked you to reflect on your learning in that chapter. You rated your knowledge of the chapter topics as beginning, developing, or leading:
>
> › Beginning: You're aware and want to try.
> › Developing: You have tried or are trying.
> › Leading: You are consistently aware, implementing changes, and making others aware.
>
> As you complete the Advocacy Focus Finder (see reproducible form on page 164), please refer back to your end-of-chapter checklists to inform your priority ratings for personal growth, professional growth, and school, district, or state needs. Total your points for each chapter topic, then circle the top three areas that you would like to address in the near future.

Now that you've identified your three advocacy focus areas, it is time to set some goals. Goals should be SMART, meaning each goal you set needs to be:

> **Specific:** What exactly are you trying to accomplish and why?
> **Measurable:** How will you know you succeeded?
> **Attainable:** Why is this a feasible goal for you?
> **Relevant:** How will this goal make positive change for underserved gifted learners?
> **Timebound:** What is your time frame for accomplishing this goal, and how will you do it within this time frame?

A SMART goal for inclusive identification from chapter 1 might be:

By the end of the fall semester, I will collect information on my school's current gifted-identification practices that influence underserved gifted learners and present this information, along with practical recommendations and a rationale for these recommendations, to my grade-level team.

A chapter 2 goal for building meaningful connections with families might look something like this:

By the second week of school, and with the help of a Spanish interpreter, I will have contacted all my students' families through mail or email to find out what their goals are for their children this year. By the end of the first month of school, again with the help of an interpreter, I will have personally talked to each family, via phone or in person, to discuss how we can work together to support their child's success.

For connecting learning to students' lives in chapter 3, a goal focused on learning materials might be:

By the time school starts, I will identify at least two engaging resources that tie specifically to contributions made by females from my students' cultural backgrounds in the field of science. I will determine how to embed these resources into the appropriate unit to supplement the textbook we use.

And a goal to embed curriculum compacting into learning units from chapter 4 could be:

By next semester, I will do the following:

- *Create a preassessment for at least one of my social studies units.*

- *Identify at least two engaging and relevant resources or activities that could be used to provide additional challenge for my underrepresented gifted students who have already mastered the concepts in the unit (or who pick them up and finish with work quickly).*

- *Create a contract that includes sections for what concepts were mastered, the acceptable alternative activities, and the appropriate working conditions.*

> **TOOLKIT STRATEGY**
>
> ### Setting SMART Advocacy Goals
> Use the reproducible SMART Advocacy Goal Worksheet on page 165 to write a SMART goal for one of your three focus areas. Once you've completed the worksheet for one focus area, put your responses together to write a single, manageable goal. Repeat this process for each of your three focus areas.

Advocating Beyond Your Classroom

The action steps you take to reach the goals you set may require advocating beyond your classroom. This may seem daunting at first, but don't forget that *you have the power to make change* for underserved gifted learners, and *you have the potential to be a valuable resource* not only for your students, but also for others in your school, district, and state.

Advocacy outside your classroom may take many forms, such as:

› writing letters; sending emails; making phone calls to or scheduling meetings with stakeholders at your school, within your district, or at the state level

› preparing and giving professional learning presentations to teachers and staff at your school or to parents in your community

› providing indirect or direct consultation to other teachers at your school

› organizing and implementing support groups for teachers or parents in your district

- addressing the people whose support you need to make changes by disseminating fact sheets or publishing articles in reputable newsletters or practitioner- or parent-friendly publications about the issue you are focused on
- presenting at local, state, regional, or national educational conferences

As you begin advocating for underserved gifted learners beyond your classroom, keep the following steps in mind:

1. Be able to articulate the need for advocacy in a specific area in a five-minute talk and identify the audience that needs to hear about this need. The "Lightning Talks" toolkit strategy below will help you with this step.

2. Identify what must happen for you to feel that the need is being addressed meaningfully.

3. Determine who can support you in your advocacy efforts (your students, their families, teachers or staff from other schools or districts, and so on).

4. Investigate and prepare for potential opposition to your goal.

5. Share your story and your students' stories. Change is more likely to happen when an audience can see the issue through the perspectives of real people. Just like your underserved gifted learners, the people you're hoping to persuade must be able to make personal connections beyond bulleted facts on presentation slides. Personal connections combined with important information can be extremely effective in engaging others in an issue about which you care deeply.

TOOLKIT STRATEGY

Lightning Talks

You can use lightning talks to inspire and motivate your colleagues to learn more about an issue in just five minutes. By contrast, asking your principal for time to give an hour-long presentation may not be a practical request. Meeting agendas tend to be full, so principals are much more likely to honor requests for short, targeted presentations.

Begin your draft for a lightning talk by focusing on the issue that matters most to you. For example, you may talk about why it is important to incorporate culturally responsive teaching strategies into daily lessons. You can provide a personal example from your classroom and the success that resulted from it. Share strategies, then restate your key idea.

Here are some tips to help you create a successful lightning talk:

- Know your audience—the subjects they teach, the experiences they have in common, and so forth.
- Find a theme for your talk and craft the content around that theme.
- Get to the point. Do not spend more than one minute on background information.
- Three is the magic number. Select no more than three strategies or key points to share.
- Repeat. Mention your key idea at the beginning of the talk and repeat it at the end of your talk.

> Practice giving your lightning talk to family members and friends before giving it to colleagues.

> Remember, a lightning talk is not for squeezing as many details as you can into a short amount of time. Don't speak at lightning speed!

REAL-WORLD EXAMPLE

At a school in Aurora, Colorado, teachers in the arts had insufficient training in how to support gifted students from historically underserved populations. After a semester of developing new talent programming through a federal grant, the arts teachers appealed to school leadership to run their own professional learning community (PLC). This group of teachers recognized their own potential as advocates, so they framed their PLC work around Donna Ford's 2014 article "Segregation and the Underrepresentation of Blacks and Hispanics in Gifted Education: Social Inequality and Deficit Paradigms." As they read and discussed the article together, the PLC determined action steps they could take to advocate for underrepresented gifted students. These steps included helping develop equitable gifted-nomination processes, providing opportunities to learn more about this issue within the PLC, and inviting alumni from underrepresented groups back into the school to serve as mentors to current underserved gifted students.

—Contributed by Kelly Ann Stiles, gifted and talented coordinator, Rangeview High School, Aurora, Colorado. Used with permission.

If you are able to advocate for underserved gifted students by conducting professional development beyond short lightning talks, use the following toolkit strategy to help you design a meaningful learning opportunity. For example, teachers in our graduate programs have designed professional development for educators in their own buildings on everything from the characteristics of giftedness in various underrepresented populations to strategies for combating implicit bias in gifted-education programs.

TOOLKIT STRATEGY

Designing a Professional Learning Opportunity

Consider the following list of questions to help you design a meaningful learning opportunity. (See the "Professional Learning Opportunity Design Template" on page 166 for a reproducible version of this list, with spaces to write in your responses.)

> What will be the overarching topic of the professional learning?

> Why is this a relevant topic for your colleagues?

> What will be your professional learning objectives?

> What will be the time frame for conducting the professional learning?

> If you meet with participants on multiple occasions, what additional topics will you address and how?

> Who will be your audience?
> What types of activities (videos, short readings, jigsawing and other small-group strategies, case studies, and so on) will you use to engage your audience in the topic?
> How will you measure participants' knowledge before and after the professional learning?
> How will you collect participants' feedback on the professional learning?

Paying your knowledge forward to other educators has far-reaching ripple effects. This type of sharing advances your own learning, your colleagues' learning, and student learning. A teacher's professional life is a four-stage learning cycle that repeats and evolves over time. Teachers learn, then implement, then reflect, then lead, which in turn sparks more learning—and the cycle begins again. See **figure 5-1** for a simple illustration of this cycle.

Figure 5-1 Teacher Learning Cycle

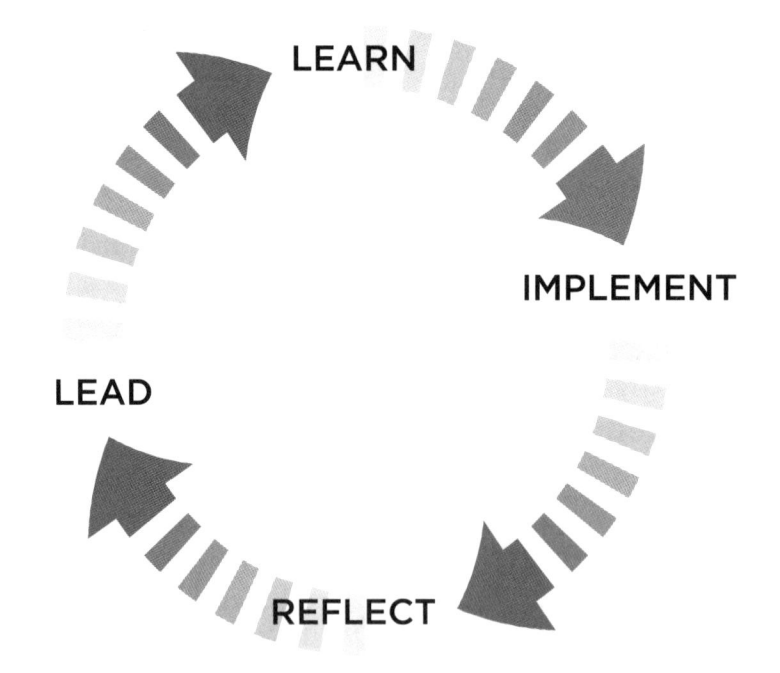

LEARN → IMPLEMENT → REFLECT → LEAD → (LEARN)

To understand how this cycle plays out in real life, consider the experience of educator Brent Braun. Braun teaches high school humanities, theater, and yearbook. His students include several underserved gifted learners. In his graduate teacher-education program, he chose to complete a passion project on creativity. Here's how the teacher learning cycle played out through his passion project:

1. He studied creativity (learn) and delivered a mini-workshop to his graduate-school classmates. During the workshop, he asked his classmates to take part in a picture completion activity, one of Ellis Paul Torrance's tests of creative thinking.

He presented his classmates with incomplete figures to which they had to add lines to create complete pictures. Next, he talked about strategies for promoting creativity in the classroom (implement). Braun was fascinated by Edward de Bono's Six Thinking Hats strategy, a creative reasoning approach that is often used to help students view an issue from various perspectives and to collaboratively generate solutions to a problem. This strategy helps strengthen students' creative thinking skills (Cramond et al. 2015).

2. Braun taught the Six Thinking Hats strategy to his theater class (implement). After implementing these strategies, he realized that he wanted to do more than the mini-workshop he'd developed for his graduate-school classmates (reflect).

3. He met with his assistant principal and began the process of planning an after-school professional learning opportunity for the teachers and staff in his building. He also developed a questionnaire to gain feedback from his colleagues at the end of the professional learning session (lead). (See **figure 5-2**.)

4. Brent is also planning on developing a "creativity community" support group at his school. By leading through professional learning and creating a support group, Brent will help his colleagues—and himself—learn a topic of their choice (learn) and try some new teaching strategies (implement).

Figure 5-2 Professional Learning Questionnaire: Cultivating Creativity in Your Classroom

---

Please be open and honest in answering the questions below.

1. Was your time today in the professional learning session well spent? Why or why not?

2. What are some suggestions for improvement on today's presentation?

3. What are some ways you would like to incorporate creativity into your classroom in the coming weeks? Please be specific.

4. Would you be interested in joining a small group of teachers in the building to become a Creativity Community to work on training other teachers in new and exciting teaching methods? Please make sure to include your name so we can set up a time to get together to discuss ideas.

—Contributed by Brent Braun, theater director, Pleasure Ridge Park High School, Louisville, Kentucky. Used with permission.

In the following spotlight, Braun reflects on this learning cycle.

SPOTLIGHT →

While I was working on the implementation ideas for my passion project, I was really struck by how complacent I had become in the classroom over the previous several years. I cannot really pinpoint when or why it began, but I had fallen into the same type of rut while I was teaching AP world history: "Here is what I normally teach now; let's just do this." One would think that my classroom could continually evolve and change, but I also fell into the trap of what was easiest, or what could get me through the next couple of weeks in class. Now I want to throw all that malaise to the side and really reinvigorate my classroom throughout the remainder of the year and start the next school year off with that same type of passion.

One of the areas that I really see that I need to grow in is the aspect of play. I usually start the year off with a lot more energy and the ability to play, but this year my energy level has diminished compared to where it normally is, so my students have not been able to play theater games and play with scenes as much as I would like them to. I have many students, especially the ones who would be considered gifted and talented in the visual and performing arts, who thrive off playing in my class, because my class is the only one that will let them express themselves outside the box. If I am not offering them that outlet, then I feel like I am not doing my job as an educator. Frankly, I also have some students who are potentially on the autism spectrum who also need play to help them decompress from their intense days inside traditional classrooms. It's my hope that as a part of this reflective process, I can incorporate more student play into my daily routine, whether that's starting every day with something or dedicating more time during the week to it.

The second part of my implementation in the building will also help me reconnect with my teacher colleagues. I work rather closely with the other fine arts teachers in the building, but I spend little to no time in general education classrooms, and it will be nice to be able to get my feet wet again in that area. It's my ultimate professional goal to remain in the classroom and teach pedagogy and instruction at the collegiate level, because I love working with new teachers and helping them establish their persona in their own classrooms and schools. I hope that by doing these trainings I can establish myself as a teacher leader in the building. This will not only help me in my relationships with my colleagues, but also establish communication as I take on coordinating programming for gifted and talented students at my school once I am done with my graduate coursework. I really think that establishing this creativity community will be a positive step at our school.

—*Contributed by Brent Braun, theater director, Pleasure Ridge Park High School, Louisville, Kentucky. Used with permission.*

Because there are few opportunities for this elsewhere, it is imperative for schools to build learning communities where teachers can acquire new strategies and exchange ideas on how to meet the needs of underserved gifted learners. Stepping up to lead a learning community, however, takes passion, commitment, and courage. By taking on this added responsibility, Braun found a way to engage his personal passion for creativity, while at the same time nurturing the creativity culture in his building.

Paying it forward by sharing your knowledge and passion through professional development is just one possible way to put your advocacy skills to work for the underserved gifted learners (and their teachers) in your building.

Although you may already have an idea of which advocacy areas you would like to focus professional learning activities on, it is always a good idea to conduct a needs assessment to fine-tune your focus.

> **TOOLKIT STRATEGY**
>
> ## Creating a Needs Assessment
>
> A needs assessment to determine priorities for professional learning often takes the form of a short survey or questionnaire. It can be distributed via paper or electronically. Many free web-based programs, such as Google Forms and SurveyMonkey, are available for designing and distributing electronic surveys.
>
> In your needs assessment, you may ask participants preference questions related to topics, learning styles, duration of professional learning activities, types of professional learning activities, and comfort level with various aspects of a topic. Including pre-assessment questions can help you ensure that you don't cover aspects of a topic that your participants already understand well. Remember to keep your needs assessment short and focused. To help you visualize what one might look like, see **figure 5-3**. For a reproducible version of this assessment that you can customize and distribute to your own colleagues, see pages 167–168.
>
> **Figure 5-3** Sample Needs Assessment

Putting the Pieces Together: Developing an Advocacy Action Plan

Once you have determined your top three advocacy priorities, set your three SMART advocacy goals, and decided the level of advocacy you're prepared to engage in (in the classroom and/or beyond the classroom), the next step is to develop an action plan. You are much more likely to work toward reaching your goals if you have a plan in place. It is important to remember that you can always modify your plan as you work through it. You may even need to modify your goals. Adjustments are a normal part of the advocacy process. You can use the "Action Planning" toolkit strategy to help you plan.

TOOLKIT STRATEGY

Action Planning

Answer the following questions for each of your three advocacy focus areas. (For a reproducible "Action Planning Template" on which you can write your answers to these questions, see pages 169–170.) You will need to decide if you want to spread your advocacy efforts over the entire school year or even longer, or if your goals need to be addressed immediately.

- What is your advocacy focus area?
- What is your SMART advocacy goal?
- Why is this goal important to you?
- What do you need to do to achieve your goal? What toolkit strategies will you try?
- When will you complete each step?
- What or who can help you reach your goal?
- What obstacles might you encounter, and how will you address them proactively?
- When will you check on your progress toward your goal and decide if you need to modify it?
- What should happen once you reach your goal? What change should you see?
- What will be your validation or reward for reaching this goal?
- How will you take time to reflect constructively on the advocacy process?

In addition to completing the "Action Planning Template," try these tips:

- Print out each action plan and keep it in a visible place.
- Set check-in points on your calendar or in your personal planner for revisiting your action plan.
- Congratulate and reward yourself when you achieve one of your goals. Although the main reward is seeing the positive impact of your advocacy on others, it is also important to acknowledge your hard work and accomplishment.
- Consider sharing your action planning process with your students and colleagues. You may even incorporate action planning into your classroom instruction.

Following is an action planning example from a teacher whose advocacy goal was implementation of Universal Design for Learning (UDL) guidelines. After completing the "UDL Strategies Checklist" in chapter 2 (pages 60–61), she realized that her students, particularly her underserved gifted learners, would benefit from a learning environment incorporating UDL principles. These would help her change the instruction and environment proactively to make the content more accessible. She then completed the "Action Planning Template" with this priority in mind.

Figure 5-4 Sample Action Planning Template: Implementing UDL Guidelines

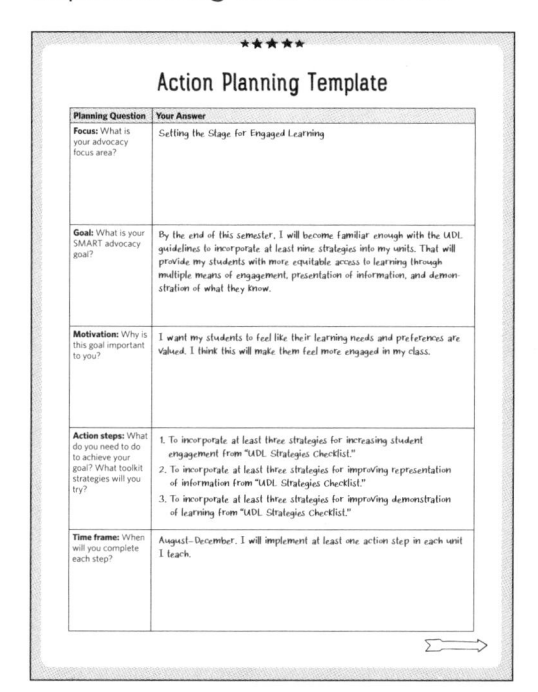

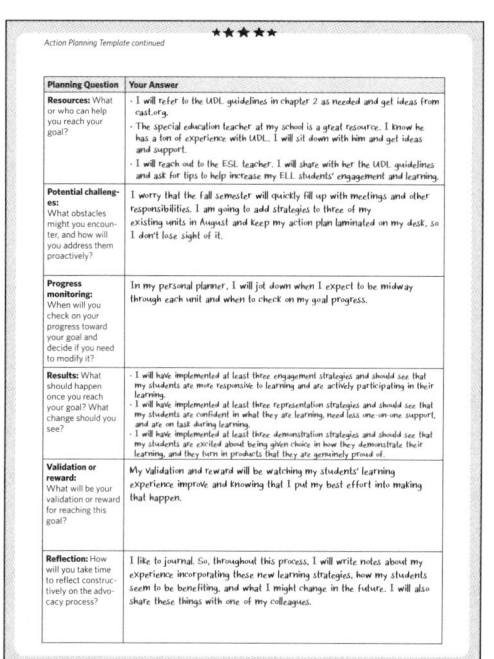

Planning Question	Your Answer
Focus: What is your advocacy focus area?	Setting the Stage for Engaged Learning
Goal: What is your SMART advocacy goal?	By the end of this semester, I will become familiar enough with the UDL guidelines to incorporate at least nine strategies into my units. That will provide my students with more equitable access to learning through multiple means of engagement, presentation of information, and demonstration of what they know.
Motivation: Why is this goal important to you?	I want my students to feel like their learning needs and preferences are valued. I think this will make them feel more engaged in my class.
Action steps: What do you need to do to achieve your goal? What toolkit strategies will you try?	1. To incorporate at least three strategies for increasing student engagement from "UDL Strategies Checklist." 2. To incorporate at least three strategies for improving representation of information from "UDL Strategies Checklist." 3. To incorporate at least three strategies for improving demonstration of learning from "UDL Strategies Checklist."
Time frame: When will you complete each step?	August–December, I will implement at least one action step in each unit I teach.

Action Planning Template continued

Planning Question	Your Answer
Resources: What or who can help you reach your goal?	• I will refer to the UDL guidelines in chapter 2 as needed and get ideas from cast.org. • The special education teacher at my school is a great resource. I know he has a ton of experience with UDL. I will sit down with him and get ideas and support. • I will reach out to the ESL teacher. I will share with her the UDL guidelines and ask for tips to help increase my ELL students' engagement and learning.
Potential challenges: What obstacles might you encounter, and how will you address them proactively?	I worry that the fall semester will quickly fill up with meetings and other responsibilities. I am going to add strategies to three of my existing units in August and keep my action plan laminated on my desk, so I don't lose sight of it.
Progress monitoring: When will you check on your progress toward your goal and decide if you need to modify it?	In my personal planner, I will jot down when I expect to be midway through each unit and when to check on my goal progress.
Results: What should happen once you reach your goal? What change should you see?	• I will have implemented at least three engagement strategies and should see that my students are more responsive to learning and are actively participating in their learning. • I will have implemented at least three representation strategies and should see that my students are confident in what they are learning, need less one-on-one support, and are on task during learning. • I will have implemented at least three demonstration strategies and should see that my students are excited about being given choice in how they demonstrate their learning, and they turn in products that they are genuinely proud of.
Validation or reward: What will be your validation or reward for reaching this goal?	My validation and reward will be watching my students' learning experience improve, and knowing that I put my best effort into making that happen.
Reflection: How will you take time to reflect constructively on the advocacy process?	I like to journal. So, throughout this process, I will write notes about my experience incorporating these new learning strategies, how my students seem to be benefiting, and what I might change in the future. I will also share these things with one of my colleagues.

Chapter Summary

This chapter invites you to begin advocating for underserved gifted learners. Becoming an advocate is an important step for both you and your students. We wholeheartedly believe that one teacher can improve the educational trajectory of a child. We have seen this happen time and time again. Underserved gifted learners, who may rarely get opportunities to shine and to show the world their talents, need champions in their lives. They need caring adults to help them envision a future they might not see for themselves—and to give them the support, love, and guidance required to get there.

Sometimes your advocacy may take place within your own educational setting. At other times you may be able to advocate at the school, district, community, state, or even national level. It is important to remember that all levels of advocacy are valuable.

The strategies in this chapter can help you focus your advocacy efforts on specific topics and causes that are important to you and the underserved gifted learners in your life. This chapter can also help you determine the level at which you are comfortable advocating (or the level at which you want to challenge yourself to advocate) for these topics and causes. Finally, this chapter can help you develop or define future goals for yourself as an advocate for underserved gifted students. To reflect on your progress on using these strategies, fill out the reproducible "'Advocate for Me' Checklist" on page 171.

After you complete the steps in this chapter, we hope that you come away with a personal advocacy action plan that you can dig into right away. We are convinced that you can be an agent of change for your underserved gifted learners. We are counting on it, and they are too.

Your Past, Present, and Future Advocacy

Past Advocacy	Present Advocacy	Future Advocacy
In past years, I supported individual underserved gifted students by . . .	This year, I have been supporting individual underserved gifted students by . . .	In the near future, I hope to support individual underserved gifted students by . . .
In past years, I supported a cause related to the needs of underserved gifted learners by . . .	This year, I have been supporting a cause related to the needs of underserved gifted learners by . . .	In the near future, I hope to support a cause related to the needs of underserved gifted learners by . . .

From *Start Seeing and Serving Underserved Gifted Students: 50 Strategies for Equity and Excellence* by Jennifer A. Ritchotte, Ph.D., Chin-Wen Lee, Ph.D., and Amy K. Graefe, Ph.D., copyright © 2020. This page may be reproduced for individual, classroom, or small group work only. For all other uses, contact Free Spirit Publishing Inc. at freespirit.com/permissions.

★ ★ ★ ★ ★

Advocacy Focus Finder

Please refer back to the checklists at the ends of chapters 1 through 4 to inform your priority ratings for personal growth, professional growth, and school, district, or state needs. Total your priority points for each chapter topic, then circle the top three areas that you would like to address in the near future.

Key:
1 = low priority
2 = medium-low priority
3 = medium priority
4 = medium-high priority
5 = high priority
N/A = not applicable

	Focus Areas	Personal Growth (1–5 or N/A)	Professional Growth (1–5 or N/A)	School/ District/ State Needs (1–5 or N/A)	Total Points
Chapter 1: See Me	Implicit bias				
	Inclusive identification				
Chapter 2: Understand Me	Building meaningful connections				
	Nurturing a safe climate				
	Setting the stage for engaged learning				
Chapter 3: Teach Me	Connect learning to students' lives				
	Ability group students flexibly				
	Respectfully differentiate for students				
	Engage students in higher-level thinking				
Chapter 4: Challenge Me	Add challenge thoughtfully				
	Supply the support necessary for success				
	Provide opportunities for mentorships				
	Identify possibilities for independent investigations				
	Recognize when acceleration is vital				
	Embed curriculum compacting into learning units				

From *Start Seeing and Serving Underserved Gifted Students: 50 Strategies for Equity and Excellence* by Jennifer A. Ritchotte, Ph.D., Chin-Wen Lee, Ph.D., and Amy K. Graefe, Ph.D., copyright © 2020. This page may be reproduced for individual, classroom, or small group work only. For all other uses, contact Free Spirit Publishing Inc. at freespirit.com/permissions.

SMART Advocacy Goal Worksheet

Advocacy Focus Area: _____

SMART Goal Element	Question	Your Response
Specific	What exactly are you trying to accomplish and why?	
Measurable	How will you know you succeeded?	
Attainable	Why is this a feasible goal for you?	
Relevant	How will this goal make positive change for underserved gifted learners?	
Timebound	What is your time frame for accomplishing this goal, and how will you do it within this time frame?	

Your SMART Goal:

_____

_____

_____

_____

From *Start Seeing and Serving Underserved Gifted Students: 50 Strategies for Equity and Excellence* by Jennifer A. Ritchotte, Ph.D., Chin-Wen Lee, Ph.D., and Amy K. Graefe, Ph.D., copyright © 2020. This page may be reproduced for individual, classroom, or small group work only. For all other uses, contact Free Spirit Publishing Inc. at freespirit.com/permissions.

Professional Learning Opportunity Design Template

Questions to Consider	Your Responses
What will be the overarching topic of the professional learning?	
Why is this a relevant topic for your colleagues?	
What will be your professional learning objectives?	
What will be the time frame for conducting the professional learning?	
If you meet with participants on multiple occasions, what additional topics will you address and how?	
Who will be your audience?	
What types of activities (videos, short readings, jigsawing and other small-group strategies, case studies, and so on) will you use to engage your audience in the topic?	
How will you measure participants' knowledge before and after the professional learning?	
How will you collect participants' feedback on the professional learning?	

From *Start Seeing and Serving Underserved Gifted Students: 50 Strategies for Equity and Excellence* by Jennifer A. Ritchotte, Ph.D., Chin-Wen Lee, Ph.D., and Amy K. Graefe, Ph.D., copyright © 2020. This page may be reproduced for individual, classroom, or small group work only. For all other uses, contact Free Spirit Publishing Inc. at freespirit.com/permissions.

Sample Needs Assessment

Introduction: _____
_____
_____
_____

Write an *X* in the box that best indicates your level of agreement with each statement.

	Strongly agree	Agree	Disagree	Unsure
1. I feel comfortable in my knowledge of gifted education in general.				
2. I feel comfortable in my knowledge of _____ learners in general.				
3. I understand the challenges involved in identifying _____ students for gifted services.				
4. I understand the unique learning needs of _____ students who have gifted potential or are identified as gifted.				
5. I know how to differentiate my instruction to meet the unique learning needs of my _____ students who have gifted potential or are identified as gifted.				
6. I know how to embed _____ strategies into my instructional practices.				
7. I consistently embed _____ teaching strategies into my instructional practices.				
8. I know how to challenge my _____ students who are gifted.				

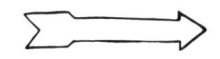

From *Start Seeing and Serving Underserved Gifted Students: 50 Strategies for Equity and Excellence* by Jennifer A. Ritchotte, Ph.D., Chin-Wen Lee, Ph.D., and Amy K. Graefe, Ph.D., copyright © 2020. This page may be reproduced for individual, classroom, or small group work only. For all other uses, contact Free Spirit Publishing Inc. at freespirit.com/permissions.

Sample Needs Assessment continued

Please rank the following subtopics with the numbers 1 through 4 to indicate your priorities for professional learning from first to last.

_____ overview of gifted education and diversity in gifted education

_____ identifying _____ gifted learners

_____ learning and affective needs of _____ gifted learners

_____ instructional strategies for _____ gifted learners

Please note any other priorities you have for professional learning on culturally and linguistically diverse gifted learners:

_____
_____
_____
_____

Please rank the following learning activities with the numbers 1 through 5 to indicate your preferences from first to last.

_____ working with case studies of students you teach or have taught in the past

_____ presentation or mini-lecture

_____ video clips

_____ short readings

_____ modifying lesson plans

Please note any other learning activities you'd prefer:

_____
_____
_____
_____

Thank you for completing this needs assessment survey!

Action Planning Template

Planning Question	Your Answer
Focus: What is your advocacy focus area?	
Goal: What is your SMART advocacy goal?	
Motivation: Why is this goal important to you?	
Action steps: What do you need to do to achieve your goal? What toolkit strategies will you try?	
Time frame: When will you complete each step?	

From *Start Seeing and Serving Underserved Gifted Students: 50 Strategies for Equity and Excellence* by Jennifer A. Ritchotte, Ph.D., Chin-Wen Lee, Ph.D., and Amy K. Graefe, Ph.D., copyright © 2020. This page may be reproduced for individual, classroom, or small group work only. For all other uses, contact Free Spirit Publishing Inc. at freespirit.com/permissions.

Action Planning Template continued

Planning Question	Your Answer
Resources: What or who can help you reach your goal?	
Potential challenges: What obstacles might you encounter, and how will you address them proactively?	
Progress monitoring: When will you check on your progress toward your goal and decide if you need to modify it?	
Results: What should happen once you reach your goal? What change should you see?	
Validation or reward: What will be your validation or reward for reaching this goal?	
Reflection: How will you take time to reflect constructively on the advocacy process?	

From *Start Seeing and Serving Underserved Gifted Students: 50 Strategies for Equity and Excellence* by Jennifer A. Ritchotte, Ph.D., Chin-Wen Lee, Ph.D., and Amy K. Graefe, Ph.D., copyright © 2020. This page may be reproduced for individual, classroom, or small group work only. For all other uses, contact Free Spirit Publishing Inc. at freespirit.com/permissions.

"Advocate for Me" Checklist

Use this checklist to reflect on where you are as an advocate for your underserved gifted students. Review your results to become more aware of your areas of strength and your areas for growth.

Key:
Beginning: You're aware and want to try.
Developing: You have tried or are trying.
Leading: You are consistently aware, implementing changes, and making others aware.

Determining Your Focus for and Level of Advocacy	Beginning	Developing	Leading
I have identified at least one area where I want to advocate for underserved gifted learners.			
I can succinctly explain the need for and the desired outcomes of this advocacy to others.			
I make a concerted effort to talk to my building colleagues about the strengths and needs of underserved gifted learners.			
I try to advocate beyond my building for causes related to underserved gifted learners.			
I have designed an action plan to focus my advocacy efforts for underserved gifted learners.			
I am working actively to achieve the SMART goals associated with my action plan.			

From *Start Seeing and Serving Underserved Gifted Students: 50 Strategies for Equity and Excellence* by Jennifer A. Ritchotte, Ph.D., Chin-Wen Lee, Ph.D., and Amy K. Graefe, Ph.D., copyright © 2020. This page may be reproduced for individual, classroom, or small group work only. For all other uses, contact Free Spirit Publishing Inc. at freespirit.com/permissions.

References

Anderson, Lorin W., and David R. Krathwohl, eds. 2001. *A Taxonomy for Learning, Teaching, and Assessing: A Revision of Bloom's Taxonomy of Educational Objectives.* New York: Pearson Education.

Assouline, Susan G., Nicholas Colangelo, and Joyce VanTassel-Baska, eds. 2015. *A Nation Empowered: Evidence Trumps the Excuses Holding Back America's Brightest Students.* Iowa City: Belin-Blank Center.

Baldwin, Lois, Susan Baum, Daphne Pereles, and Claire Hughes. 2015. "Twice-Exceptional Learners: The Journey Toward a Shared Vision." *Gifted Child Today* 38 (4): 206–214. doi.org/10.1177/1076217515597277.

Betts, George. 2016. "The Whole Gifted Child." nagc.org/blog/whole-gifted-child.

Carson, Jessica A., Marybeth J. Mattingly, and Andrew Schaefer. 2017. "Gains in Reducing Child Poverty, but Racial-Ethnic Disparities Persist." scholars.unh.edu/cgi/viewcontent.cgi?article=1301&context=carsey.

Colangelo, Nicholas, Susan G. Assouline, and Miraca U. M. Gross, eds. 2004. *A Nation Deceived: How Schools Hold Back America's Brightest Students.* Iowa City: Belin-Blank Center. accelerationinstitute.org/nation_deceived.

Cramond, Bonnie, Sarah Sumners, Dong Gun An, Sarah Marie Catalana, Laura Ecke, Noparat Sricharoen, Suehyeon Paek, Hyeri Park, Burak Türkman, and Sonya Türkman. "Cultivating Creative Thinking." 2015. In *Methods and Materials for Teaching the Gifted*, edited by Frances A. Karnes and Suzanne M. Bean, 345–378. Waco, TX: Prufrock Press.

Cristodero, Damian. 2018. "Mason Research Helps Boost Students of Underserved Populations." gmu.edu/news/513246.

Finn, Chester E., and Amber M. Northern. 2018. "Narrowing the Gifted Gap for Disadvantaged Students." nagc.org/blog/narrowing-gifted-gap-disadvantaged-students.

Ford, Donna Y. 2014. "Segregation and the Underrepresentation of Blacks and Hispanics in Gifted Education: Social Inequality and Deficit Paradigms." *Roeper Review* 36 (3): 143–154. doi.org/10.1080/02783193.2014.919563.

Ford, Donna Y. 2015. "Multicultural Issues: Recruiting and Retaining Black and Hispanic Students in Gifted Education: Equality versus Equity Schools." *Gifted Child Today* 38 (3): 187–191. doi.org/10.1177/1076217515583745.

Ford, Donna Y., Tarek C. Grantham, and Gilman W. Whiting. 2008. "Culturally and Linguistically Diverse Students in Gifted Education: Recruitment and Retention Issues." *Exceptional Children* 74 (3): 289–306. doi.org/10.1177/001440290807400302.

Fredricks, Jennifer, Wendy McColskey, Jane Meli, Joy Mordica, Bianca Montrosse, and Kathleen Mooney. 2011. *Measuring Student Engagement in Upper Elementary Through High School: A Description of 21 Instruments.* (Issues & Answers Report, REL 2011–No. 098). Washington, DC: US Department of Education, Institute of Education Sciences, National Center for Education Evaluation and Regional Assistance, Regional Educational Laboratory Southeast. ies.ed.gov/ncee/edlabs/regions/southeast/pdf/REL_2011098.pdf.

Graefe, Amy Karol. 2017. "Gifted Students' Perceptions of Empowerment Within High School Classrooms" Ph.D. diss. University of Northern Colorado. digscholarship.unco.edu/cgi/viewcontent.cgi?article=1437&context=dissertations.

Isakson, Scott G., and Donald J. Treffinger. 1985. *Creative Problem Solving: The Basic Course.* Buffalo, NY: Bearly Limited.

Jensen, Eric. 2013. *Engaging Students with Poverty in Mind.* Alexandria, VA: ASCD.

Jensen, Eric. 2016. *Poor Students, Rich Teaching: Mindsets for Change.* Bloomington, IN: Solution Tree Press.

J Taylor Education. 2016. "Depth and Complexity Framework: Understanding the Pieces." jtayloreducation.com/wp-content/uploads/2016/06/General-DC-Handouts-from-SA-Concordia-PD.pdf.

Kena, Grace, Lauren Musu-Gillette, Jennifer Robinson, Xiaolei Wang, Amy Rathbun, Jijun Zhang, Sidney Wilkinson-Flicker, Amy Barmer, and Erin Dunlop Velez. 2015. *The Condition of Education 2015* (NCES 2015-144). National Center for Education Statistics, U.S. Department of Education. Washington, DC. nces.ed.gov/pubs2015/2015144.pdf.

Lee, Seon-Young, Paula Olszewski-Kubilius, Rob Donahue, and Katrina Weimholt. 2007. "The Effects of a Service-Learning Program on the Development of Civic Attitudes and Behaviors Among Academically Talented Adolescents." *Journal for the Education of the Gifted* 31 (2): 165–197. doi.org/10.4219/jeg-2007-674.

Lee, Seon-Young, Paula Olszewski-Kubilius, and George Peternel. 2010. "The Efficacy of Academic Acceleration for Gifted Minority Students." *Gifted Child Quarterly* 54 (3): 189–208. doi.org/10.1177/0016986210369256.

National Association for Gifted Children (NAGC). 2010. *NAGC Pre-K–Grade 12 Gifted Programming Standards.* Washington, DC: NAGC. nagc.org/resources-publications/resources/national-standards-gifted-and-talented-education/pre-k-grade-12.

National Center for Education Statistics (NCES). 2017. "Table 203.50: Enrollment and Percentage Distribution of Enrollment in Public Elementary and Secondary Schools, by Race/Ethnicity and Region: Selected Years, Fall 1995 Through Fall 2027." nces.ed.gov/programs/digest/d17/tables/dt17_203.50.asp.

National Center for Education Statistics (NCES). 2018. "Fast Facts: Back to School Statistics." nces.ed.gov/fastfacts/display.asp?id=372.

National Center for Education Statistics (NCES). 2019a. "Children and Youth with Disabilities." nces.ed.gov/programs/coe/indicator_cgg.asp.

National Center for Education Statistics (NCES). 2019b. "English Language Learners in Public Schools." nces.ed.gov/programs/coe/indicator_cgf.asp.

National Paideia Center. n.d. "Paideia Socratic Seminar." Accessed July 15, 2019. paideia.org/our-approach/paideia-seminar/index.

Olszewski-Kubilius, Paula, Saiying Steenbergen-Hu, Dana Thomson, and Rhoda Rosen. 2017. "Minority Achievement Gaps in STEM: Findings of a Longitudinal Study of Project Excite. *Gifted Child Quarterly* 61 (1): 20–39. doi.org/10.1177/0016986216673449.

Peterson, Jean Sunde. 1999. "Gifted—Through Whose Cultural Lens? An Application of the Postpositivistic Mode of Inquiry." *Journal for the Education of the Gifted* 22 (4): 354–383.

Regional Education Laboratory (REL) Northwest. 2018. "Soaring to College: Accelerating Learning Access, Outcomes, and Credit Transfer in Oregon." ies.ed.gov/ncee/edlabs/regions/northwest/pdf/soaring-to-college.pdf.

Ridnouer, Katy. 2011. *Everyday Engagement: Making Students and Parents Your Partners in Learning.* Alexandria, VA: ASCD.

Ritchotte, Jennifer A., and Amy K. Graefe. 2017. "An Alternate Path: The Experience of High-Potential Individuals Who Left School." *Gifted Child Quarterly* 61(4): 275–289. doi.org/10.1177/0016986217722615.

Ritchotte, Jennifer A., Hasan Zaghlawan, and Chin-Wen Lee. 2017. "Paving the Path to Meaningful Engagement for High-Potential Children." *Parenting for High Potential* 6(2): 8–13.

Showalter, Daniel, Robert Klein, Jerry Johnson, and Sarah L. Hartman. 2017. "Why Rural Matters 2015–2016: Understanding the Changing Landscape." ruraledu.org/user_uploads/file/WRM-2015-16.pdf.

Snyder, Thomas D., Cristobal de Brey, and Sally A. Dillow. 2019. *Digest of Educational Statistics 2017 (NCES 2018-070).* National Center for Education Statistics, Institute of Education Sciences, US Department of Education. Washington, DC. nces.ed.gov/pubs2018/2018070.pdf.

Sparks, Sarah D., and Alex Harwin. 2017. "Too Few ELL Students Land in Gifted Classes." edweek.org/ew/articles/2017/06/21/too-few-ell-students-land-in-gifted.html.

US Department of Education. 2016. "Non-Regulatory Guidance: English Learners and Title III of the Elementary and Secondary Education Act (ESEA), as Amended by the Every Student Succeeds Act (ESSA)." ed.gov/policy/elsec/leg/essa/essatitleiiiguidenglishlearners92016.pdf.

US Department of Education Office for Civil Rights. 2018. "Civil Rights Data Collection for the 2015–2016 School Year." ed.gov/about/offices/list/ocr/docs/crdc-2015-16.html.

Vygotsky, Lev S. 1978. *Mind in Society.* Cambridge, MA: Harvard University Press.

Resources

Books

Tomlinson, Carol Ann. 2017. *How to Differentiate Instruction in Academically Diverse Classrooms.* This book is a must-have for teachers. It includes many strategies that teachers can use right away to meaningfully differentiate instruction for gifted students in mixed-ability classrooms.

Winebrenner, Susan, and Dina Brulles. 2018. *Teaching Gifted Kids in Today's Classroom: Strategies and Techniques Every Teacher Can Use.* This book is another fantastic resource. It's filled with practical strategies that educators can use immediately to differentiate instruction for gifted students in mixed-ability classrooms.

★★★★★

Websites

Acceleration Institute • accelerationinstitute.org. Here you'll find resources for parents, educators, policy makers, and researchers regarding academic acceleration.

The Curriculum Project • curriculumproject.com/product_guide_kits_product.php. At this web page, you'll find affordable product guide kits to help develop guidelines and rubrics for authentic classroom assessments.

How to Choose Outstanding Multicultural Books • scholastic.com/teachers/articles/teaching-content/how-choose-best-multicultural-books. This resource published by Scholastic offers excellent advice for choosing multicultural books, as well as numerous book recommendations and additional resources.

IRIS Center • iris.peabody.vanderbilt.edu/module/div. The IRIS Center offers a free online learning module to increase your knowledge about classroom diversity.

J Taylor Education • jtayloreducation.com. Visit this website for a wealth of resources on incorporating depth and complexity.

National Center for Research on Gifted Education • ncrge.uconn.edu/resources. Find more studies on English language learners at the Resources page of this website, sponsored by the University of Connecticut.

The National Mentoring Partnership • mentoring.org. This organization provides resources for people who want to become mentors or for people who want to start a mentoring program. It also has a network for regional mentorship advocates.

Our Nation's English Learners • ed.gov/datastory/el-characteristics/index.html#intro. This website offers information on the characteristics and locations of ELL students in the United States.

Renzulli Center for Creativity, Gifted Education, and Talent Development • gifted.uconn.edu/schoolwide-enrichment-model/sem3rd. Drs. Joseph Renzulli and Sally Reis provide links to dozens of reproducible forms from the third edition of their book *The Schoolwide Enrichment Model* to help you incorporate enrichment and independent investigations into your classroom.

SMART Goals for Gifted Students • freespiritpublishingblog.com/2018/01/04/smart-goals-for-gifted-students. This blog post by Richard Cash offers guidance on and ideas for setting high-quality, meaningful learning goals for gifted students.

UDL Center • medium.com/udl-center. The UDL Center provides resources and support for educators interested in implementing Universal Design for Learning.

Index

Bold entries indicate reproducible forms.

A

Ability
    grouping students by, 69, 73–76
    teachers placing emphasis on, 8
Academic acceleration. *See* Acceleration
Academic Challenge Support Tips (toolkit strategy), 106, 107–108
Academic language skills, social language skills *vs.*, 9
Acceleration, 122–130
    content, 122–125
    at Greeley Central High School, Colorado, 129–130
    report on, 122
    research on, 122
    for underserved gifted learners, 122, 128–129
    whole-grade, 125–127
Achievement, teachers placing emphasis on, 8
Achievement test scores, 18
Action Planning (toolkit strategy), 160
Action Planning Template, 160, **169–170**
Action plans, for service learning, 66–67, 68
Active listening, 78–79
Additive approach to service learning, 66
Administrators, race of, 7
Advanced Placement (AP) courses, 122, 124, 126, 128, 129, 149
Advancement Via Individual Determination (AVID) program, 129
Advocacy
    Action Plan for, 160–161
    determining main focus areas of, 151–153
    examples of, 147, 148–149, 150–151, 155
    Lightning Talks, 154–155
    needs assessment determining your focus for, 159
    outside of the classroom, 153–159
    professional learning communities (PLCs) and, 155–156, **166**
    SMART goals, 152–153
    steps for, 154
    two types of, 148
Advocacy Focus Finder (toolkit strategy), 151, 152, **164**
"Advocate for Me" Checklist, 162, **171**
African cultural heritage, 7
Alaska Native students, 7, 8
American Indian students, 7, 8
AP courses. *See* Advanced Placement (AP) courses
AP exams, 129, 130
Applying UDL Principles to Create an Inclusive Classroom (toolkit strategy), 45, **60–61**
Artistic interpreter, in literature circles, 77
Asian/Asian American students
    overrepresentation in gifted programs, 13–14
    projections on number of, 7
    subgroups within, 14
ASPIRE acronym, 3, 105
Assessment. *See also* Rubrics; Tests and testing
    best practices for identification and, 20–21
    curriculum compacting and, 132
    differentiation and, 85–86
    formative, 86
    for gifted program, culturally and linguistically diverse learners and, 8, 9
    needs, for professional learning, 159, **167–168**
    needs grouping and, 73
    preassessments, 85
    summative, 85–86
Assessments of Giftedness Special Interest Group (SIG), 150
Assouline, Susan G., 122
Audio recordings, 114
Aurora, Colorado, 155

B

Background checks, for mentors, 110
Baldwin, Lois, 150–151
Banks, James A., 66
Behavioral engagement, 42
Best Practices in Identification Checklist, 20, **29–30**
Betts, George, 17
Big Brothers Big Sisters (BBBS) program, 109
Big ideas, creating depth in lessons with, 89
Black children, poverty among, 10
Bloom's Revised Taxonomy, 87, 101
Board games, 70
Boards of Cooperative Educational Services (BOCES), 90
Bookmark, higher-level thinking, 87, **100**
Boredom, in gifted students, 106
Bowen Elementary, Louisville, Kentucky, 116
Braun, Brent, 156–157, 158
Breakfast with Stars (toolkit strategy), 11
Building RAFTs (toolkit strategy), 83
Building Step-by-Step Project Timelines (toolkit strategy), 85, **98**
Building Supply Costs and Order Form, **95**
Burch, Steve, 130
Bureau of Labor Statistics Career Exploration, 65

C

CARE acronym, 3, 63–64
Career fields, learning about, 64–65, 108–109
Challenges/being challenged, 104–146
    "Challenge Me" Checklist, 132, **145–146**
    identifying students' readiness for, 105–106
    importance of, 104
    Multi-Tiered System of Support (MTSS) model for, 105
    in rural areas, 120–121
    support tips for teachers on, 106–107
    through acceleration, 122–130, **140–144**
    through curriculum compacting, 130–132
    through independent investigations, 112–117, **138–139**
    through mentorships, 108–112, **133–137**
    through Young Chautauqua (YC) program, 117–120
Charles, Lisa, 116
Charts, emotional literacy, 107
Chautauqua Lake, New York, 117
Check-ins, for independent investigations, 114–115
Checklists
    about, 4
    "Advocate for Me," 162, **171**
    Best Practices in Identification, **29–30**
    "Challenge Me," 132, **145–146**
    Empowered-to-Learn, 40, **56–58**
    Group Work Self-Reflection, 76, **96**
    for nomination process for gifted education, 16–17
    Safe Climate, 38–39, **54–55**
    "See Me," 23, **31**
    "Teach Me," 91, **103**
    UDL Strategies, 46, **60–61**
    "Understand Me," 46, **62**
Choice boards, 80–82
Choices, differentiation through student, 80–84
Choosing Content Acceleration Options Thoughtfully (toolkit strategy), 124–125
Choosing Whole-Grade Acceleration Options Thoughtfully (toolkit strategy), 126–127
Chunking assignments and projects, 84–85, 114
Church, Jodi, 121
Civil Rights Data Collection website, 14
Classroom(s)
    culturally responsive, 32
    grouping within. *See* Grouping students
    honoring small requests in your, 41
    positive classroom norms in, 39
    Safe Climate Checklist for, **54–55**
    safe climate in, 38–39
Classroom observations
    ability grouping and, 73
    determining learner readiness for challenge and, 106
Cognitive Abilities Test (CogAT), 19
Cognitive engagement, 42
Colangelo, Nicholas, 122
Collaboration. *See also* Grouping students
    in culturally responsive classroom, 32
    curriculum compacting and, 131
    service learning and, 65, 66, 68
    Socratic seminars and, 87–88
    supporting challenges with, 107
Collaborative teaching, meaningful engagement and, 42
College credits, acceleration programs and, 128–129
College, early entrance to, 127
Colorado Humanities, 118
Colorado Legacy Foundation Grant, 129
Colorado public school district, 90–91
Community, the
    mentorships and, 109
    service learning in the, 65–68
Community-wide survey, 66–67
Complexity, in lessons, 89–90
Concurrent enrollment, 122, 128, 215
Conflict resolution, 78
Connector, in literature circles, 77
Content acceleration, 122–125
Contracts, for curriculum compacting, 131–132
Contributions approach to service learning, 6
Coronado Hills Elementary School, Denver, Colorado, 74
Creating a Needs Assessment (toolkit strategy), 159
Creating a Plan for Service Learning (toolkit strategy), 66–67
Creating Choice Boards (toolkit strategy), 81
Creating Interest Groups (toolkit strategy), 70, 71–72
Credit by examination, 125
Cultural background
    connecting learning to students', 64
    culturally responsive classroom and, 32
    safe classroom and, 38, 41
Cultural capital, 11
Cultural lens, 8

177

Culturally and linguistically diverse (CLD) learners, 1. *See also* English language learners (ELLs); Underserved gifted learners
    about, 7–8
    curriculum compacting for, 130
    questions for teachers about, 8
Culturally responsive classroom, creating a, 32
Culturally responsive feedback, 42
Culturally responsive literature circles, 77–79, **97**
Culturally responsive teaching, connecting learning to students' lives and, 64
Culture explorer, in literature circles, 77
Curriculum compacting
    about, 130–131
    content acceleration and, 124
    contracts, 131–132
    independent investigations pairing with, 116
    pretests, 116, 131, 132
    SMART goal for, 153
Curriculum Compacting Steps (toolkit strategy), 131

D

De Bono, Edward, 157
Decision-Making and Social Action approach to service learning, 66
Denver Public Schools (DPS), 36
Depth and Complexity Framework training, 90–91
Depth, in lessons, 89–90
Designing a Professional Learning Opportunity (toolkit strategy), 155–156
Details, creating depth in lessons with, 89
Determining Learner Readiness for Challenge (toolkit strategy), 106
Differentiation, 63, 79–86
    assessment and, 85–86
    breaking larger assignments into smaller steps, 84–85
    Colorado's professional development program for, 90–91
    content acceleration and, 124
    with respect, 79–80
    through RAFTs, 83–84
    through student choice, 80
Disabilities. *See also* Twice-exceptional (2e) students
Discussion leader, in literature circles, 77
Diversity, 1, 6, 14
Dominant culture, 8
Dual credit, 122
Dual enrollment, 122, 125, 128

E

Early College High School (ECHS), 127
Economically disadvantaged learners, 7
    about, 10–11
    academic acceleration for, 122
    independent investigation by, 116
    mentorships and, 109
    questions for teachers about, 11
    in rural area, regional programming for, 120–121
Edgerton, Thelma Bear, 118–119
Education Week, 14
Educators. *See also* Teacher(s)
    affirming mentality of, 40–41
    creating a culturally responsive classroom, 32
    lightning talks to, 154–155
    personal experiences of. *See* Spotlights
Emotional engagement, 42
Emotional literacy, 107
Emotional needs, grouping by, 73
Empowered-to-Learn Checklist (toolkit strategy), 40, **56–58**
Empowerment, learner
    choice boards, 80–81, 82
    independent investigations and, 112, 114
    in a safe classroom community, 39–41
    service learning and, 65, 66
    students choosing group members and, 76
English language learners (ELLs), 1
    about, 8–9
    accelerated learning and, 128
    content acceleration and, 123
    gaps in equity goals for, 14–15
    long-term, 10
    questions for teachers about, 10
    real-world example of, 9–10
    safe learning environment for, 38, 39–40
    20 percent threshold for determining access to gifted education, 14
Enrichment cluster, 74, **93–95**
Enrichment options, accelerated learning options with, 131–132
Estis, Alicia, 74
Ethics, creating depth in lessons with, 89
Evaluation rubric, 86
Examples, classroom. *See* Real-world examples
Exemplars, for independent investigations, 116
Expert groups, 71
Explicit bias, 21

F

Families
    Denver Public Schools' efforts on getting to know, 36
    involved in mentorships, 110
    learning about your students, 34–35
    Recipe for Success for, 35, **51**
Family focus groups, 36
Family Identity Survey (toolkit strategy), 34–35, **49–50**
Family nights, 36
Federation of State Humanities Councils, 117
Fences (Wilson), 108
Field trip, 108
First grade, early entrance into, 126
Fiz, Bertie, 36
Flexible ability grouping, 69. *See also* Grouping students
Ford, Donna, 14, 155
Format, for RAFTs, 83, 84
Formative assessments, 86
Frames: Differentiating the Core Curriculum (Kaplan and Gould), 89

G

Genius Hour, 116
Geographic location, underserved category and, 7
Gifted and talented coordinator position, advocacy for, 149
Gifted education programs
    identification for. *See* Identification
    inequity in. *See* Underrepresentation of students in gifted education; Underserved gifted learners
    regional programming in rural areas, 120–121
    20 percent threshold to determine access to, 14–15
Gifted identification. *See* Identification
Giftedness
    in ELL students, 9
    looking different in underserved populations, 16–17
    masking, 12
    seen through different cultural lenses, 8
Giftedness Knows No Boundaries campaign, pillars of, 1–2
Gifted students. *See also* Underserved gifted learners
    creating positive classroom norms, 39
    in underresourced rural and urban areas, 7
Gilbert, Therese, 35
Goals, advocacy, 151–153, **165**
Goal-setting, 44, **59**, 67
Gould, Bette, 89
Grade-skipping (whole-grade acceleration), 125–127
Graefe, Amy, 4, 130
Greeley Central High School, 129–130
Greeley-Evans Schools, Colorado, 35, 119
Gross, Miraca, 122
Grouping students, 42, 63, 69–79
    by ability, 69, 73–76
    with culturally responsive literature circles, 77–79
    flexible ability grouping, 69
    individual accountability and, 43, 63, 75–76
    by interest, 69–72
    by need, 72–73
    working alone instead of, 76
Group Work for Self-Reflection Checklist, 76, **96**

H

Helping Students Connect with the Future (toolkit strategy), 64–65
Hickam, Homer, 64
Higher-level thinking, 63–64, 86–91
    asking higher-level questions for, 87, **100–102**
    by incorporating depth and complexity in lessons, 89–91
    for independent research group, 72
    with Socratic seminars, 87–89
Higher-Level Thinking Bookmark (toolkit strategy), 87, **100**
High expectations, conveying and supporting, 32, 37–38
Hispanic cultural heritage, 7
Hispanic learners
    poverty among, 10
    projections on number of, 7
    underrepresented in gifted education, 14
Historical figures, in Young Chautauqua (YC) program, 117–119
Home building exercise, 74, **93–95**
Honoring Small Requests (toolkit strategy), 41
Honors classes, 120, 129, 149

I

Identification
    Best Practices in Identification, 19, 20, **29–30**
    challenges for underserved gifted learners, 18, 19
    implicit bias and. *See* Implicit bias(es)
    nonverbal and performance-based options, 11
    restrictive criteria for, 18, 19–20
    "See Me" checklist for inclusive, **31**
    SMART goal for inclusive, 152
    Talent Hunt Inventory for, 18–19, **27–28**
    twice-exceptional students, 12–13, 19
Identification Plan Investigation (toolkit strategy), 19, 20–21
Identity
    cultivating students' intellectual, 107
    Family Identity Survey, 34, **49–50**
    My Memory Timeline, 33, **47**
Implementing Socratic Seminars (toolkit strategy), 88–89
Implicit Association Test, 24
Implicit bias(es), 16, 21–25
    accelerated learning and, 128
    hidden in social media, 23–24
    Implicit Association Test, 24
    potential bias recognition, 24–25
    real-world examples of, 22
    "See Me" Checklist for Inclusive Identification, 23, **31**
    word-association activity on, 23
Independent Investigation Planning Guide (toolkit strategy), 115, **138**
Independent investigations, 112–117
Independent Investigation Self-Evaluation, 117, **139**
Independent research group, 72
Individuals with Disabilities Education Act (IDEA), 12–13, 150
Inner-city schools, 7
Intellectual identity, cultivating, 107
Intentional guidance, 105
Interests, student
    grouping students by, 69–72
    independent investigations, 112
International Baccalaureate (IB) classes, 126, 127, 128
Inventory, Talent Hunt, 18–19, **27–28**
Iowa Acceleration Scale (IAS), 126
IQ scores, focus on, 8, 18

J

Jacob K. Javits Gifted and Talented Students Education Program, 90
Jigsaw strategy, 42

K

Kaplan, Sandra, 89
Kendig, Karen, 91
Key passage locator, in literature circles, 77
Kindergarten, early entrance into, 126

L

Lacy, Margie, 116
Language of the disciple, creating depth in lessons with, 89
Language skills, social *vs.* academic, 9
Latinx gifted community, 6, 36, 74, 129–130
Leadership, service learning and, 66
Learning activities, connecting to students' lives, 63, 64–68
  to be used in real-life career fields, 64–65
  creating something for a real audience and, 64
  SMART goal for, 153
  through problem-based learning, 68
  through service learning, 65–68
Learning contract, 72
Learning environment. *See* Classroom(s)
Learning Goal Plan strategy, 44, **59**
Learning More About My Classroom and Implicit Bias, 24–25
Learning More About Myself and Implicit Bias, 23–24
Learning Needs Survey, 73, **92**
Learning preference, grouping students by their, 73
Lee, Harper, 83
Lesson plans
  on self-awareness and identity, 38, **52–53**
  on using higher-level questioning, 87, **101–102**
Lightning Talks (toolkit strategy), 154–155
Literature circles, culturally responsive, 77–79

M

Masking phenomenon, 12
Mathematics
  ability grouping project, 74, **93–95**
  content acceleration and, 123–124, **140–144**
McGuire, Paula, 121
McKinney, Rebecca, 36
Meaningful connections with students, 33–36, 152
Meaningful engagement in underserved gifted learners, 41–46
Medina, Jacqueline, 91
Memory timeline, 33, **47**
Mentorship Evaluation Rubrics (toolkit strategy), 111
  Mentorship Evaluation Rubric 1: For the Mentor, **136**
  Mentorship Evaluation Rubric 2: For the Mentee, **137**
Mentorship Questionnaire (toolkit strategy), 110, **133–135**
Mentorships, 65, 108–112, **133–137**
Middle Eastern cultural heritage, 7
Mini-Lesson Ideas for Culturally Responsive Literature Circles (toolkit strategy), 78–79
Mini-lessons, embedded in culturally responsive literature circles, 77–79
Minority students, underrepresentation and, 13–14
Modeling
  for independent investigations, 113–114
  meaningful engagement and, 42
  respectfully disagreeing with another person's opinion, 78
Monologue, for Young Chautauqua (YC) program, 117
Morey Middle School, Denver, Colorado, 36
Morman-Burke, Amber, 19
Multicultural education, service learning and, 66
My Memory Timeline, 33, **47**

N

National Association for Gifted Children (NAGC) conference (2012), 150
  pillars of Giftedness Knows No Boundaries, 1–2
National Center for Education Statistics (NCES), 7
National Paideia Center, 87–88
National Twice-Exceptional Community of Practice (2e CoP), 12, 150
A Nation Deceived: How Schools Hold Back America's Brightest Students (Colangelo, Assouline, and Gross), 122
A Nation Empowered: Evidence Trumps the Excuses Holding Back America's Brightest Students (Assouline, Colangelo, and VanTassel-Baska), 122
Need, grouping by, 72–73
Needs assessment, 159
Nevada, 15
Nomination for gifted program
  advocacy efforts and, 149
  checklists for, 16–17
  cultural experiences/backgrounds and, 8
  economically disadvantaged students and, 16–17
Nonverbal-based options for assessment, 9

O

Observations. *See* Classroom observations
October Sky (film), 64
Opportunities to Lead (toolkit strategy), 43

P

Pacific Islanders
  Asian Americans *vs.*, 14
  overrepresentation in gifted programs, 13–14
  projections on number of, 7
Patterns, creating depth in lessons with, 89
Pereles, Daphne, 150–151
Perseverance, 104, 106, 108, 113, 116
Personal Financial Literacy standards, 74
Perspectives group, 71
Peterson, Jean Sunde, 8
Planning guide, independent investigation, 115, **138**
Pleasure Ridge Park High School, Louisville, Kentucky, 158
Positive Classroom Norms (toolkit strategy), 39
Potential, belief and support in students', 17, 37
Poverty, 11. *See also* Economically disadvantaged learners
Presentations
  for independent investigations, 114, 115
  Young Chautauqua (YC) program, 118, 119–120
Preservice teacher education program, 75
Pretests, for curriculum compacting, 116, 131, 132
Problem-based learning (PBL), 68
Problem-solving approach, meaningful engagement and, 43
Problem-solving skills
  independent investigations and, 113
  project timelines and, 85
Process Evaluation Rubric (toolkit strategy), 86, **99**
Products, independent investigation, 115–116
Professional growth, advocacy goals and, 151
Professional learning community (PLC), 155
Professional learning opportunity, 155–156, 157–159, **166**
Professional Learning Opportunity Design Template, 155, **166**
Professional learning questionnaire, 157
Project Timeline, 85, **98**
Public service announcements (PSAs), 66, 67
Public speaking, for Young Chautauqua (YC) program, 117–120

Q

Questions/questioning
  creating depth in lessons with unanswered, 89
  higher-level, 87, **100–102**
  for independent investigation, 115
  research, for independent investigations, 113–114
  in Socratic seminars, 87–88

R

RAFTs (Role, Audience, Format, and Topic), 83–84
Rangeview High School, Aurora, Colorado, 155
Reading strategies, for culturally responsive literature circles, 78
Real audiences, creating products for, 64
Real-world examples
  on ability grouping, 75
  about, 3
  on advocacy, 155
  on conveying high expectations for twice-exceptional student, 37
  on creating a safe learning environment, 38
  ELL gifted student, 9–10
  on exposure to career options, 108
  on giftedness looking different in underserved populations, 16
  on grouping by interest, 69–70
  on honoring small requests, 41
  of implicit bias, 22
  on independent investigations, 112–113
  on restrictive identification criteria, 19
  on service learning, 65
  on student choice, 80
Recipe for Success (toolkit strategy), 35, **51**
Reflection
  after independent investigation, 116–117
  Group Work Self-Reflection Checklist, 76, **96**
  in higher-level questioning lesson, 102
  in self-awareness and identity lesson, 53
  service learning and, 65, 67
Regional programming, in rural areas, 120–121
Renaissance Secondary School, Colorado, 65
Research
  on acceleration, 122, 125
  choice board on conducting, 82
  for independent investigations, 113–114
  with interest groups, 72, 73
  for RAFTs, 83
  for Young Chautauqua (YC) program, 117, 118
Research questions, 113–114
Resources
  on acceleration, 122
  for higher-level questioning lesson plan, 101
  for independent investigations, 114
  for mentorship program, 109
  for Not Just Math lesson, 140
  for self-awareness and identity lesson, 52
Right 4 Rural (R4R) project, 90–91
Robotics club, 109
Roles, for RAFTs, 83, 84
Rube Goldberg machines, 113
Rubrics
  for independent investigations, 115, 117, **139**
  Mentorship Evaluation, 111, **136–137**
  process evaluation, 86, **99**
  Young Chautauqua presentation, 119–120
Rules, creating depth in lessons with, 89
Rural areas
  gifted students in underresourced, 7
  independent investigation project for students in, 116
  regional gifted programming in, 120–121
  Right 4 Rural (R4R) project for, 90–91
Russian cultural heritage, 7

S

Safe Climate Checklist (toolkit strategy), 38–39, **54–55**
Sample Curriculum Unit: Not Just Math, 123–124, **140–144**
Sample Lesson Plan: Self-Awareness and Identity, **52–53**
Sample Lesson Plan: Using Higher-Level Questioning to Guide Inquiry, 87, **101–102**
Sample Needs Assessment, 159, **167–168**
Samples
  Action Planning Template, 161
  Choice Board, 82
  Empowered-to-Learn Checklist, 40
  Learning Goal Plan, 44
  My Memory Timeline, 33
  RAFT, 83–84
  Recipe for Success, 35
  Safe Climate Checklist, 39
  Student Evaluation of Cultural Connections in Texts, 79

Talent Hunt Inventory, 19
Talent Tree, 34
Scaffolding, 37, 42, 114, 128
"See Me" Checklist for Inclusive Identification, **31**
Self-awareness, sample lesson plan, 38, 52–53
Self-concept
    supporting high expectations and, 37
    Talent Tree and, 34, **48**
Self-paced instruction, 124
Service learning, 65–68
Setting SMART Advocacy Goals (toolkit strategy), 153, **165**
Six Thinking Hats strategy, 157
Skits, 114, 115
Small requests from students, honoring, 41
SMART Advocacy Goal Worksheet, 153, **165**
SMART goals, 3, 152–153
Social language proficiency, 9
Social media, implicit biases hidden in, 23–24
Social needs, grouping by, 73
Social-skills strategies, for culturally responsive literature circles, 78–79
Socratic seminars, 87–89
South Asian Americans, 14
Spanish-speaking learners/families, 36, 130
Speak Up (toolkit strategy), 15
Special Populations Network, 150
Spotlights
    on ability grouping, 74
    about, 3
    on accelerated learning, 129–130
    on advocacy, 150–151
    on Depth and Complexity Framework professional development, 90–91
    on getting to know families, 35, 36
    on mentorships, 111–112
    on regional planning for economically disadvantaged rural schools, 121
    on teacher learning cycle, 158
    on Young Chautauqua (YC) program, 118–119
Stereotypes, implicit biases and, 22, 23
Stiles, Kelly Ann, 149, 155
Strengths, Talent Tree exercise on a student's, 45
Student-centered instruction, 32, 43
Student choice, differentiation through, 80–84
Student Evaluation of Cultural Connections in Texts (toolkit strategy), 79, **97**
Students, treating equitably *vs.* equally, 6. *See also* Gifted students; Underserved gifted learners
Summarizer, in literature circles, 77
Summative assessments, 85–86
Surveying Learning Needs (toolkit strategy), 73, **92**
Surveys
    community-wide, 66–67
    Family Identity Survey, 34, **49–50**
    Learning Needs Survey, 73, **92**
    Mentorship Questionnaire, 110

T

Talent Hunt Inventory (toolkit strategy), 18–19, **27–28**
Talent Tree (toolkit strategy), 34, **48**
Teacher(s). *See also* Educators; Spotlights
    advocacy by. *See* Advocacy
    building meaningful connections with students. *See* Meaningful connections with students
    caring about students, 63–64
    challenging their students. *See* Challenges/being challenged
    commitment to underserved gifted learners, 1
    connecting learning to students' lives, 64–68
    cultural lens of white, middle-class, 8
    Depth and Complexity Framework training for, 90–91
    differentiation by. *See* Differentiation
    efforts to get to know their students and their families, 11 (*See also* What I Want You to Know About Me)
    engaging students in higher-level thinking, 86–91
    goal of equity *vs.* equality, 6
    grouping by. *See* Grouping students
    implicit bias in. *See* Implicit bias(es)
    learning cycle of, 156–157
    modeling by. *See* Modeling
    questions about culturally and linguistically diverse learners for, 8
    questions about economically disadvantaged learners for, 11
    questions about ELL students for, 10
    questions about twice-exceptional learners for, 13
    race of, 7
    in rural schools, 120
    supporting development of the whole child, 17
Teacher on special assignment (TOSA), 149
Teaching tools, 2. *See also* Toolkit strategies
"Teach Me" Checklist, 91, **103**
Technical education, 127
Telescoping, 124
Temperature readings, on emotions, 107–108
Tests and testing. *See also* Assessment
    ability grouping and, 73, 75
    gifted identification issues with, 18, 19
    implicit bias, 24
    pretests for curriculum compacting, 116, 131, 132
    teacher bias for gifted nomination process and, 149
    whole-grade acceleration and, 126
Thermometer, range of emotions on a, 107–108
Three-times rule, 108
Tier 1 of MTTS, 105
Tier 2 of MTTS, 105
Tier 3 of MTTS, 105
Tips to Promote Meaningful Engagement (toolkit strategy), 42–43
To Kill a Mockingbird (Lee), 83
Tomlinson, Carol Ann, 79–80
Toolkit strategies, 3. *See also* What I Want You to Know About Me; individual titles of toolkit strategies
Topic(s)
    for independent investigations, 112, 115
    for RAFTs, 83, 84
    when grouping by interest, 70–72
Torrance, Ellis Paul, 156
Transformative approach to service learning, 66
Trends, creating depth in lessons with, 89
Tully Elementary, Louisville, Kentucky, 19
Turk, Lisa, 126
Twenty percent threshold, 14–15
Twice-exceptional (2e) students, 1
    about, 12–13
    advocacy for, 150–151
    conveying high expectations to, 37
    definition of, 12, 151
    masking phenomenon, 12
    questions for teachers about, 13
    20 percent threshold for determining access to gifted education, 15
2e CoP Summit, 150

U

Unanswered questions, creating depth in lessons with, 89
Unconditional positive regard, 17
Unconscious biases. *See* Implicit bias(es)
Underrepresentation of students in gifted education
    determining, 13–15
    factors contributing to, 15–25
Underresourced rural/urban areas, gifted students in, 7
Underserved gifted learners, 6. *See also* Culturally and linguistically diverse (CLD) learners; Economically disadvantaged learners; English language learners (ELLs); Gifted students; Twice-exceptional (2e) students
    accelerated learning for, 122, 128–129
    accomplishing challenging goals. *See* Challenges/being challenged
    adapting strategies for, 4
    advocating for. *See* Advocacy
    building meaningful connections with, 33–36
    challenging. *See* Challenges/being challenged
    connecting learning to lives of, 63, 64–68
    creating a safe learning environment for, 38–41
    denied access to gifted programs, court cases on, 15
    giftedness looking different in, 16–17
    grouping. *See* Grouping students
    high expectations of, 37–38
    identification issues for, 18–21
    list of potential characteristics of, 17
    meaningfully engaged, 41–46
    notes about themselves from. *See* What I Want You to Know About Me
    opportunities to lead, 43–44
    teachers' commitment to, 1
Underserved, use of term, 1
Understanding How Implicit Bias Works (toolkit strategy), 23
"Understand Me" Checklist, 46, **62**
Universal Design for Learning (UDL) principles, 44–46, **60–61**, 73, 161
Urban areas
    gifted students in underresourced, 7
    poverty in, 10
    rural schools *vs.* schools in, 120
US Department of Education
    Civil Rights Data Collection website, 14
    Jacob K. Javits Gifted and Talented Students Education Program, 90
    Office for Civil Rights, 12–13, 15
US Department of Justice Case Summaries website, 15

V

VanTassel-Baska, Joyce, 122
Video games, 69–70
Vygotsky, Lev, 43, 75

W

What I Want You to Know About Me, 4, 18, 32, 33, 37, 38, 43, 64, 69, 76, 80, 105
Whole child, the, 17
Whole-grade acceleration, 125–127
Wilson, August, 108
Wordsmith, in literature circles, 77
Writing, 37, 80, 112–113

Y

Young Chautauqua Presentation Rubric (toolkit strategy), 119–120
Young Chautauqua (YC) program, 117–120
Your Past, Present, and Future Advocacy (toolkit strategy), 150, **163**

Z

Zone of proximal development (ZPD), 43, 75, 104

Digital versions of all reproducible forms and lesson plans can be downloaded at **freespirit.com/seeing-forms**. Use password **2serve**.

About the Authors

Jennifer Ritchotte, Ph.D., is an associate professor of gifted education at the University of Northern Colorado (UNC). She teaches undergraduate and graduate-level courses in both special education and gifted education. She is also the director of the Center for Gifted and Talented Education at UNC. Her research primarily examines the cognitive and affective needs of at-risk gifted student populations. Prior to completing her Ph.D. in special education with an emphasis in gifted education, Jennifer was a middle and secondary language arts teacher. Her years of teaching language arts to gifted seventh graders, in particular, inspired her advocacy in gifted education. Jennifer is also the mother of two gifted children. Her experiences as a parent have informed her work in the field and motivated her to help other parents understand the unique learning needs of their gifted children.

Chin-Wen "Jean" Lee, Ph.D., grew up in Taichung, Taiwan. English was her favorite subject in school. Because of this language learning experience and her cultural background, she identifies very much with culturally and linguistically diverse learners. She was and is encouraged by teachers who believed in her along the way, and she wants to spread the message of believing in students. She studies special education and gifted education. In 2012, Jean arrived in Colorado for her doctoral degree. She believes that she was brought to Colorado by design because Colorado has a long history of supporting twice-exceptional students and their teachers. Jean studied professional learning about twice-exceptionality, and she wrote her dissertation in appreciation of the dedicated educators in Colorado. Her mission is to help children and young adults from disadvantaged backgrounds reach their full potential and to support their teachers.

Amy Graefe, Ph.D., is an assistant professor and co-coordinator of gifted education at the University of Northern Colorado (UNC) and the director of the Summer Enrichment Program, a nationally recognized summer program for gifted learners in grades preK–12 that focuses on the whole gifted child. She is also the mother of two gifted daughters. Her primary research interests include secondary gifted education, creativity, and underserved gifted learners. Amy attended a small, rural school growing up, and prior to her work at UNC, she served for twenty-two years in various capacities as a teacher, library media specialist, instructional coach, and gifted-education specialist. In these roles, she had the privilege of working with students and teachers in grades K–12 in richly diverse public schools. These experiences formed the foundation of her passion for supporting underserved gifted learners, their families, and their teachers.

Other Great Resources from Free Spirit

The Cluster Grouping Handbook: A Schoolwide Model
(Revised & Updated Edition)
How to Challenge Gifted Students and Improve Achievement for All
by Dina Brulles, Ph.D., and Susan Winebrenner, M.S.

For teachers and administrators, grades K–8.
272 pp.; PB; 8½" x 11"; includes digital content.

Free PLC/Book Study Guide
freespirit.com/PLC

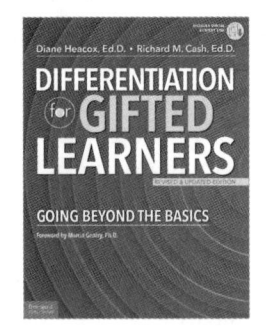

Differentiation for Gifted Learners
(Revised & Updated Edition)
Going Beyond the Basics
by Diane Heacox, Ed.D., and Richard M. Cash, Ed.D.

For K–8 teachers, gifted education teachers, program directors, administrators, instructional coaches, and curriculum developers.
264 pp.; PB; 8½" x 11"; includes digital content.

Free PLC/Book Study Guide
freespirit.com/PLC

A Teacher's Guide to Flexible Grouping and Collaborative Learning
Form, Manage, Assess, and Differentiate in Groups
by Dina Brulles, Ph.D., and Karen L. Brown, M.Ed.

For teachers and administrators, grades K–12.
200 pp.; PB; 8½" x 11"; includes digital content.

Free PLC/Book Study Guide
freespirit.com/PLC

Teaching Gifted Children in Today's Preschool and Primary Classrooms
Identifying, Nurturing, and Challenging Children Ages 4–9
by Joan Franklin Smutny, M.A., Sally Yahnke Walker, Ph.D., and Ellen I. Honeck, Ph.D.

For teachers of preschool, preK, K–3.
248 pp.; PB; 8½" x 11"; includes digital content.

Free PLC/Book Study Guide
freespirit.com/PLC

Get Gifted Students Talking
76 Ready-to-Use Group Discussions About Identity, Stress, Relationships, and More (Grades 6–12)
by Jean Sunde Peterson, Ph.D.

For teachers, counselors, youth workers, and parents, grades 6–12.
304 pp.; PB; 8½" x 11"; includes digital content.

Teaching Gifted Kids in Today's Classroom
Strategies and Techniques Every Teacher Can Use
(Updated 4th Edition)
by Susan Winebrenner, M.S., with Dina Brulles, Ph.D.

For teachers and administrators, grades K–12.
256 pp.; PB; 8½" x 11"; includes digital content.

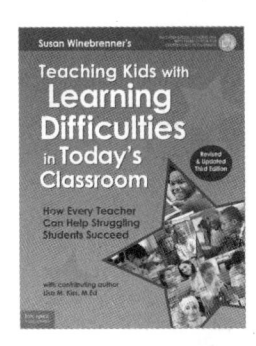

Teaching Kids with Learning Difficulties in Today's Classroom
How Every Teacher Can Help Struggling Students Succeed
(Revised & Updated 3rd Edition)
by Susan Winebrenner, M.S., with Lisa M. Kiss, M.Ed.

For K–12 teachers, administrators, and higher education faculty.
288 pp.; PB; 8½" x 11"; includes digital content.

Free PLC/Book Study Guide
freespirit.com/PLC

Buy the Set:
Teaching Twice/Multi-Exceptional (2e) Students in Today's Classroom
by Susan Winebrenner, M.S., Lisa Kiss, M.Ed., and Dina Brulles, Ph.D.

For teachers and administrators, grades K–12.

Interested in purchasing multiple quantities and receiving volume discounts?
Contact edsales@freespirit.com or call 1.800.735.7323 and ask for Education Sales.

Many Free Spirit authors are available for speaking engagements, workshops, and keynotes.
Contact speakers@freespirit.com or call 1.800.735.7323.

For pricing information, to place an order, or to request a free catalog, contact:
Free Spirit Publishing Inc. • 6325 Sandburg Road, Suite 100 • Minneapolis, MN 55427-3674
toll-free 800.735.7323 • local 612.338.2068 • fax 612.337.5050
help4kids@freespirit.com • freespirit.com